The Concept of Modern Law

Lex et Res Publica

Polish Legal and Political Studies

Edited by Anna Jaroń

Volume 11

Zur Qualitätssicherung und Peer Review der vorliegenden Publikation

Die Qualität der in dieser Reihe erscheinenden Arbeiten wird vor der Publikation durch die Herausgeber der Reihe geprüft.

Notes on the quality assurance and peer review of this publication

Prior to publication, the quality of the work published in this series is reviewed by the editors of the series.

Michał Peno, Konrad Burdziak (eds.)

The Concept of Modern Law

Polish and Central European Tradition

PETER LANG

Bibliographic Information published by the Deutsche Nationalbibliothek
The Deutsche Nationalbibliothek lists this publication
in the Deutsche Nationalbibliografie; detailed bibliographic
data is available in the internet at http://dnb.d-nb.de.

This publication was financially supported by the University of Szczecin.

Translated by Sylwia Zawadzka, Justyna Zahorska,
Agnieszka Kotula and Agnieszka Nowosad

ISSN 2191-3250
ISBN 978-3-631-78325-2 (Print)
E-ISBN 978-3-631-78580-5 (E-Book)
E-ISBN 978-3-631-78581-2 (EPUB)
E-ISBN 978-3-631-78582-9 (MOBI)
DOI 10.3726/b15622

Peter Lang – Berlin· Bern · Bruxelles · New York ·
Oxford · Warszawa · Wien

This publication has been peer reviewed

www.peterlang.com

Preface

The monograph contains texts prepared by representatives of various branches of law, philosophers and dogmatists who link a general reflection on law with caselaw. This ensures that the presented approaches are versatile and insightful, and that the addressed issues vary, the most important of which is the oeuvre of the Polish jurisprudence and its contribution to building a modern state. The context exceeds beyond a simple report on or presentation of this oeuvre and in many cases it only refers to it.

The content of this volume is as follows. The monograph begins with the issue of policy of law in historical, theoretical and dogmatic-legal aspect. The policy of law is a modern project 'par excellence' which provides a coherent framework of a specific tradition the legal thought of the beginning and the end of the 20th century. Petrażycki's policy of law was the culmination of the great project of the scientific theory of law based on psychological grounds, in a sense descriptive (empirical) threads have never been forsaken for philosophical speculation. Although axiology played here a role, over the previous century it was considered a science of morality with all its (neo-positivist) consequences. These issues are addressed in a text titled *Leon Petrażycki's policy of law and Jerzy Wróblewski's theory of law* (J. Jaśkiewicz PhD). It seems that there was an *iunctum* between the general reflection on law and detailed jurisprudence (dogmatists). A successful attempt to indicate such relations is found in the text titled *Theories and views of Leon Petrażycki and the formation and development of labour law* (M. Rylski PhD).

The programme of modern and scientific policy of law culminates in *de lege lata* regulations on lawmaking, which oftentimes draw inspiration from the experience of modernist trend of economic law analysis. In fact, it would be hard to find more scientific tools in lawmaking than those provided by economic sciences. In Polish law, one can notice a trend to make Western ideas integrated in law and jurisprudence to the greatest extent possible, which is typical of post-socialist countries. This is proved by a compiled work titled *Assessment of outcomes of regulations in Poland as an example of law economisation: evolution, problems, prospects for development* (Ass. Prof. K. Nizioł).

The bridge between criminal law, modern constitutionalism and the policy of law would be an article by K. Burdziak *Article 31 Section 3 of the Polish Constitution and Leon Petrażycki's concept of the policy of law*. It is worth paying attention to texts on the relationship between criminal law and theory and the philosophy of law. Both chapters also refer to L. Petrażycki. These are chapters titled *From the psychologism of Leon Petrazycki to the model of subjective criminal liability in the Polish law* (M. Kowalewska-Łukuć PhD, M. Nawrocki PhD) and *Scope of moral evaluation of a man's act as a co-creating element of intuitive law and positive law as regards the model structure of a sanctioned norm in criminal law (a contribution to the possible impact of Leon Petrażycki's theory of criminal law)* (Professor Łukasz Pohl).

The compilation on civil law is dedicated to the relation between the theory of law and specific jurisprudences. The chapter titled *Sensus spiritualis of the Polish civil law: a few words on the autonomy of will* (S. Słotwinski PhD) presents the idea of a prominent Polish civil law specialist Andrzej Stelmachowski. The legislator created a coherent structural regulation of the autonomy of civil law entities. Particularly interesting is the relation between types of this autonomy distinguished by Stelmachowski, namely, functional autonomy and structural autonomy. These semantic treatments, and detailed analyses of legal institutions will undoubtfully reflect some tradition and tendency of the Polish jurisprudence.

The second part of this volume concerns the application and statutory interpretation of law. It is the subject of interest of the Polish theory of law consideration of which is particularly well developed and in many aspects can compete with the theory of law of western states. This framework covers two texts: *Values in the statutory interpretation (from tradition to the latest approach in the Polish theory of law)* (Ass. Prof. O. Bogucki) and *Learning facts and using law based on Wróblewski's concept of judicial application of law* (M. Żbikowska PhD).

The volume closes the study on an important problem linking Polish and Western theory of law and philosophy about *the Concept of Conventional Actions in Law* (K. Gmerek PhD, M. Peno PhD).

K. Burdziak, M. Peno

Contents

M. Peno, consulted with M. Zieliński

Introduction: The Idea of Modern Law in the Light of Polish Legal Doctrine and Theory of Law

The monograph contains texts pertaining to the most important issues from the field of research on the forming, shaping (reshaping) and evolution of modern jurisprudence in Central European legal tradition (here, this term will be applied intuitively to characterise countries such as Poland, Bulgaria, the Czech Republic, Romania, Slovakia, Hungary and probably Belarus or Ukraine, and partially also the Baltic States). It should be noted at the very beginning that Polish jurisprudence serves here as the fundamental reference point. The very notion of legal tradition may give rise to certain concerns that are not definitively resolved in the monograph. The indirect objective of this book is to answer the question whether such a tradition exists and what is the role it plays in the globalising world of legal though that remains influenced by Western sciences (particularly the Anglo-Saxon ones). This question can be answered in reference to the innovative character of ways in which research problems can be solved, the historical continuity (identity) of concepts, theories, schools and research institutions, as well as a certain type of cultural connections with Central European jurisprudence. It should be noted that Polish jurisprudence in a broad sense collects in its history, present day and ambitions all the characteristics that are typical of the central part of Europe, namely, (a) pluralism of sources and inspirations (related to long-term absence of statehood and the resulting employment of researchers at various research institutions), (b) relatively late, yet highly intense implementation of Enlightenment ideas that took on in the legal thought and legislature of newly formed or reborn states (at the turn of the 20th century or in the early 20th century) the form of a fully developed modernism (with the specific Neo-Positivist admiration, naturalistic approach to research and their subject), (c) a specific type of social progressiveness (e.g. voting rights for groups that were previously discriminated) and (d) the experience of Marxist ideology different to the West, for real and not just imaginary.

Nonetheless, historically, the Polish legal thought has drawn inspiration from traditions that were sometimes contradictory (e.g. the Franconian and the German ones), formulated at Russian, German, Austrian or French universities. This formulation covered detailed knowledge of the binding law (legal dogmas – knowledge of the criminal law, the civil law, the administrative law, etc.), but also a general reflection on law.

One can seek in this book the answer to the question about the modern character of science or in jurisprudence. However, the role of the Szczecin centre should be described here in detail, particularly the Szczecin school of the theory of law that usually influences texts incorporated to this book and its effect on the development of modern theory of law in this part of Europe. One should note, that from the perspective of theoretical, methodological grounds and the vision of law (as a certain system of norms), authors of this monograph are linked to the Szczecin centre of the theory of law, historically embedded in the achievements of the Poznań school of the theory of law that was formed in the 1960s around Prof. Zygmunt Ziembiński, student of Czesław Znamierowski (a lawyer and a philosopher) and Kazimierz Ajdukiewicz (logic and methodology). The Szczecin theory of law is centred on statutory interpretation issues developed systematically as a derivative concept of interpretation by Maciej Zieliński and his students. The high scientific level is also achieved in works by Stanisław Czepita that pertain to, among others, the original concept of conventional activities. Another person linked to the Szczecin centre was Aleksander Peczenik. Although for most of his life he acted in Lund, in the last years of his life he worked as a professor of the theory of law at the University of Szczecin.

The general jurisprudence referred to in the post-war period in Poland as the theory of the state and the law stems from the Marxist tradition (which assumed that these two factors are inseparable). It was understood as general considerations regarding law exercised in Socialist states. However, in fact, the term 'jurisprudence' did not and does not refer to considerations enmeshed in a certain ideology but declares a certain method – the method of exercising certain considerations about the law modelled on empirically oriented sciences aiming at formulating collections of properly organised general theorems (similar to model scientific theories known from empirical sciences). This is an ambitious scientific programme that ascribes the task of building law-describing theories to jurisprudence. It can be said that this is a traditional approach to jurisprudence that can be attributed to Ziembiński and the Poznań theory of law of its prime time (the 1960s).

In turn, Aleksander Peczenik, despite being associated with the Szczecin centre that continued traditions of the Poznań centre, postulated a different approach. Peczenik claimed that although jurisprudence aims at obtaining knowledge of the law, it is part of the law and thus takes part in its formation. In the traditional model, law is a set of legal norms and jurisprudence is a set of coherent and well-justified theorems about the law. The distinction between law and jurisprudence is hence easily observable. Nonetheless, in Peczenik's approach, this distinction becomes blurry, as it is relativised with regard to a certain convention determined by legal culture in a broad sense. A judge somewhat transforms the rules of reasoning, moral intuition, etc. into the 'binding law' compliant with the expectations of jurisprudence and even those of a broader audience. Jurisprudence formulates postulates pertaining to what law should be like and affects the shape of law. In particular, jurisprudence formulates normative concepts of legal reasoning and statutory interpretation, as well as sources of law and their hierarchy. Obviously, courts must take due account of these rules, i.e. reasoning and interpretation, as well as sources of law.

These two ways of interpreting jurisprudence should not be considered contradictory. One could attempt to prove that the other model fits the contemporary state of knowledge of law better, as it is more modern. However, it is important that the issue of how jurisprudence and law were understood at the centres in Szczecin and Poznań played a significant role, which is distinctive to some extent in the modern Polish jurisprudence dominated by eclectic philosophy of law (although one can obviously indicate other strong theoretical and legal traditions, such as those formulated in Kraków, Łódź and Wrocław).

Attachment to a certain jurisprudential tradition can be noticed in all texts included in this volume. At the same time, the open character of the assumptions employed in jurisprudential studies allows one to include then into the scope of philosophical or philosophical-legal considerations. These are however characterised by a deep attachment to methodology and detailed terminological and conceptual grounds. This should be given a proper value. The general Polish consideration pertaining to law was born in the Modern Era. It had no strong Enlightenment background or an in-depth perception of Enlightenment ideas (due to the loss of independence and orientation towards the Romanticist though). This does not mean that it was not given though, but that it was developed outside the borders of the national state. This can be exemplified by Leon Petrażycki, the father of the theory of law in this part of Europe, and his travels from Russia to Germany, which ended in his employment at the University of Warsaw.

It can be said that the theory of law in Poland has been modern from the very beginning. Born in the era of paroxysm of implementation of philosophical positivist postulates, it remained influenced by Neo-Positivism despite the experience of the world war and occupation (which obviously affected the adopted meta-ethical attitudes). In turn, in the time of the People's Republic of Poland under the communist regime, the theory of law and also jurisprudence *per se* were directed towards the Marxist ideology. Paradoxically, it was a highly fruitful time when undoubtfully modern concepts and theories on methodology, application and interpretation of law were developed. It was also the time of development of legal dogmas. The Modern Era can be understood here as an attachment to certain (logocentric) vision of the world, systematised scientific work and a precise research method. Jurisprudence was intended as a science of precisely this kind in the proper sense, although obviously there was a dispute on the scientific nature of jurisprudence, particularly legal dogmas. However, the very fact that such a dispute was held (with the participation of, i.e. Peczenik) shows a certain approach to the modern jurisprudence and attachment to the theory of law and not philosophical methods (which is discussed further in the book).

The geographical origin of considerations in the central-eastern region of Europe may give rise to questions on mutual relations between jurisprudence in the region. Although this issue has not been yet examined in depth, it is not a direct objective of this book to make any conclusions in this regard. Nonetheless, the fact that this problem was signalled seems to be of an inherent value. Particularly when considering that there are arguments that for cultural, social, geopolitical or historical reasons, such links were present and still are, and allow themselves to be examined in categories that exceed beyond contingency. Nonetheless, these relations most probably weakened after the system transformation and the demise of socialist states (at the turn of the 1990s). This was due to the fact that the reality of socialist states formed a certain (more or less forced) community with individual jurisprudences functioning within its borders. The very fact that, i.e. the University of Sophia subscribed until the end of the 1980s *Państwo i Prawo* (the most influential polish legal journal) confirms that there was a certain platform for exchanging thoughts. This is also confirmed by initial research on quotations of papers from various states of the so-called Eastern Bloc. The Eastern bloc states were not the only ones that were influenced by the achievements of prominent Polish representatives of jurisprudence. One can mention here works by Jerzy Wróblwski, translated in Roman countries. However, sadly, the part of Polish theoreticians of law in the global circulation was forces with the change of their place of functioning, as in the case of Peczenik, who years ago had to leave Poland as a result of the dramatic political turmoil of the 1960s.

After all, due to the research areas of the general reflection on law, it also has some application usefulness for any legal system and any jurisprudence. This is the case for, i.e. the concept of statutory interpretation, the issue of dynamics or statistics of the legal system or various particular jurisprudential concepts (e.g. conventional activities), particularly philosophical-legal matters in a broad sense. At the same time, one cannot omit the input resulting from legal dogma considerations in the forming of the modern law.

Symptomatically, from the birth of modern and independent Polish jurisprudence, which should be linked to the regained independence (which is typical of states in Eastern Europe), this science was involved in the philosophical project of modernity. This project envisaged that a modern state, law and society will be built based on scientific knowledge. Not surprisingly then, the first modern Polish penal code (the so-called Makarewicz's Code) was formed based on the best models determined by the sociological school of criminal law. Studies conducted by Leon Petrażycki, Bronisław Wróblewski and Czesław Znamierowski are well-known – these studies were carried out in line with the vision of modern science with psychology and sociology involved, while the idea of integrating legal sciences with social sciences seemed to somewhat determine the research paradigm in legal sciences. One of these implemented projects is undoubtfully the science of the politics of law (similar to the philosophical assumptions of Nathan Roscoe Pound, although significantly different and original). Already at the philosophical congress of 1936 in Kraków, general jurisprudence was considered a theory of law, while the main issue discussed at the legal part of the congress was the problem of 'juridisation of sociological categories'.

In this sense, also the jurisprudence of the second half of the 20th century was also assumed to be modern, which allowed it to maintain high methodological levels, at times with the use of verbal means that embedded studies in reality governed by the Marxist-Lenninist ideology, usually considering this method and methodology a stronghold not to be accessed by censorship or constraints of the official philosophical line. In turn, from the times of the system transformation, that is, for the last 30 years, one could notice some transformations in the way law is considered. These transformations cover a change or a relief of previous rigoristic methodological approach or methodological pluralism. Thus, the approach to scientific matters changes. Self-reflection on the condition and direction of these changes is important, however, it does exceed beyond the framework of this paper as well, as these are post-modern tendencies.

It can be said that the notion of modernity of jurisprudence is understood in this monograph as science implemented in line with specific methods in compliance with an approach characterised by a positivistic (meaning the philosophical positivism) methodological awareness directed at formulating general theorems about law. A great contribution to the creation of this model of jurisprudence, particularly the general reflection on law, was made by Leon Petrażycki, the creator of the theory of law as a science in the truest sense of the term. Ideas or concepts developed by Petrażycki are what constitutes the important reference point for the texts included in this volume, although the characteristics of various legal institutions or concepts in view of their role as the foundation of the model law in a broad sense exceeds Petrażycki's thought. In a sense, Petrażycki's theory of law is the origin and the model for the modern jurisprudence *per se*.

The attempt to define the 'modern law', particularly when speaking of the modernity of a particular jurisprudence ("modern criminal law", "modern civil law"), gives rise to numerous research problems. The relation between modernity and the Polish legal tradition stems undoubtfully from the direction of scientific interests of authorities (e.g. the role of Petrażycki and Polish theoreticians of law in the shaping of modern jurisprudence) and also objective geopolitical conditions in which the modern Polish legal thought formed. Hence, the pluralism of sources and ideas, including philosophical assumptions, the strength of logical grounds and the attachment to studies on legal phenomena (sociology of law), as well as the specific progressiveness (e.g. in the area of constitutional law and election law – voting rights for women or criminal law – modern solutions drawing from the sociological achievements of the criminal law school).

The works included in this volume pertain to issues spread over time. This is because issues or problems of modern law can be considered in view of a period from the final decades of the 19th century to the late 20th century. One cannot fail to emphasise that the issues were covered in a broad range and the subject of Polish tradition was placed next to European traditions that are leading in certain aspects. The texts pertain to main problems addressed by representatives of the Polish jurisprudence presented in their historical context and in a broader philosophical, social, cultural context as the core of a certain legal tradition that was born in very difficult conditions, yet also integrating various schools or directions in jurisprudence.

The subject of the book concerns modernity understood as the Modern Era or modernisation. Modernity should not be identified with the contemporary times. This is rather to indicate the roots of modernity, to juxtapose them with the fruit they gave. Here, an important role is played hence by the comparative-historical factor and the theoretical, philosophical, historical, cultural or social context of the shaping of law in the Modern Era. In other words, firstly, each of the essays refers to the Post-Modern image and vision of the world, which can be described using terms such as determinism, universalism, scientism, objective and methodological naturalism; secondly, an attempt is made to confront this image or vision with the current state of contemporary Poland and, thirdly, to identify sources of modernist solutions in the Polish law while making references to primarily Polish authors.

Modernism can be understood as a certain era (industrialisation, scientism, naturalism of subject and the method of research). Modernism can be also perceived as an intellectual trend, including that which fuels jurisprudence, based on a scientific vision of the world. To a considerable extent, modernism constitutes a continuation of philosophical positivism.

There are many ways for perceiving modernism or modernity in law. A superficial analysis of texts included in this volume already allows one to distinguish some approaches to this problem. The first one may refer to thoughts of prominent lawyers of the 20th century such as Petrażycki, Wróblewski, Ziembiński or even Peczenik. These are perfect examples and one can also add prominent dogmatists (such as Stelmachowski, the achievements of whom the article in this volume refers to).

The other approach seems to reach to the shaping of a certain paradigm of scientific nature of law, i.e. a vision of law as such. Scientific nature may be considered in the category of an attempt to build modern jurisprudence in the proper sense of the word 'jurisprudence (as a collection of properly outstanding and justified theorems on law), which corresponds to, e.g. the reflection on the policy of law or the scientific theory of law. On this background, frictions on the normativism-naturalism line can be observed.

Thirdly, one can perceive modernity also as modernisation, i.e. transformation (somewhat in Weber's approach) from the traditional model to the modern one, and a reflection on the process of modernisation, as well as inclusion or application of solutions from a more advanced (in certain terms) jurisprudence. This can be exemplified by elimination of custom law from sources of law (in Poland, this is exceptionally vivid from the late 1940s). Although this may be a more recent transformation – transformation as entering liberal democracy and market economy of the 1990s, or an older one, i.e. transplantation of new solutions in the Poland of the 19th century until the 1920s/1930s. The first one should be linked to development of economic analysis of law founded on capitalistic liberal economy that is difficult to imagine in socialist reality, and which currently plays the key role in the lawmaking process (for instance, in the aspect of assessing results of regulations). This also covers somewhat natural outcomes of industrialisation and scientific development (e.g. psychologism in law – theory of declarations of will or subjective rights or objectification of civil liability in relation to industrialisation of societies).

Here, it is worth to remember that the idea of modern law and scientific approach to implementation of jurisprudence has a long tradition in the central European region that reaches far back to Petrażycki, but the level of political-criminal or socio-legal studies in socialist modernism was anything but low.

This pertains also to the original methodology, theory of law or statutory interpretation.

Fourthly, from a philosophical perspective, one can notice consequences of the Enlightenment thought, rationalistic and focused on emancipation of humanity, also by means of law, from any restrictions. However, Enlightenment ideas were rather transplanted (and somewhat late) and not produced on the grounds of Polish philosophy or jurisprudence. The attachment to the idea of social agreement and democracy in a broad sense characterised lawyers, politicians and regular citizens both after independence was regained and after World War One, as well as after the system transformation at the turn of the 1990s. Obviously, building a civil society, which is the safeguard of democracy, takes time and experience of several generations living in peaceful urban conditions and a stable public sphere.

Modernisation of European law meant in principle codification of this law (initially considered discovering or noting rules of nature that can be learned and accessed by any human). In this very way one can consider the issue of modernisation from the view of codification of private law (civil law) and the theoretical or philosophical grounds of that law. As a rule, in the Euro-Atlantic area modernisation was accompanied by the formation of a state and national state, however, in the case of many Central European countries, the formation of a national state made it necessary to take swift legislative action aiming to create legal order almost instantly *ex nihilo*. This oftentimes gave rise to the necessity to apply foreign solutions. It also gave a chance for creating comprehensive and modern legal solutions from scratch, although this required development of an effective research method – this explains the development of comprehensive theory of law. Could this law form and also remain independent and valuable? This question is answered implicitly by some texts included in the volume.

J. Jaśkiewicz

Legal Policy by Leon Petrazycki vs. Theory of Law by Jerzy Wróblewski

1 Introduction

Nearly all scientific publications on the policy of law[1] begin with a presentation of Leon Petrazycki's ideas. It is not only due to the fact that Petrazycki is believed to be a pioneer of this discipline, but also due to the expansiveness and longevity of his concept of creating a certain superscience, incorporating nearly all aspects of normative, economic and psychosocial functioning of law. Petrazycki was a renowned representative of the German school of law, an equally exquisite member of the academic society of the Russian Empire and a pioneer and symbol of a sovereign Polish science – recovering after more than a century of foreign rule. During his academic work in Germany and Russia (until the Bolshevik revolution) he was a popular and renowned scholar. He was treated with great esteem at the beginning of his scientific career in Poland. However, he cannot be described as a scholar praised by politicians and decision-makers. Petrazycki remained uncompromising and independent in his scientific work, what is emphasized in a sense by the circumstances of his life decisions and tragic death[2].

Innovation and multitude of dimensions in Petrażycki's programme was an original, controversial and – above all – unknown phenomenon for many of his contemporary researches, who functioned in different cultural or linguistic circle. It was also due to his personal and scientific peregrinations, as Petrazycki, unlike any of his contemporary prominent lawyers, had been entangled in the

1 The term "polityka prawa" does not have one English equivalent. The most common translation, also proposed in this work, is "legal policy", cf. e.g. H. W. Babb, *Petrażycki: Science of Legal Policy and Theory of Law*, Boston University Law Review 1938 and *Politics of Law and Legal Policy Between Modern and Post-Modern Jurisprudence*, T. Biernat, M. Zirk-Sadowski (eds.), Warsaw 2008; Editors of Petrażycki's works also use such translation, cf. L. Petrażycki, *O nauce, prawie i moralności. Pisma wybrane*, Warsaw, 1985, p. 199.

2 Szerzej A. Kojder, *Leon Petrażycki's socio-legal ideas and their contemporary continuation*, "Journal of Classical Sociology" 2006, vol. 6, no. 3 and J. Woleński, *Leon Petrażycki o prawie i moralności*, Roczniki Polskiej Akademii Umiejętności, 2016/2017.

twists of history of the Central and Eastern Europe at the turn and early years of the 20th century.

However, it is hard to overestimate Petrazycki's importance for the Polish 20-century science. There are references to Petrazycki in the works of the most renowned Polish philosophers, including Kazimierz Twardowski, Kazimierz Ajdukiewicz, Tadeusz Kotarbiński and many other outstanding representatives of the humanities, social sciences or law. The prominent Polish philosophers, social scientists and law theorists dealing with the issues of legal policy included, for example, Maria Borucka-Arctowa, Kazimierz Opałek, Adam Podgórecki, Sławomira Wronkowska and Jerzy Wróblewski.

Jerzy Wróblewski is one of the most exquisite representatives of the Polish post-war theory of law. The analytical acquis of the Lviv-Warsaw school is significant for Wróblewski's methodology and scientific research tools[3]. However, there are traces of fascination with Petrazycki's concepts in the text and resources of the most significant of Wróblewski's works. Wróblewski was familiar with those works of Petrazycki which survived the war. Even more important for Jerzy Wróblewski's work was activity of the scholars Bronisław Wróblewski (Jerzy's father) and Jerzy Lande, who knew Petrazycki directly.[4].

Wróblewski's works are set in the analytical trend characteristic for the Polish post-war theory of law[5]. Wróblewski' scientific activity constitutes a consistent and coherent system built throughout many years, comprising theoretical, methodological, semiotic and axiological aspects of law. Wróblewski's main areas of

---

3 First of all the concepts by Kazimierz Ajdukiewicz.

4 After the World War Two, the activity continued only by Lande at Jagiellonian University in Cracow (Wróblewski was Lande's assistant).

5 Polish post-war theory of law was fundamentally different from the philosophy of law in terms of objectives and principles. The primary objective of the theory of law was to formulate scientific theorems or methodological directives referring to legal phenomena, whereas the philosophy aimed at explanation of the ontological, gnoseological or eschatological assumptions of these phenomena. Theoretic works of that time are characterized by: philosophical minimalism, emphasising the scientific nature of law studies and jurisprudence, as well as linguistic and logical methodology. While remaining theoretical, Wróblewski avoided straightforward philosophical declarations, although he accused Petrazycki's theory - and, indirectly, the positivist theory of law - of aphilosophism, cf. J. Wróblewski, *Leon Petrażycki - pozytywizm filozoficzny i antypozytywizm prawniczy*, Studia Prawnicze 1982, z 3–4, pp. 7–8. According to Wróblewski, any theoretic orientation has philosophical grounds; the same *Postawa filozoficzna i afilozoficzna we współczesnej teorii prawa,* Studia Prawnicze, 1966, z. 13, p. 84 et seq.

interest in this field were the scientific nature and normativity of legal studies, languages related to law and normative or optimisation modelling of law making and application processes; in the last period of his work, also the axiology of law.[6].

The subject matter and concept of the scientific programme, consistency and passion in its implementation, as well as the breadth and multi-faceted nature of the area of Wróblewski's research remind Petrazycki's legal policy project. It can be assumed that for Wróblewski, the concept of legal theory was a source of inspiration and later a reference point for theories he created and developed throughout decades of his scientific activity. Philosophical and theoretical aspects of relation between Petrazycki's legal policy and Wróblewski's theory of law are subject of further considerations, where – as it should be emphasized – the issue of relations and competitiveness of both concepts was treated as a contribution to a full analysis of the associations between the concepts of both scientists.

2 Genesis and Assumptions of Petrazycki's Legal Policy

The idea of the science which Petrazycki later named legal policy originated in one of his earlier works, written in German at that time – „Die Fruchtverteilung beim Wechsel der Nutzungsberechtigten"[7]. The analysis of the rules of the distribution of income between the owner and the bona-fide holder as well as the division of dowry under the Roman law led Petrazycki to conclude that legal regulations are strictly associated with politics and economic practice of the Roman Empire. Demonstrating the link between the rules on the distribution of income under Roman law and the activities of latifundia owners, drew attention to the issue which the other researchers had not previously recognized, namely the motivational function of the law.

The key to formulating the scientific programme of the new discipline turned out to be Petrazycki's observation that the solutions adopted by Roman legislators were solely the result of the impact of environmental phenomena or external pressure on jurisprudence and not the outcome of conscious legislation.

---

6 Wróblewski focused on the problem of law making and application of law especially in the end of his scientific career, publishing (regardless of numerous articles) three monographies focusing solely on these issues: *Teoria racjonalnego tworzenia prawa*, Wrocław 1985, *Zasady tworzenia prawa*, Warsaw 1989 and *Sądowe stosowanie prawa*, issue I, Warsaw 1972; issue II, Warsaw 1988.

7 Berlin 1982. At that time Petrazycki was a holder of a scholarship by Russian government in Berlin, a seminarist of an outstanding Roman and civil law scholar, Heinrich Demburg.

Petrazycki, in a way reversing the perspective of the relations analysed, indicated the possibility to consciously enact such a law whose validity would produce real effects, planned and intended by the legislator (mental, social, economic or other). What is more – and proves the uniqueness and primacy of his concept – Petrazycki claimed (and aimed at proving it in his further works) that it was possible to create science whose focus would be learning all the aspects of psycho-social operation of law in order to construct a scientific, ethical and praxeological model of the legislator.

Petrazycki developed the theses fundamental for the commencement of the project of establishing legal policy in „Die Lehre vom Einkommen[8]", where the civil law institutions, well-known to the lawyers contemporary to Petrazycki, became a starting point and a contribution to reflect on the importance of the legislator's expertise in the process of making law and forecasting the results of the legislator's social activity. In „Die Lehre vom Einkommen" Petrazycki introduced the ideas fundamental for his concept: social ideal, tasks and methods of (civil) politics[9] and formulated the thesis that it is possible to build civil politics (later named legal policy), based on scientifically justified knowledge on the effects of law on human psyche. He wrote: "conscious politics should lead to faster and qualitatively better development than common law"[10]. It takes a long time before the countless repetitive social facts gradually crystallize into certain feelings and instinctive aspirations, and such aspirations gradually condense into legal views, finally turning into positive law; this time is lost in vain and can

8 *Die Lehre wom Einkommen.Vom standpunkt des gemeinen Civilrechts unter Berücksichtigung des Entwurfs eines bürgerlichen Gesetzbuche für das Deutsche Reich*, vol. 1 and II, Berlin 1893 and 1895.

9 Petrazycki used the term: motivationspolitik (Introduction to volume 2 Die Lehre vom Einkommen).

10 It has been emphasised that it is not accidental that the first works of Petrazycki which referred to this concept were written in Germany, as - according to Petrazycki - German scientific community was better prepared (than the Russian community) for this innovative idea. As emphasised by Petrazycki himself, the main aim of his monographes in German was not solving any particular issues but proving the need for creation and effective operation of legal policy, cf. А.В. Малько, В.А. Затонский, Правовая политика: основы теории и практики. Учебно-методический комплекс, Москва 2015, s. 86 (A.V. Malko, V.A. Zatonsky, Legal policy: the fundamentals of theory and practice. Training and metodological complex, Moscow 2015, p. 86).

only be saved if we are aware of the need to create a proper legal norm (progress acceleration).[11].

It is astonishing that those early German works of Petrazycki, less than 30 years old at that time, already contained all elements and ideas significant for his future scientific career[12]. From that point on, the main scientific aim of Petrazycki (considering his immense involvement and extensive achievements, one might say it was also his life goal) has been the construction of the science (theory) of law policy. Such autonomous and multifaceted discipline required, according to Petrazycki, changes in the practice (paradigm) of legal sciences, psychological ethics, social sciences and methodology, so that they constituted an adequate foundation for the proposed discipline[13]. Petrazycki has devoted nearly all his later works to this task.

The essence of legal policy issues, Petrazycki wrote in "Introduction to the teachings of law and morality", was supposed to consist in "scientifically sound anticipation of the consequences to be expected in the event of the introduction of certain legal provisions and the development of rules whose introduction into the legal system would give rise to certain desired effects"[14]. The mission of the future science, on the other hand, was to "consciously lead humanity in the same direction which it had hitherto followed on the path of unconscious empirical adaptation, as well as to properly accelerate and rectify the pursuit of the "great luminous ideal of the future" (meaning the ideal of love)"[15].

Implementing the intention of reconstructing the science announced in the earliest works, Petrazycki proposed introducing new method to the area of legal sciences; he called it a legal-political method, consisting in combining

---

11 L. Petrażycki, Polityka cywilna a prawo zwyczajowe [in:] Leon Petrażycki, *O prawie, nauce i moralności. Pisma wybrane,* Warsaw 1985, p. 359.

12 It is characteristic that a note has been preserved, written by Petrażycki, coming from the "Berlin" period of his creative path (i.e. first half of the 90s of the 19th century) "The development takes place in an unconscious way. Legal policy is supposed to operate consciously through studying the motivational and educational impact of the legal norms"; (J. Licki, *Motywacyjne i wychowawcze działanie prawa jako podstawa naukowej polityki prawa* in *Prawo w społeczeństwie,* ed. J. Kurczewski, Warszawa 1975, s. 233 i 234).

13 As regards various areas of law, such as for example the criminal or civil law, Petrazycki underlined the universal nature of the legal policy programme, but emphasised that each of these areas may be a subject to separate policy constituting an element of the whole legal policy system.

14 L. Petrażycki, *Wstęp do nauki prawa i moralności,* Warsaw 1968, p. 13.

15 Ibidem,, p. 16.

two empirical areas of studies of the psycho-social aspects of law, specified by the author as motivational and educational functions of law. In accordance with these two types of the impact of law on the human psyche, the tasks of the legislator practising law policy based on scientific premises narrowed down – according to Petrazycki – to the rational management of individual and social behaviour by inducing motives for desired behaviour and perfecting the human psyche and cleansing it from the antisocial features and habits.

Therefore, Petrazycki moved towards the psychosocial functions of law which in a way resulted in his questioning and rejecting the positivist paradigm of legal sciences and considering law a psychic phenomenon in the original form of psychological theory of law, familiar not only to the researchers of his legacy. Rejecting his contemporary understanding of law and modernization of the manner of practising legal sciences required that Petrazycki constructed an appropriate theory and terminology – the issue Petrazycki was very aware of, as he emphasized that the current science is not and may not constitute a foundation for building the science of legal policy. To implement this task, Petrazycki claimed the following steps necessary:

- establishing the scientific model of law and preparing adequate scientific methodology for legal sciences,
- revision of the current manner of understanding law and examining particular legal phenomena (law as a real phenomenon accessible for scientific cognition), associated with creating new theory of law, ethics, social science,
- constructing methodology of legal policy.

These tasks were consistently implemented in Petrażycki's works. Unfortunately, only a few are known and quoted, as "Sociology" – the work which was the complement, and maybe the greatest and, at this time, the most innovative element of this monumental project, was lost.

3 Methodology of Science According to Petrazycki

Methodology of Petrazycki's science is the original contribution of the author in the field of social sciences. Petrazycki rejected his contemporary classification of science and based his proposal on the semantic characteristics[16]. Observation was supposed to be the basic research method in learning and creating the

16 J. Wróblewski, *Język a nauka w teorii Leona Petrażyckiego* in: *Z zagadnień teorii prawa i teorii nauki Leona Petrażyckiego. Studia opracowane dla upamiętnienia stulecia urodzin*, ed. K. Opałek, Warsaw 1969, pp. 179–180.

concepts of particular psychic phenomena, thus Petrazycki's concept of legal terms. Petrazycki points out to introspection as the appropriate method of observation. Further stage in shaping scientific theories is constructing general terms, specified as class terms in Petrazycki's terminology. Thus, according to Petrazycki, a scientific theory could only be a judgement (statement) or a group of true judgements (statements) referring to the class defined by the concept, whereas the statements in the group should be adequate. According to Petrazycki, not all class statements were of scientific value. Only the adequate statements – "neither the limping, nor the jumping ones", as he vividly described – had this value. The aim of adequacy theory was to create class terms independent of the names applied in colloquial language and free from their vagueness. According to Petrazycki, the appropriate (adequate) legal theory allowed to draw the correct conclusions regarding the impact of legislative actions[17].

4 Psychological (Psycho-social) Foundations and Functions of Law According to Petrazycki

The scientific policy of law was supposed to derive the knowledge necessary to construct teleological directives from the psychological theory of law. For Petrazycki, law was a psychic phenomenon, whose designate was a certain phenomenon occurring in the person's consciousness, which Petrazycki called impulsion. Psychic dimension of the legal or moral principles consisted in the fact that the perceived or imagined behaviour of a person, according to Petrazycki, released appropriate emotion, which, in turn, modified the intellectual content of this behaviour, giving the judgement a practical characteristic of an obligation. Modified characteristics of someone's judgement were projective in nature, originating in the inner world of a person. For Petrazycki, the only real equivalent (designate) of law was the experience which included the image of certain behaviour and the accompanying impulsion. If it was only an obligation which was the content of the mental experience, Petrazycki considered it a legal norm. If the experience was accompanied by entitlement (understood as possibility to demand certain conduct from another person), it was considered a legal norm[18].

17 L. Petrażycki, *Tworzenie pojęć klasowych i budowanie teorii naukowych* in: L. Petrażycki, *O nauce, prawie i moralności…*, p. 37 et seq.

18 L. Petrażycki, *Teoria prawa i państwa w związku z teorią moralności*, vol. 1–2, Warsaw 1959–1960.

Thus, law had a real and attributive-imperative dimension for Petrazycki. According to Petrazycki, law and morality complemented each other, although Petrazycki claimed that more complex nature of legal norms contributes to shaping social attitudes to a much greater extent than morality does. The power of motivational pressure, according to Petrazycki, stemmed from the fact that "the sense of duty of action in the human psyche was accompanied by the conviction that someone is entitled to these actions, even though they constitute realization of a duty." According to Petrazycki, this additional motivational pressure did not occur in morality, whose casual function he perceived to be of a lesser importance.

The legal policy required revising the current understanding of law (its creation and development) as the product of social adaptation, i.e. not only a psychological issue. Petrazycki discussed the issues of psychological, or rather psycho-social functioning of law in his next work, "Sociology" – unfortunately lost during World War Two. Certain concepts presenting the assumptions of Petrażycki's sociology of law may be reconstructed from his earlier works. In this field, Petrazycki distinguished the social functions of law, such as: division and exchange of material and cultural goods and the organisation of a society for production, exchange of social tasks and other tasks. He considered other functions of law to be derivative. These included motivational and educational function, important from the point of view of legal policy.

For Petrazycki, enacting legislation with a specific content caused certain legal experience in the human psyche, which in turn resulted in the emergence of certain social – not only individual – attitudes and behaviours. In his opinion, educational function was socially integrating, allowing individuals to adapt better in the increasingly larger groups, as well as fostering cultural or civilizational progress. In such an approach to the function of the law, the legislative activity should not be limited to ordering or prohibiting such conducts, but having such influence on the addressees of the law that the implementation of the factual situation assumed by the legislator has become their preferred action due to the dispositions imprinted by law in the human psyche. Petrazycki, despite the strong psychologism of his concept, noticed the important relation between the legal experience and their projections in the form of legal norms and the social phenomena shaped by cultural conditions.[19].

19 K. Frieske, *Leona Petrażyckiego teoria czy socjologia prawa* in: *Prawo w społeczeństwie…*, p. 128.

5 Petrazycki's Ethics and Social Ideal Imperative

Petrazycki understood the legislative activity based on a political and legal method as a measure to achieve overall objective, a social ideal specified as the love ideal which the other instrumental objectives are subordinate to. Petrazycki, who believed in ethical and social progress of humankind and was inspired by the theory of evolution and Darwinism, claimed that individual adaptation to life by a human being, similar to other species, had taken place due to unconscious association of the repetitive apulsive or repulsive experience. He believed that stimulating those processes was supposed to lead to – as it is in the case of organisms avoiding harmful substances – a better social adaptation of human beings and, consequently, progress of mankind. According to Petrazycki, the ultimate developmental aim of the human psyche was the love ideal.

Although Petrazycki's optimism may seem unjustified, he pointed out to the communicative and non-normative dimension of law much more often than his contemporary scholars. However, he perceived the dimension in the environmental and behavioural conditions characteristic for positivists. According to Petrazycki, the constant communication and exchange of experience between people resulted in certain fixed emotional adaptations being imprinted in their minds. This process, according to Petrazycki, has so far been spontaneous, although its result was the cultural and ethical progress, different in every historical period.

The human circle where the exchange of information and experience occurred has expanded during his times. He perceived this a positive phenomenon, which, through exchange of information and mutual experience (and, given the social functions of law indicated by Petrazycki, the tangible and intangible goods as well) would lead to abolishing all social divisions and the triumph of the ethics based on love ideal in the future. He wrote that the process of the emergence of "the subjective power of the good" in the minds of the individuals, as well as in the collective psyche, in the form of "permanently crystallized creations of love" constituted the essence of progress and culture[20].

In Petrazycki's projection, the realization of this ideal and the eradication of individual egoisms was to result in the disappearance of legal and moral norms[21]. Thus, law and morality were necessary to Petrazycki only due to inadequate adaptation of human psyche to the real social relations. Hence, scientific legal policy was only to serve rationalization and acceleration of the adaptation processes in

20 L. Petrażycki, *Wstęp do nauki polityki prawa,* Warsaw 1968, pp. 43–44.
21 L. Petrażycki, *O filozofii,* Warsaw 1939, p. 20.

the period of transition in order to eliminate social costs of the evolution, carried out in a spontaneous manner so far. He emphasized at this point that the legal policy (in order to be effective) has to take into account the achieved level of social development and the legal system it is supposed to function in, thus rejecting the possibility to formulate ahistoric laws and statements. Neither he absolutized the legal values, pointing out that from the educational and motivational perspective not every law may have a positive impact. In certain conditions, law may be demoralising, encouraging the progress that is socially harmful.

6 Policy of Law According to Wróblewski

The concept of legal policy is based on assumption that the activity of an employer or the entity applying the law is a deliberate and rational activity. Similar to Petrazycki, Wróblewski held the view that rational creation or adaptation of law is necessary to obtain the desired social effects, or at least better than expecting their spontaneous realization. As pointed out by Wróblewski, these elements highlighted the rational basis for each of the concepts of legal policy, consisting in the possibility of reasonable human activity leading to achievement of the social objectives through the appropriate creation and application of the law[22].

For Wróblewski, legal policy, constituting a selected (also in scientific terms) part of social policy, was a broader field than the theory of law and the field of jurisprudence which constituted a subject of his interest[23]. Undoubtedly, as Wróblewski wrote himself, he did not share part of Petrazycki's ontological and epistemological concepts, rejecting especially psychologism and the psychological manner of perception, in favour of an analytical, directive concept of language. In turn, the issue of methodology and scientific accuracy of the constructed theories was at least as important for Wróblewski, as it was for Petrazycki and although Wróblewski had the opportunity to use the assistance of much better developed and mature methodology, he did not reproach Petrazycki for that. On the contrary, he emphasized that the scientific significance of Petrazycki's concepts lies in the fact that they form a system whose elements stimulate scientific reflection, although some of the ideas or claims are

---

22 K. Opałek, J. Wróblewski, *Zagadnienia teorii prawa*, Warsaw 1969, p. 191 et seq.

23 Thus, in his concepts, Wróblewski did not use the term "legal concept"; instead, within the field of his research interests, he replaced it with the terminology he considered scientifically adequate and relevant to his concepts: theory, rules, system.

no longer valid.[24]. However, Wróblewski did not agree with Petrazycki's psychologism and considered it useless in the analytical approach to law. He noticed and appreciated the potential contained in Petrazycki's concepts which stepped beyond the areas of linguistic-logical, semantic or normative justification of legal norms and reasoning.[25]

Wróblewski considered "legal policy" in a broad manner, namely, as "using the law" to achieve the aims set by some socially relevant entity. Scientific or legal policy claims (or statements, as specified by Wróblewski) may be instrumentally or systemically relativized; consequently, a minimalistic (technical, instrumental) or maximalistic (evaluatory) scope of this discipline is specified[26].

In the minimalistic version, the tasks of legal policy would be limited to the instrumental assessments and requirements, i.e. indication which legal rules constitute the most instrumentally appropriate measure to achieve the intended aim. Thus, legal policy in the minimalistic version constituted a set of instrumentally relativized expressions, remaining in logical relations with each other, bound with the intended aim. Wróblewski perceived the scientific nature of that version of legal policy similarly to the issue of the scientific nature of any technique.[27]

In Wróblewski's concept, the minimalistic legal policy, apart from instrumental aims, included indicating axiology of the system. The expressions of the maximalistic version of legal policy contain the systemically relativized expressions (statements), as well as the non-relativized claims which are not of scientific nature whatsoever. The foundations of the systemic axiology of legal policy were supposed to be the statements and evaluations formulated in them, justified by the system of values in force in a given social system, as well as the statements and evaluations that could be derived from the former ones (using Wróblewski's terminology – instrumentally relativized). In Wróblewski's opinion, the conformity of the statements with particular elements of the axiological system is expressed in the formulation of appropriate phrases stating this conformity or the occurrence of an inference relationship.

Wróblewski claimed that a maximalistic version of the legal policy is also possible to be developed scientifically, however in the sphere of axiology only

---

24 Wróblewski considered Petrażycki a pioneer of the theory of law; J. Wróblewski, *Filozofia, metodologia i antypozytywizm prawniczy Petrażyckiego*, Studia Filozoficzne 1983, no.10, p. 23.

25 Ibidem.

26 Ibidem. Cf. also K. Opałek, J. Wróblewski, *Zagadnienia teorii prawa…*, p. 90 and 91.

27 J. Wróblewski in: K. Opałek, J. Wróblewski, *Prawo, metodologia, filozofia, teoria prawa*, Warsaw 1991, p. 45.

the statements that are systemically relativized to the system of values adopted by the legislator (secondary evaluation). According to Wróblewski, the primary evaluation constructing the system and catalogue of values, into which relativization occurred, was not an element of legal policy, but a part of ethics or social policy.[28].

7 Theories of Rational Lawmaking and Application of Law

Policy of law in Wróblewski's concept has been divided into three sections:

1) policy of lawmaking,
2) policy of applying law,
3) policy of using the competence granted to specific entities, other than the bodies making or applying competence law, denoted as "law implementation policy"[29].

The lawmaking policy was supposed to consist in establishing legal norms (rules, as specified by Wróblewski) used for realization of the objectives intended by the legislator[30]. For Wróblewski, the policy of applying law was closely correlated and, in a way, assigned to the policy of lawmaking as an area of normative and praxeological implementation of the objectives adopted by the legislator.

The third type of policy, i.e. the law enforcement policy, remained beyond the interest of the lawmaker, as it concerned the sphere not subject to systemic modelling and scientific stimulation. The "law enforcement" policy depended, to a large extent, on the activity of various entities or bodies which were granted some autonomy or freedom in competence by law. The author indicated civil law, due to its dominant method of regulation consisting in a broad use of competences, and criminal law, in the sphere of execution of punishment, as the fields of law where such a policy would apply.[31].

The models presented in Wróblewski's works – a model of rational legislation and the model of law application – were supposed to create theoretical, scientific and methodological foundations of two classic areas of the positivistic concept of legal policy: lawmaking and operative and non-operative application of law. The suggested division was based on a formal and normative

28 Ibidem,, p. 120.
29 J. Wróblewski, *Teoria racjonalnego*.... pp. 50, 51 oraz *Zasady tworzenia prawa*..., p. 36.
30 J. Wróblewski, *Teoria racjonalnego*..., p. 50
31 Ibidem, p. 51 and p. 37 and 38.

distinction between the spheres of making and applying law, classic in terms of legal positivism. Such a distinction, characteristic for continental law systems at the times when Wróblewski's concept was formed, had ideological and doctrinal grounds. Wróblewski has not directly questioned the validity of this convention in the Polish legal doctrine, however stressed that the issue of separating lawmaking from application of law is very questionable. Neither he found any justification for such delimitation of normative and dogmatic arguments. Therefore, the criterion of separation of the spheres of lawmaking and law application adopted by Wróblewski was different from the one functioning in the legal dogmatics.

Wróblewski considered lawmaking to be "establishment of rules which are abstract and general (enough)" and application of law as "establishing individual and specific rules based on the abstract and general rules"[32].

From the point of view of the feasibility of achieving legal policy assumptions and objectives, Wróblewski emphasized the primacy of statutory law, underlining that it is the law – acting as a measure of social control – which has a motivational effect on the addressees. Only in the case when it is not (motivationally) effective or there are doubts regarding qualification of certain situation, there are premises for launching judicial application of law[33]. In his model, Wróblewski assumed (as idealization) a full and in a way one-direction communication between a general and abstract legal rule formulated in a lawmaking decision and an individual and specific rule contained in the decision of the operative application of law. For Wróblewski, the main area of application of the law enforcement policy were cases of discretional freedom in examination proceedings (*sensu stricto* application of law) or enforcement proceedings (e.g. enforcement of judgments of criminal courts or civil courts)[34] and by private entities (*sensu largo* application of law)[35].

---

32 J. Wróblewski, *Sądowe stosowanie prawa…*, pp. 403 and 404. However, Wróblewski noticed and broadly discussed the issue of "judicial lawmaking" (especially in terms of interpretation of law and freedom of decision), pointing out not only the theoretical significance of this division, but the relation between both spheres. J. Wróblewski, *Problems of judicial reasoning in civil law and common law systems: some reflections on Julius Stone's approach*, Bulletin of the Australian Society of Legal Philosophy, v.10, no.38/39, 1986, pp.187–202.

33 J. Wróblewski, *Sądowe stosowanie prawa…*, pp. 373 and 374.

34 For Wróblewski, judicature is the most important field of law application policy.

35 Szerzej J. Wróblewski, *Sądowe stosowanie…*, chapter 13, p. 357 et seq.

8 Rationality as the Foundation of Policy of Law

The rationality of human actions binds the theories of Petrazycki and Wróblewski. For Petrazycki and Wróblewski alike, action meant intended activity, deliberately focused on achieving certain aim. The consciousness of action and its objectives was a derivative of knowledge.[36] For Petrazycki, the science able to provide an adequate theory describing psychosocial functions and effects of law (scientific criterion, empirical criterion) was the most important determinant of rationality.

Analytical concepts, especially the views of K. Ajdukiewicz, affected Wróblewski's perception of rationality[37]. For Wróblewski, learning (discovering) law and its application (impact) are done through language (normative criterion, communication criterion[38]). The concept of rationality used by Wróblewski remains in a significant relation with the structure and use of language, especially the rationality constituting the assumption of the normative theory of interpretation.

The notion of rationality functioning in Polish law studies can be specified as a counterfactual assumption that an entity making a socially or legally important decision is guided by knowledge and preferences that can be ascertained and justified by scientific methods.[39] Such knowledge included strict and verifiable methodological assumptions concerning the discernment of the decision-maker in a regulated or interpreted environment. Analytical and logical knowledge bases, e.g. assumptions of non-contradictory statements, exclusion, asymmetry, transient preferences, etc. play an important role here. The logical structure of

---

36 Methodological requirements of rationality, including the accuracy of expression, respecting the requirements of logic and appropriate empirical justification. Reference to the standards of rationality in Polish science - cf. K. Szaniawski, *Racjonalność jako wartość* in: *O nauce, rozumowaniu i wartościach*, Warsaw 1993, p. 532 et seq.

37 Whose views are considered to be an important source foe the scientific inspiration of Wróblewski. According to Ajdukiewicz, these are: intersubjective communication of the content of scientific opinions using a clear and explicit language, as well as intersubjective verifiability of these opinions by recreation and review of the conditions they function in. For Ajdukiewicz, the criterion of intersubjectivity, assuming the social and deliberative nature of scientific knowledge, was an indicator of rationality.

38 M. Zirk-Sadowski, *Pozytywizm prawniczy a filozoficzna opozycja podmiotu i przedmiotu poznania* in: *Studia z filozofii prawa*, ed. J. Stelmach, Kraków 2001, pp. 84–85; (the same) *Legal Epistemology and Transformation of Legal Cultures* in: *Epistemology and Methodology of Comparative Law*, Brussel 2004.

39 Cf. L. Nowak, *Interpretacja prawnicza. Studium z metodologii prawoznawstwa*, Warsaw 1973, p. 39 et seq.

knowledge is developed in particular groups of assumptions intellectual and axiological (e.g. linguistic rationality, juridical rationality) and other assumptions concerning general or specific knowledge.[40]

From a sociolinguistic perspective close to Wróblewski, rationality may be perceived as a certain structure (system) displaying certain features, adding sense to the actions undertaken within its scope, in which certain statements, assessments and values co-exist, relevant to the making of legal decisions. There are various factors determining this sense, where various interactions occur between the sensorigenic structures and their subjects (institutional approach to rationality). Rationality may also be considered as a certain idealistic aim of the cognitive process. In such approach rationalization of law consists in adopting certain criteria jointly determining its safety and security, implementing methodological directives on the one hand and restricting the freedom to use it on the other[41].

Constructs of methodological rationality used by Wróblewski in the theory of lawmaking refer to justification of the decision (methodological rationalism)[42]. He indicates rational lawmaker as a lawmaker who selects proper means for the assumed aim due to possessed knowledge and assumed preferences[43]. Wróblewski emphasizes that the assumption of lawmaker's rationality is not specific for law and relates to any human activity and the conditions of its rationality.

Wróblewski distinguishes two types of rationality of the lawmaking process (lawmaking decisions): internal rationality and external rationality. The internal rationality of a decision is a situation in which a decision is justified due to the knowledge and preferences of the legislator. External rationality is granted to those legislative decisions which have been accepted (justified) by a critic[44].

---

40 More: Z. Ziembiński, *Wstęp do aksjologii dla prawników*, Warsaw 1990, pp. 162–169; J. Wróblewski, *Teoria racjonalnego…* pp. 60–64. Wróblewski acknowledges the benefits resulting from the construct of rational legislator, but criticises the assumption of its ideal, emphasising the necessity to include the subjective elements of the legal system and the role of dogmatics and legal practice in exposing the imperfections of the statutory law, cf. J. Wróblewski, *Teoria racjonalnego…*,. 63.

41 Cf. J. Wróblewski, *Wartości a decyzja sądowa*, Wrocław 1973, chapter 4; *Funkcje prawa a pewność prawa*, Studia Prawno Ekonomiczne, 1974, vol. 13, pp. 12–14, *Sądowe stosowanie…*, p. 326–332.

42 K. Opałek, J. Wróblewski, *Zagadnienia teorii prawa…*, p. 89, J. Wróblewski, *Teoria racjonalnego…*, p. 65 et seq.

43 J. Wróblewski, *Teoria racjonalnego….*, p. 57.

44 J. Wróblewski, *Proceduralne wartości tworzenia prawa*, Studia Prawno-Ekonomiczne, 1981, col. XXVII, p. 49 et seq.

For Wróblewski, if a decision is justified, it is synonymous to rationality[45]. In terms of internal rationality, it covers the correctness of reasoning constituting elements of the decision-making process in the circumstances of the premises accepted by the court. In terms of external rationality, it covers the elements referring to the legislator, case law, legal practice, the rule of law or elements outside the system.[46] Apart from the difficulty in differentiating the criteria of internal and external rationality of applying law, the assessment of rationality of the judicial application of law undoubtedly combines various methodological, normative and axiological elements discussed in the aforementioned assumptions of the so-called deep structure of lawmaking. The consequence of adopting such stance is the conclusion that any decision by the legislator or the entities applying the law aimed at realization of various social aims, even if such decisions seem rational or effective to some extent, may not be considered legal policy until they are based on properly justified assumptions or will not comply with the sociotechnical directives based on these claims.

The rational legislator relies on the assumption that the aim they are pursuing is valuable due to a certain perspective[47]. For Wróblewski, science is the depository of knowledge as a premise for a rational decision.[48]

Knowledge, which is both a foundation and an instrument of rationalization (including the application of law) of lawmaking (justification or criticism of lawmaking decisions) comprises two resources in Wróblewski's concept: factual knowledge and instrumental knowledge. Factual cognition is strictly scientific and results in the statements allowing to justify the instrumental rules providing the knowledge about how to achieve given goals. Instrumental cognition (knowledge) serves to formulate social engineering directives based on the regularities established in factual cognition. A factor complicating instrumental

---

45 J. Wróblewski, *Uzasadnienie aktu prawodawczego*, Państwo i Prawo, 1987 z. 1, p. 22 et seq *Uzasadnienie i wyjaśnienie decyzji sądowej*, Studia Prawno-Ekonomiczne, vol. XVI, 1976, p. 7 et seq *Justicication of Legal decision*, Revus Intern. Philospohie, 1979, pp. 127–128; *Meaning and Truth of Judicial Decision*, Helsinki 1983, pp. 56–59.

46 Cf. J. Wróblewski, *Sądowe*…, pp. 262–268.

47 The choice of particular aim depends on the knowledge of the reality phenomena and the measures available to the legislator, as well as on the assumed preferences (Wróblewski indicates that the rational legislator does not set themselves any goals which may not be attained on the grounds of the available knowledge or are in conflict with other aims or system of values the legislator relies on).

48 J. Wróblewski, *Polityka tworzenia prawa a hierarchia wartości*, Państwo i Prawo, z. 9, 1983, p. 27.

cognition is the fact that, according to Wróblewski, technical directives can be assessed both from the point of view of their effectiveness, efficiency, accuracy, as well as from the perspective of a certain system of values. The factual cognition, instrumental cognition and their axiological conditions constitute three dimensions of the basis for lawmaking.[49]

Wróblewski, in a manner characteristic for all his works, modifies and complements his earlier concepts with new threads. Inspired by the achievements of cybernetics, he presents the processes of lawmaking and application as elements of a complex cybernetic system, which serves to achieve homeostatic and instrumental goals (law as a social homeostasis[50]). In such modelling, the aim of a rational legislator is for the law to become an instrument providing an optimal level of control within a given social system.

In the later works, the communicative dimension of law became increasingly important for Wróblewski. In this dimension, lawmaking was perceived as a complex and multidirectional "dialogue" between the legislator and the addressees as the entities equipped with, according to Wróblewski, "appropriate" communicative rationality.[51] In this aspect Wróblewski notices the function of science in a positivistic aspect. In the complex, dynamic relations between the legislator and the addressees, science was supposed to be a rationalizing and optimizing factor, serving the purpose of verification of the cognitive assumptions adopted in the lawmaking process. The ongoing revolution fosters the growth of managerial tendencies exposing the role of science in solving social issues (social engineering).

For Wróblewski, science is something more than just a tool for supplying an instrumental/socio-technical knowledge. Scientific nature is to serve both the formal values such as rationality and efficiency, but also the material aims.[52] This approach emphasizes not only the function of knowledge and science understood in a subjective manner, but, first and foremost, the socially involved and responsible role of researchers as rationalizing (external) lawmaking experts. As

---

49 J. Wróblewski, *Zasady tworzenia…*, pp. 73.

50 J. Wróblewski, *Prawo a homeostaza społeczna*, Państwo i Prawo, z. 12 Z. 1982, p. 30 et seq.

51 J. Wróblewski, *Materialne i proceduralne aspekty prawa*, Studia Prawno-Ekonomiczne, vol 9, 1990, p. 27. In this communicative perspective, the concept of a rational legislator may be perceived as idealization indicating the necessary conditions of the acts of speech formulated in the legal discourse (cf. M. Zirk-Sadowski, *Prawo a uczestniczenie w kulturze*, Łódź 1998, pp. 87–92).

52 J. Wróblewski, *Proceduralne wartości tworzenia…*, p. 55.

emphasized by Wróblewski, in his defence of the objective value of legal policy, "the scientic ideology of lawmaking assumes a scientific value, not as politically entangled as democracy"[53].

Similar formulas and conditions of rationality in Wróblewski's works refer to the sphere of the application of law, although the scholar notices the differences between the requirements and expectations justifying the decision to make law and to apply law[54]. He remains on the grounds of a classic separation between the spheres of making and applying law, denying the possibility of basing the decision of applying law solely on the other judicial decision or scientific opinion (doctrine). For Wróblewski, rationality was not only the domain of experience and empirical and methodological criteria of justifying the decision of the operative application of law, but also the issue of socially approved and verifiable conditions in which these beliefs have been formulated and communicated (communicative and social aspect)[55].

9 Axiology of Lawmaking and Application of Law

Scientific (linguistic-logical) and normative element of substantiation of the decision is bound by axiology. When discussing the issues of axiology of lawmaking and application of law, Wróblewski avoids the involvement and taking sides of one ethics[56]. According to Wróblewski, the question of valuation in the legal policy refers to the determinants of the choice of objectives adopted by the legislator and the selection of criteria and the evaluation of the measures leading to this objective[57]. The content of this assessments in historical scale is determined by the type of the system of law and particular stage of social development. This includes in particular the base values. In certain legislative phenomena, the assessments are formulated by groups determining the content of legal norms and the values they serve. Generally speaking, such groups are

---

53 Ibidem.

54 J. Wróblewski, *Uzasadnienie aktu prawodawczego*, Państwo i Prawo, 1987, z. 1, p. 22 et seq.; *Justicication of Legal decision*, Revus interne Philospohie, 1979, pp. 127–128; *Meaning and Truth of Judicial Decision*, Helsinki 1983, pp. 56–59.

55 Corresponding to verification criteria formulated in the works of K. Ajdukiewicz, (the same) *Zagadnienia i kierunki filozofii. Teoria poznania, metafizyka*, Warszawa 1983 (2nd edition), p. 72 et seq.

56 M. Ossowska exhibits the accuracy of such allegation towards Petrazycki in: *Socjologia moralności. Zarys zagadnień*, Warszawa 1963, p. 256.

57 J. Wróblewski, *Polityka tworzenia prawa….*, p. 28 et seq

political decision-makers who are in certain specific relations to other social groups, which limit the freedom of legislative decisions.

As indicated by Wróblewski, a perfect solution for the policy of creating the law would be a (scientific) development of such axiological system that would be complete, coherent and hierarchically and systemically ordered. Based on such idealization, it would be possible to formulate requirements to be followed by a rational legislator. They narrow down to the assessment of law as a measure to reach the assumed objectives and the expression of fundamental principles. The first approach leads to the instrumental approach to law, the second – according to Wróblewski – exceeds the model of rational lawmaking, however he emphasizes that instrumentalization of law may not be carried out excluding the fundamental values[58].

Wróblewski characterizes the axiological determinants of the legislator by introducing the concepts of formal values and material values. The formal values consist of: the formal values in the strict sense (rationality and optimality of legislative decisions); the formal resulting values (effectiveness and efficiency of decisions taken by the legislator) and the other formal values (legality). What they have in common is the fact that the legislator should adopt them regardless of the substantive objectives of their activities. Material values, in turn, are all values assumed by the legislator in their activity, except formal values[59].

Addressing the issues of axiology, Wróblewski refers to the social context of the functioning of law, underlining how the "public" policy of law depends on the distribution of attitudes to law in a given society. He considers the knowledge of this distribution – and thus the empirical research on these aspects – as a component of the resource database the rational legislator should rely on. Thus, the evaluatory attitude of the legislator is both rationalized and communicative. At the same time, Wróblewski emphasizes that the use of negative sanctions, which is characteristic for a state coercion, is an effective measure of a social control. However, directly referring to Petrazycki's ideal, the law understood in this way does not have a direct impact even on shaping altruistic attitudes, as it primarily controls the behaviour, not experiences[60].

---

58 Ibidem, p. 36.

59 J. Wróblewski, *Proceduralne wartości tworzenia…*, p. 51 et seq

60 J. Wróblewski, *Teoria racjonalnego…*, p. 58.

10 Models of the Policy of Law

For Polish theorists representing the analytical school, modelling was the basic tool for constructing a scientific theory. As concluded by Wróblewski, the positivistic models shaped by empirical sciences were subject to increasing pressure from "relativistic" models of humanistic models, treating science as a cultural phenomenon.[61] The main criterion differentiating the positivist and neopositivistic scientific concepts was the issue of verification and falsification of the subject of theory (modelling), obviously from a non-cognitive perspective. Wróblewski noticed and accepted the fact that the legal sciences stepped beyond the framework of a positivistic paradigm, which should be associated with rejecting certain positivistic assumptions regarding the essence and functioning of law.

In Wróblewski's works, similar to other Polish legal theorists, modelling is of idealizing nature.[62] The aim of modelling the theory of lawmaking was to systematize and justify the statements or technical directives on how the legislator should proceed. Thus, the scientific model of lawmaking was to contain the minimal conditions to be fulfilled by legislation and specified the directions of solutions based on formal and material values adopted by the legislator. In Wróblewski's concept – similar to Petrazycki's legal policy – the model of rational creation was supposed to be praxeological model, formulating the conditions of effective action. Wróblewski specifies the determinants and sequence of construction of this model as follows:

1) assuming the aim and specifying it to the extent precise enough for the selection of measures serving its achievement,
2) establishing relations between the objectives and the means of achieving them,
3) determining which of the possible means of achieving the stated objective may constitute legal measures,
4) selecting a particular legal measure,
5) determining the form of the legal regulation,
6) establishing legal norms[63].

Wróblewski underlined that the model of rational lawmaking may serve cognitive and practical function. The first is descriptive, the latter normative and thus may be

---

61 Ibidem,, p. 36.

62 With reference to the assumptions and aims of modelling in the Polish theory of law, cf. A. Malinowski, L. Nowak, *Problemy modelowania w teorii prawa*, Państwo i Prawo 1972, z. 2, p. 91.

63 J. Wróblewski, *Teoria racjonalnego…*, p. 132 et seq.

considered a model for the actual legislative activity, therefore serving the assessment of the actual legislative processes.

The aim of legislation is a certain state of affairs the legislator should achieve. From a substantive and, as can be noticed, most general point of view, the author divides the aims into homeostatic, serving to maintain a certain social *status quo*, or instrumental, indicating the directions of transformation of social relations. The aim may be treated as a value itself – in such a case, it is not scientifically justified. The aim, on the other hand, may be justified due to its systemic relativization to a certain system of values or an instrumental relativization to hierarchically higher objectives.

The rational legislator relies on the assumption that, for particular reasons, the pursued aim is valuable to the legislator. The choice of a particular aim depends on the knowledge of the actual events and the measures which the legislator has at hand, as well as on the preferences the legislator adopts. J. Wróblewski indicates that the rational legislator does not set goals which are not attainable on the grounds of available knowledge or in conflict with other aims or systems of value the legislator relies on.

Another component of rational lawmaking is description of the regularities between the objective and the means of achieving it. According to Wróblewski, such regularities are described in the so-called rules of science, linking a number of phenomena using various relations – from the logical, causative to the probable ones. Specifying the legal measures, from all other measures available to the legislator, is at least a two-stage process: a selection of the measures accepted within the conducted policy and from the point of view of a specific legal policy. Wróblewski emphasizes that the legislator should first of all consider whether the legal norms of the objectives, due to axiological or praxeological reasons, will be the best measure to carry out the intentions.

The choice of a certain legal measure takes place once the catalogue of alternative means of action has been established. A specific choice depends on the optimal measure, due to similar selection criteria as in the case of the selection of the legal measures.

Determination of the form of regulation, following the choice of a given legal measure, should be understood as including a given regulation in one of the branches of law.

Formal legislative process provided for in a given legal system and establishing and announcement of a legal act ends the process of rational lawmaking[64].

64 J. Wróblewski, *Teoria racjonalnego…*, p. 75.

In the field of application of law, Wróblewski has distinguished three types of models: descriptive, normative and mixed. Descriptive model constitutes an idealistic presentation of a process or a decision of the judicial application of law in two models. The first is of empirical background – based on theoretical assumptions adopted in this model (a descriptive-generalizing model). The second consists in a description of a judicial application of law as "application of the theory of a higher degree of generalisation" than the theory of the recognized phenomena. The other type – the normative model – constructs the judicial model of application of law. The components of both models constitute a mixed model, with two subtypes: legal and ideological. The legal model is reconstructed based on the norms regulating the judicial application of law, which the legal dogmatics has been responsible for in the first place. Judicial application of law, formulating the directives regulating court activity, determines the features and content of the ideological model[65].

The models referring to the material and procedural aspects of law are worth noting in the concept of modelling the application of law presented by J. Wróblewski. For Wróblewski, the relations between the material and procedural law constituted a significant issue which determined the modelling. Wróblewski, distancing himself from the dogmatic characteristics and the criteria it adopted, considered the delimitation of material law and procedural law as an insurmountable problem and therefore used the terms "material and procedural aspects of law"[66]. As the material aspect he understood the content qualification of the act or conduct, constituting a material element of the assessment made by a particular entity; as a procedural aspect, he meant application of a procedural rule (logical, formal, institutional) to qualification of the importance of this act or conduct, thus constituting – on the grounds of a given procedure – the rule of acknowledgement[67].

Material decision-making model comprises the issues the court has to solve in order to justify its decision. In that sense it is a model of rational decision in application of law. Procedural model treats application of law as the application of procedural rules establishing particular phases of court proceedings. In the material model, the material law (substantive norms) are the resolutory norms (the legal grounds of the final judicial decision regarding application of

---

65 J. Wróblewski, *Sądowe stosowanie*... p. 34–35.

66 As Wróblewski wrote: "it is not justified to include any finite set of rules (standards) in only one of the given types of law"; *Materialne i proceduralne aspekty prawa*..., p. 21.

67 Ibidem.

law). Procedural norms are various type of rules used to establish and clarify all elements necessary to make this decision[68].

In the material model, the final decision of the choice of legal consequences consists in applying the material law (provisions) understood solely as substantial norms (such model has been specified by J. Wróblewski as "clean")[69]. The final decision establishes the substantive and legal consequences of the facts deemed proven in judicial proceedings in a binding manner. Substantive termination of judicial recognition occurs only when the knowledge acquired in judicial recognition is sufficient to apply the substantive law norm(s) as the resolutory norms. The proper procedural model characterizes the judicial proceedings as applying procedural provisions in particular stages of the proceedings. The "clean" version of the model assumes application of substantive law norms in the termination phase of the proceedings, however leaving this aspect aside (ibid.)

The substantive-decisive model assumes correspondence between the content (sense) of the information and its substantive qualification (the case of isomorphy), leaving aside the relation between the manner and conditions of transmission, transfer and reception of information (formal and conventional of its acknowledgement). Thus, substantial idealization does not refer to conventional conditions of recognition. In Wróblewski's concept, substantive correspondence is an expression of the possibility of semantic adequacy of cognition[70].

11 Summary

Petrazycki began the discourse on the possibility to construct the science that would formulate, organize and justify the statements or directives rationalizing and optimizing the processes of lawmaking and law application (legal policy as science)[71]. The reflections of Petrazycki's concept appear in numerous works not only by his students, but also the aquis of Polish philosophy, theory and

68 Ibidem, p. 26.

69 J. Wróblewski, *Sądowe stosowanie*..., p. 42.

70 However, Wróblewski does not address the issue of whether and to what extent the procedural aspects of law determine the sphere of substantive recognition, cf. J. Jaśkiewicz, *Poznanie faktów postępowaniu cywilnym*, Warszawa 2013, pp. 42–43.

71 Petrażycki's reflections on legal awareness, social aims and functions of law and the possibility of using theoretical knowledge of psychophysical processes for practical applications should be regarded as particularly important contribution to the development of contemporary concepts of legal sciences. Petrazycki was also one of the pioneers of the modern methodology of legal and social sciences.

sociology of law. Particularly, such relations are visible in Wróblewski's works on lawmaking and application of law. It is due to the fact that it was Wróblewski who has probably taken up the theoretical and methodological topics discussed in Petrazycki's works to the greatest extent; he did so, however, from the analytical perspectives and in line with his own, autonomous scientific programme[72]. Thus, the content of this works may be, to some extent, considered Wróblewski's answer to Petrazycki's legal policy programme. There are the following common assumptions and requirements present in the concepts by both scholars, referring to the issue in question:

- the requirement of scientific nature (scientism),
- voluntarism,
- possibility of rationalization of law through science,
- acknowledgement of the fact that law is a measure of social control,
- acknowledgement of the fact that law is an expression of legislator's will,
- inclusion of axiology in the field of legal policy.

The issue of the value of knowledge, and the scientific cognition in the first place, is a project of Enlightenment and positivistic philosophy. According to positivists, experience and science were supposed to serve understanding and transformation of the world. Positive philosophy abandoned contemplation in favour of active action and proposed a programme of practical actions based on systematic and scientifically verified knowledge. Like in Comte's adage – *savoir pour previor* – the benefits of this knowledge were to foster social progress. The society of the future was supposed to be rational, their life programmed and organized by science – objective, free from theological restrictions, speculations or other "subjectivity". The scientific and cognitive basis of knowledge were promoted by utilitarianism in particular, with special emphasis on the empirical justification of science, ethics and also law, considered by positivists as one of the most important factors and instruments of action. [73].

72 It should also be remembered that this specific "discourse" between the scholars, who had no chance of meeting each other in person, determined not only ideas and inspirations different in certain aspects, but also the time and conditions of Wróblewski's work

73 Bentham's programme emphasised the causal and, at the same time, motivational functions of law in implementing the supreme aim - providing a maximum amount of happiness to a maximum number of people. It is therefore not without reason to claim that Petrazycki's concept of legal policy was inspired by Bentham's ideas.

Although both Petrazycki and Wróblewski criticized positivism, their concepts refer to the scientific cognitive assumptions of positivism to a large extent. For Petrazycki, the scientific nature, cognitive scientism was first of all a set of methodology tools, a process of objectivization – based on the paradigm of natural sciences – of the subject of cognition and justification of knowledge of the studied phenomena, where empirical evidence: experiments, observation and logical reasoning play the key role. For Petrazycki, law was a real psychosocial phenomenon, studied and recognized using scientific methods[74]. Petrazycki's drew the will to act, faith in the reason and causative power of science and the social progress of humanity from the philosophers of the Enlightenment and positivists. In his opinion, the basis of the planned discipline was to be the fullest possible understanding of the causal action of the law. Such knowledge was supposed to constitute the basic content of that science. Legal policy, similar to other social sciences, should, as Petrazycki emphasized, accumulate the knowledge on the rules of effectiveness of predictions concerning the effects of specific lawmaking, using empirically acquired knowledge concerning the causal and consequential action of law.

Scientific nature and rationalization of the processes of lawmaking and application of law also form a solid foundation of Wróblewski's theory. The determinants of rationality of lawmaking or application of law formulated by Wróblewski constitute the core of the scientific nature of legal policy. Holding analytical ground, Wróblewski refuses Petrazycki's psychologism, without questioning the psychosocial functions and aspects of law. From the non-cognitive perspective, he allows the possibility of scientific description and explanation of factual phenomena creating the resources of knowledge on the legal policy.

For Petrazycki, legal policy was a practical science – not only descriptive. Rationality, viewed from the scientific perspective, was not only a method, but nature and destiny of human beings, who were supposed to use science in their pursuit of perfection regarding themselves and the surrounding world. Rationalization of making and applying law through scientific cognition – thus the legal policy – was a social programme in which exposing the nature of the world through science served its positive transformation[75].

---

74 Petrazycki's scientific and cognitive orientation reflected the assumptions of classic positivism, although his concept of law was anti-positivistic, cf. *A Treatise of Legal Philosophy and General Jurisprudence.* Volume 12, *Legal Philosophy in the Twentieth Century: The Civil Law World*, Tome 1: *Language Areas*, ed. E. Pattaro, C. Roversi, Springer 2016, p. 556.

75 In certain aspects, Petrazycki's programme exhibits similarities to the currents of Marxism criticising the non-activist scientism and formulating a thesis that scientific

For Petrazycki's theory it was also important to liberate from the restrictions of contemporary science and dependency on professional jurisprudence and its mindset. Wróblewski did not put so much emphasis on these aspects, however criticized the programme of legal positivism from the point of view of modernism and neopositivism. Although Wróblewski avoids ideological involvement and does not disclose any assumptions or preferences other than strictly methodological, his understanding of rationality contains positivistic belief that it is possible to improve social reality through science. Thus, he shares Petrazycki's voluntarism and optimism that the spontaneous, particular lawmaking processes can be replaced by rationalized legislation. Hence, both concepts assume the possibility of cause-and-effect operation of law in the social space and implementation of normative projects on a social scale (volunteerism, social engineering).

Focusing on the lawmaking policy, significant for both concepts, assumes the normative system functioning in a classic legislator-addressees' convention, whereas the position of the legislator is sovereign in this system. The knowledge and preferences of a society may be corrected by scientists who program the optimum model of social life and indicate the measures to achieve it[76]. Institutionalized, rational legislator fits the modernistic model of exercising public power where the efficiency and rationality is a feature of administration consisting of professionals and experts precisely executing their professional and social roles.

Rationalization is a process of value judgment for Petrazycki and Wróblewski alike. For Petrazycki, the supreme objective of the legal policy was to improve the human psyche in the direction set by the social ideal, i.e. the ideal of love. Similarly to Kant, or maybe Kant-inspired, Petrazycki believed in progress and solidarity of species[77]. The knowledge constituting the scientific policy of law was supposed to be the highest measure of evaluation of the statutory law and the results obtained through this law accessible for human cognition. In Petrazycki's

cognition is not a practice of creating social awareness understood as objective knowledge of the world, but creating a social self-consciousness which should result in objective, however historically relativized, knowledge of the world. Wróblewski considered this aspect of Petrazycki's concept as Marxist (cf. J. Wróblewski, *Leon Petrażycki: pozytywizm filozoficzny i antypozytywizm prawniczy…*, p. 11). Wróblewski, in turn, referred to the Marxist concept of vanishing of the state and law in his fist works from the 1950s, cf. K. Opałek, J. Wróblewski, *Zagadnienia teorii prawa…*, p. 89.

76 Cf. M. Zirk-Sadowski, *Polityka fiskalna a polityka prawa*, Acta Universitatis Lodziensis, Folia Iuridica 75/2105, p. 15.

77 Cf. I. Kant, *Uzasadnienie metafizyki moralności,* Warsaw 1971, p. 68 et seq.

concept, natural law was replaced by rationality and reason founded on Enlightenment foundation, although not distant from the naturalists' concept.[78]

Axiology (defined as ideology in some works) is also an important aspect of Wróblewski's theoretical concepts, although he neither formulates nor introduces any catalogue of supreme values or imperative[79]. Although Wróblewski can be considered a relativist in the field of axiology, he does not deny the possibility to adopt a certain intersubjective axiological system which would justify the aims, assumptions and claims of the legal policy. The issue of justifying the non-instrumental (independent) values is beyond science, however it may be assumed that Wróblewski considers the "scientific nature" of legal policy and rationality of decisions taken within its framework as independent values. This is because science is more than only a tool of delivering instrumental or socio-technical knowledge. According to Wróblewski, scientific nature is to serve both the formal values such as rationality and efficiency, but also strictly material aims.[80]

For Wróblewski, rationality is a value as such, as it is the source of progress and social homeostasis. Voluntaristic concept of rationality which Wróblewski used in his works combines deterministic and empirical aspects (instrumental rationality) with communicative aspects (discoursive rationality[81]). Wróblewski's works on lawmaking (especially the earlier ones) are dominated by a voluntaristic-instrumental model of law, with the monopoly of an enlightened and rationalized – however fully sovereign – legislator supported by expert knowledge. The scholars, holding various functions at different stages of the lawmaking process, are the guardians of rationality and depositaries of the value which the legislator serves and which is constituted by rationality.

As construed in his later works, with time Wróblewski started to consider the issue of rationality not only on the axis of instrumental communicative relations between will (personified by a sovereign) and reason (represented by science), but also in a broader discoursive perspective between the legislator and the entities applying the law (especially courts). Being well-familiar with the western

78 M. Szyszkowska, *Filozofia prawa i filozofia człowieka,* Warsaw 1972, p. 200.

79 Wróblewski describes himself as a supporter of intersubjectivism, non-cognitivism and "historic relativism of socially determined assessments" (the same) *Materialne i proceduralne aspekty prawa…*, p. 29.

80 J. Wróblewski, *Proceduralne wartości….*, p. 55.

81 On the subject of instrumental and discursive rationality, cf. W. Cyrul, *Idea racjonalności w dyskursie prawniczym* in: *Prawo-Władza-Społeczeństwo-Polityka. Księga jubileuszowa profesora Krzysztofa Pałeckiego*, Toruń 2006, p. 138 et seq

views, especially the concepts of hermeneutics and the communicative concepts of law, as well as aware of the symptoms of the crisis of a post-war legal doctrine in the countries of the Soviet bloc, Wróblewski defended the role of science, as he was concerned – not without reason – that the juridisation of the application of law and social relations will negatively affect the quality and effectiveness of law, to the detriment of the progress and good that could arise from implementation of the (scientific) legal policy.

M. Rylski

The Theories and Views of Leon Petrażycki and the Creation and Development of Labour Law

1 Introductory Remarks

Leon Petrażycki (1867–1931), considered to be one of the most outstanding and well-recognised Polish lawyers in the world[1], became famous primarily as the

---

1 The interest in L. Petrażycki's views and theories is constantly growing, as evidenced by the number of publications devoted to this lawyer or those which present his thoughts in a more extensive way (119 such publications were published in the period 1932–1951, 183 in the years 1952–1971, 255 in the period 1972–1991, and 282 in the years 1992–2009 - cf. A. Kojder, E.V. Timošina, *Bibliografi ja opublikowanych trudov L.I. Petražickogo*, [in:] L.I. Petražickij: Teorija i polityka prava. Izbrannyje trudy. Sankt-Peterburg 2010, p. 966–1012). Those currently considered to be the continuators of his concepts include e.g. P. Sorokin (the creator of the first Chair of Sociology at Harvard University), see especially P.A. Sorokin, *Doroga dalniaia: Awtobiografia (Дорога дальняя: Автобиография)*, Moscow 1992, p. 56, as cited in: A. Mereżko, *Teoria Leona Petrażyckiego w kontekście rosyjskiej filozofii prawa (uczniowie i kontynuatorzy)*, Przegląd Prawno-Ekonomiczny 2009, No. 6, p. 6), M. Rejsner (University in Sankt Petersburg, see especially M.A. Rejsner, *Sowremennaia jurisprudencjia i uczenie L.I. Petrażyckogo (Современная юриспруденция и учение Л.И. Петражицкого)*, Russkoje bogatstwo (Русское богатство) 1908, p. 59, as cited in: A. Mereżko, *op. cit.*, p. 8), G. Gurvitch (University of Paris, see especially G. Gurvitch, *Le Temps Présent Et l'Idée du Droit Socia*, Paris 1931[1932]), N. Timasheff (Fordham University in New York, see especially N. Timasheff, Право как коллективно-психологическая реальность, [in:] Труды русских ученых за границей. Берлин, Berlin 1923, vol. 2) and M. Laserson (US Department of Justice, University of Columbia, see e.g. M. Laserson, *The Work of Leon Petrazhitsky*, Columbia Law Review 1951, No. 1, p. 59–82), and in Poland e.g. A. Podgórecki, A. Peretiatkowicz, J. Licki, J. Lande, H. Piętka and A. Kojder. The views and theories of L. Petrażycki are also evoked by modern scientists – see e.g. E. Fittipaldi, *Everyday legal ontology. A psychological and linguistic investigation within the frame of Leon Petrazycki's theory of law*, Milan 2016; R. Banakar, *Who Needs the Classics? – On the Relevance of Classical Legal Sociology for the Study of Current Social and Legal Problems*, [in:] Retssociologi, eds. O. Hammerslev and M.R. Madsen, Copenhagen 2012, and a bit older publications of R. Poli, M. Libardi, *Logic, Theory of Science and Metaphysics According to Stanislaw Lesniewski*, Grazer Philosophische Studien 1999, No. 57, pp. 183–219.

author of the psychological theory of law[2], creator of the scientific politics of law and political economy[3], father of the sociological approach to the analysis of issues of law and legal issues[4], and, in the light of the latest discoveries, also as the

---

2 Admittedly, researchers stress that Petrażycki was not the only one, or even the first who tried to use the psychological approach to law. Nikolai Korkunov is considered to be the precursor of such optics in the countries of the eastern bloc (like e.g. J. Stanek, *Rosyjski realizm prawny. Psychologiczna koncepcja prawa – powstanie i rozwój*, [in:] Naturalizm prawniczy. Stanowiska, eds. J. Stelmach, B. Brożek, Ł. Kurek, K. Eliasz, Warsaw 2015, p. 222; *Eadem*, *Teoria Nikołaja Korkunowa. Pierwsza próba psychologicznego ujęcia prawa*, [in:] *op. cit.*, p. 233 ff., whereas in western countries, the germs of this approach may be found in the works of Rudolf von Jhering, Otton von Gierke, and later also Georg Jellinek – see more in A. Bosiacki, *Wstęp*, [in:] Leon Petrażycki, Polityka prawa cywilnego i ekonomia polityczna, ed. A. Bosiacki, Warsaw 2017, p. 27. L. Petrażycki was, nevertheless, definitely the first one to give this idea the shape of a "truly general, systematic and methodologically developed" theory of law (A. Walicki, *Filozofia prawa rosyjskiego liberalizmu*, Warsaw 1995, p. 249).

3 According to L. Petrażycki, thanks to the use of pleasant and unpleasant emotions, it is possible to strengthen or weaken certain human inclinations, leading to a gradual socialization of individuals, understood as raising the general moral level of humanity. This process and the directions of its development can be properly planned with the law playing a fundamental role in their implementation. The use of law in this way (for the purpose of social evolution) was referred to by Petrażycki as the policy of law (L. Petrażycki, *O ideale społecznym i odrodzeniu prawa natury*, [in:] L. Petrażycki, O nauce, prawie i moralności. Pisma wybrane, Warsaw 1985, p. 153; More in: L. Petrażycki, *Wstęp do nauki polityki prawa*, Warsaw 1968).

4 L. Petrażycki was appointed the Head of the Department of Sociology at the Faculty of Law and Political Sciences at the University of Warsaw (it was the first Department of this type in Poland and one of the first in Europe). He was also the Vice-President of the International Institute of Sociology (IIS) in Paris. K. Motyka wrote e.g. that: "Petrażycki's merit is that he empirically oriented the Polish legal science and contributed to overcoming of its dogmatism and formalism. He also initiated large-scale, socio-technical research on the functioning of law and legal awareness as well as on the rationalisation of the lawmaking process. The beginning of the discussion on the ontological status of law and the methodological status of legal sciences should also be attributed to him." (K. Motyka, *Wpływ Leona Petrażyckiego na polską teorię i socjologię prawa*, Lublin 1993, p. 205). In his works, Petrażycki pointed to the social genesis and functions that human experiences and emotions perform in collective life, emphasized how legal norms affect the society and its individuals as well as how the so-called intuitive law is transformed in the course of the so-called emotional contagion into norms of a positive nature (more on the subject A. Kojder, *Idee społeczno-prawne Leona Petrażyckiego i ich współczesne kontynuacje*, [in:] Klasyczna socjologia polska i jej współczesna recepcja, eds. J. Mucha and W. Wincławski, Toruń 2006, pp. 57–90.

precursor of the economic analysis of law[5], especially the so-called behavioural trend" (*behavioural law and economics*)[6]. Few contemporary researchers, however, are aware[7] that L. Petrażycki should also be credited with the intellectual and moral merits in the process of gradual crystallization of labour law (as we

---

5 See e.g. Giaro T., *Leon Petrażycki i ekonomiczna analiza prawa. Materiały do dalszych rozważań*, [in:] Nauka i nauczanie prawa. Tradycja i przyszłość. Konferencja na dwóchsetlecie Wydziału Prawa i Administracji Uniwersytetu Warszawskiego, ed. H. Izdebski, Warsaw 2009, pp. 221–239.

6 In order to explain and predict how people react to the establishment of certain legal norms, the original representatives of the economic analysis of law referred to neoclassical theories of economics (demand and supply, market equilibrium, theory of games – R. Cooter, T. Ulen, *Ekonomiczna analiza prawa*, Warsaw 2009, pp. 18–67, or the so-called maximization of expected utility– J. Neumann, O. Morgenstern, *Theory of games and economic behavior*, Princeton 1947, as cited in M. Peterson, *An introduction to decision theory*, Cambridge 2009, pp. 3–4). Then, however, it was observed (in the course of various experiments) that the decisions taken by rational entities differ significantly from the predictions based on neoclassical theories of economics. (cf. e.g. J. Arlen, E. Talley, *Experimental law and economics*, NYU Law and Economics Research Paper 2008, No. 08–30, *passim*; C. Jolls, C. Sunstein, R. Thaler, *A behavioral approach to law and economics*, Stanford Law Review 1998, No. 5, pp. 1471–1480). As a result of these discoveries, some authors of the *law and economics* trend considered descriptive decision-making theories, in particular the so-called prospect theory by Tversky and Kahneman, as the ones better describing the reality. (D. Kahneman, A. Tversky, *Prospect Theory: An Analysis of decision under risk*, Econometrica: Journal of the Econometric Society 1979, No. 2, pp. 263–291; A. Tversky, D. Kahneman, *Judgment Under Uncertainty: Heuristics and Biases*, Science 1974, No. 4157, pp. 1124–1131). A closer analysis of L. Petrażycki's views (e.g. on the role of psychology in legal sciences or his conviction about the influence of legal reality on the decision-making process of the addressees of legal norms) leads to the conclusion that they not only coincide in many places with the views of the representatives of behavioural economic analysis of law, but may also provide it with a strong basis for more mature research, both from the subjective side (e.g. related to the influence of cultural factors on the process of making decisions by legal entities - cf. L. Petrażycki, *O dopełniających prądach kulturalnych i prawach rozwoju handlu*, Warsaw 1936, as well as contemporary R. Zyzik, *Czy Leon Petrażycki był prekursorem behawioralnej ekonomicznej analizy prawa?* as well as methodologically (M. Małecka, *O behawioralnym podejściu do badania prawa, paradoksie, do którego prowadzi i sposobie jego przezwyciężenia*, Nauka i Szkolnctwo Wyższe 2013, No. 1, pp. 36–39).

7 The exception in this respect is A. Kojder, who, in the foreword to the Polish edition of L. Petrażycki's works (*O nauce, prawie i moralności…*, s. XXXIV) emphasizes his pioneering views on labour law.

know it now). His original, bold, revolutionary and surprisingly accurate (given the time they were expressed) views on the need to increase the legal protection of people pursuing gainful employment and even to create a separate area of civil law for this type of social relations, which did not yet exist at that time – labour law – received a lot of attention in the legal world of that time. The reason for this was not only the high intellectual and cognitive value of the arguments presented by L. Petrażycki, but also the fact that they were presented and extensively justified on the occasion of criticism of the project of the German Civil Code – BGB, being of general interest, (in a work called *Die Lehre vom Einkommen*[8], or more precisely in its final part entitled *Civilpolitik und politische Oekonomie*[9]). It should be emphasised that it was 1895, i.e. long before the formal separation of labour law from civil law (not only in Poland, but also in other European countries)[10] and

8 L. Petrażycki, *Die Lehre von Einkommen: Vom Standpunkt des gemeinen Civilrechts unter Berücksichtigung des Entwurfs eines bürgerlichen Gesetzbuches für das Deutsche Reich*, Berlin 1895, vol 2.

9 Further in this study, the author will use the above mentioned Polish translation of the work – L. Petrażycki, *Polityka prawa cywilnego i ekonomia polityczna*, ed. A. Bosiacki, Warsaw 2017.

10 The historical sources of the construction of a contract of employment can be found in the Roman *locatio conductio operarum* (F. Zoll, *Prawo pracy w biegu wieków*, Rocznik Prawniczy Wileński 1930, pp. 3–4), and even, as some claim, in the Hammurabi's Code (see K. Koranyi, *Powszechna historia państwa i prawa. Tom I. Starożytność*, Warsaw 1961, p. 26) Nevertheless, labour legislation has been formally recognised as a separate area of law from civil law relatively recently. This process was long and led through various stages. From the above mentioned ancient times, through patronage agreements, various forms of serfdom and the so-called guild law in the Middle Ages. Then the Napoleon's Code, based on liberal ideology, which elevated freedom of contract to the rank of a fundamental principle of private law, followed by many social and economic processes in the world, which led to the creation of the trade union movement and the creation of an increasing number of norms protecting working people against exploitation by employers, accidents at work, occupational diseases and other risks waiting for employees in the work process (this was facilitated, among others, by the universal social insurance in Germany introduced by Otto von Bismarck). Until the creation of the first Labour Code in France in 1910 (although its regulations focused mainly on work in industry, based at that time on the Taylor model, which was propagated mainly by the American entrepreneur Henry Ford) and the adoption of the Weimar Constitution in Germany in 1919, which officially granted labour law the status of an independent field of law (more on the history of European labour law can be found in *The Making of Labour Law in Europe. A comparative Study of Nine Countries up to 1945*, ed. B. Hepple, London – New York 1986; in L. Weddeburn, M. Rood, C. Lyon-Caen, W. Däubler, P. Van Der Heijden, *Labour law in the Post-Industrial Era. Essays in*

even long before the introduction of the first significant regulations protecting representatives of the world of work against exploitation by the beneficiaries of the next stage of the successively expanding industrial revolution[11].

Honour of Hugo Sinzheimer, Dartmouth 1994 and *The Transformation of Labour Law in Europe. A comparative Study of Nine Countries 1945–2004*, ed. G. Hepple, Oregon 2009). At the international level, the most important event in this process seems to have been the establishment, under the Treaty of Versailles, of the International Labour Organisation in 1919, now an agency of the United Nations, of which Poland was a co-founder. In Poland, the process of separating labour law from civil law gained momentum only after the country regained independence in 1918, and its formal ending is usually dated back to 1964. It was then that the provisions introducing the Civil Code (Article XII § 1) stated explicitly that its regulations do not violate the labour legislation. Undoubtedly, however, in the minds of Polish lawyers, labour law was considered a discipline separate from civil law much earlier. This is evidenced by the works of Z. Fenichel (*Zarys polskiego prawa robotniczego*, Krakow 1930, p. 1 ff.), A. Raczyński (*Polskie prawo pracy*, Warszawa 1930, p. 1 ff.), J. Bloch (*Kodeks pracy. Ustawy, rozporządzenia, dekrety, orzecznictwo. Komentarz*, Warszawa 1936, p. 1 ff.), as well as the fact that, as early as in 1938, at a conference of Deans of the Faculties of Law, the legal community supported the introduction of a separate subject called "labour law" into the curriculum of studies. (S. Grzybowski, *Wspomnienia*, Krakow 1999, p. 609), and the first Department of Labour Law was established in Łódź in 1950. Moreover, although the first Polish Labour Code entered into force only in 1975, attempts to codify this branch of law took place already in the 1940s. (more in A. Giedrewicz-Niewińska, *Projekt kodeksu pracy z 1949 r.*, Oświęcim 2015, p. 1 ff.; J. Piątkowski, *Prawo do Kodeksu pracy czy konieczność jego posiadania*, Studia z zakresu prawa pracy i polityki społecznej 2017, No. 1, pp. 1–16).

11 The first significant and widespread legal regulations, which actually improved the situation of workers in the work process, were only introduced at international level by the International Labour Organisation in 1919. (e.g. an eight-hour working day). In Poland, the most important regulations protecting working people were introduced by the issue of two Regulations of the President of 16th March 1928 on the contract of employment of blue-collar and white-collar workers (Journal of Laws of the Republic of Poland of 1928, No. 35, items 324 and 325), and previously the Act of 16th March 1922 on Holiday Leave (Journal of Laws of the Republic of Poland of 1922, No. 40, item 334). The latter covered workers employed by the industry and trade, providing for even one month's leave for white-collar workers, which was one of the most favourable holiday leave entitlements in Europe at that time (more in: W. Organiściak, *Prawo pracy II Rzeczypospolitej. Szkic dla celów dydaktycznych*, Prace Naukowe Uniwersytetu Śląskiego 2009, No. 2704, pp. 233–257; W. Muszalski, *Ogólna refleksja o rozwoju prawa pracy i jego uwarunkowaniu*, Studia Iuridica Lublinensia 2015, No. XXIV, p. 59 ff.). These observations do not, of course, mean that there have been no legislative changes in Europe before aimed at increasing the protection of people

The above-mentioned postulates, which are rather general and systemic in nature, are not the only ones that deserve special attention of labour law representatives. For it appears that L. Petrażycki's arguments concerning, among others, the limitation of the debtor's liability for damages caused to the creditor, the need to keep a written form when concluding contracts in business transactions or the question of immediate (i.e. by virtue of law, without prior notice by the creditor) maturity of certain property claims are of paramount importance for labour law regulations (although Petrażycki himself did not sometimes refer them directly to the employee-employer relationship). If we add the original and expressive, against the background of the world of law and politics at that time, views of this lawyer on the equality of women, including their right to work, it can be said that, in this way, the threads of Petrażycki's thought have been outlined, to which the doctrine of labour law should now pay special attention.

However, if we stop with the above-mentioned list, it is difficult not to get the impression that it is still incomplete. It seems that L. Petrażycki's "universal" theories may prove to be equally useful for learning of labour law. These theories do not relate directly to labour law relations, or even to any specific legal relations. This involves primarily the Petrażycki's postulate of the "rebirth of natural law" as well as the "social ideal" outlined by this thinker in the politics of law[12]. The first of these issues can be linked to the idea of human rights and its impact on the development of labour law, as a modern axiological justification for current legislative solutions, such as safe and hygienic working conditions, holiday leaves, minimum wages, daily rest standards, maximum working time standards, protection of women, young people, children and older people in the labour market. The second issue may shed some light on the current directions of development of labour law, including the desirable ways of solving contemporary problems

pursuing gainful employment. Particularly noteworthy in this respect are regulations restricting child labour (Great Britain - 1802, Prussia - 1839, France - 1841, Austria - 1859), increasing the protection of women (Great Britain - 1844, France - 1848, Germany - 1878, Austria - 1884) or establishing the industrial inspection to supervise respecting of workers' rights (Great Britain - 1833, Prussia - 1853, France - 1874, Austria - 1885).

12 L. Petrażycki, *O ideale społecznym i odrodzeniu prawa natur…*, p. 153 ff. See also R. Zyzik, *Ideał społeczny w polityce prawa Leona Petrażyckiego. Perspektywa ewolucyjna*, Archiwum Historii Filozofii Myśli Społecznej 2015, No. 60, p. 175 ff.:; A. Szadok-Bratuń, *O dwóch koncepcjach prawa naturalnego polskich filozofów prawa okresu międzywojennego*, Przegląd Prawa i Administracji 2015, No. 3661, p. 233 ff. M. Szyszkowska, *Filozofia prawa i filozofia człowieka*, Warsaw 1989, p. 56 ff.

and challenges of the labour market, such as, for example, the phenomenon of universal replacement of employment contracts with civil law contracts, which deprive employees of increased social protection.

It is only when these two additional issues are taken into account that the subject of research into Petrażycki's thought in the context of the emergence, development and even the future of labour law seems to be properly outlined. Unfortunately, due to editorial limitations, further argumentation of this article will not take into account the subject matter indicated in the previous paragraph, but will be limited to the previously indicated issues.

2 L. Petrażycki and Dualism of Civil Law

As already mentioned, L. Petrażycki, in his criticism of the German BGB, made some observations on the need for the legislator to treat the so-called remuneration claims differently from other claims of a private law nature[13]. In order to justify this view, Petrażycki presented several arguments, most of which, in the subsequent years of labour law shaping, were developed in many scientific papers, including those of a monographic nature[14] and, nowadays, are considered almost axiomatic.

Firstly, this is supported by the fact that "remuneration creates the consumption fund of workers and their families, i.e. usually the only source of satisfaction of the most intense needs (so-called existence needs: food, housing, heating…), on the regular satisfaction of which depends the life and health". In other words, "if farmers, factory owners or merchants are not paid their debts on time, it is more or less unpleasant for these people and they are angry; but in the same

13 Analysis of the argumentation of L. Petrażycki in this respect leads to the conclusion that by the term "remuneration claims" he primarily understands employee claims on account of remuneration for work (cf. L. Petrażycki, *Polityka prawa cywilnego…*, p. 256 ff.) However, it sometimes seems that his reasoning goes further and also covers the employee's general legal situation in relation to the employer (cf. *Ibidem*, pp. 259–260).

14 H.L. Grantt, *Travail, salaires et bénéfices*, Paris 1921; H. Harmsen, *Lohnzahlungen bei Betriebsstockungen: ein Versuch zur Lösung des Problems aus dem Wesen des Arbeitsvertrages*, Berlin 1925; K. Flasche, A. Lorenz, W. Riechers, *Die Ausarbeitung, Einführung und Handbung des Gehaltsgruppenkatalogs*, Berlin 1959; M. Goldštejn, V. Korotkov, *Garantijnye i kompensacionnye vyplaty rabocim i sluzascim*, Moscow 1960; M. Špiljak, *La repartition du revenu de l'entreprise et le systeme de remuneration en Yougoslavie*, Belgrad 1961; M. Święcicki, *Prawo wynagrodzenia za pracę*, Warsaw 1963; J. Skoczyński, *Prawna ochrona wynagrodzenia za pracę*, Warsaw 1995.

case, a worker with his wife and children is starving or, out of this misery, will be released for the spoil of evil temptations"[15].

It is worth emphasising here that, currently, the doctrine of labour law commonly distinguishes the so-called alimony (maintenance) function of remuneration for work, which is expressed in the fact that "remuneration is the main, and often the only source of income for employees and their families"[16]. This type of feature of the remuneration for work is now considered to be the most important justification for the existence of many protective labour law provisions[17]. These include, for example, an order to pay an employee remuneration for work at least once a month, on a fixed and pre-determined date (Art. 85(1) of the Act of 26 June 1974 - the Labour Code[18], further referred to as the LC), or prohibitions or restrictions on the possibility of making deductions from remuneration by the employer (Art. 87, Art. 87^1, Art. 88, Art.91 of the LC), or even its seizure by a bailiff in enforcement proceedings (Art. 821^1, Art. 829(5), Art. 833 of the Act of 17 November 1964, Article 87, Article 88, Article 91 of the Code of Civil Procedure[19], further referred to as the CCP)[20]. The authors of the original legislative solutions in the BGB criticised by L. Petrażycki did not see the need to differentiate the level of protection for this type of property claims, probably because they followed too closely the concepts that once existed in Roman law, often without taking into account the realities of social and economic life in Germany at that time[21]. However, under Roman law, the remuneration for the

15 L. Petrażycki, *Polityka prawa cywilnego…*, p. 256.

16 Resolution of the Supreme Court of 2013, II PZP 4/2012, LEX no. 1281360. See also Ulman P., *Praca człowieka i godne jej wynagradzanie w świetle encykliki Centesimus annus*, [in:] Polityka społeczna wobec „rzeczy nowych". 25-lecie encykliki Centesimus annus św. Jana Pawła II, ed. Jan Mazur, Krakow 2016, p. 302.

17 See J. Wratny, *Prawo do wynagrodzenia za pracę w świetle zasad sprawiedliwości i równości*, Annales Universitatis Mariae Curie-Skłodowska 2015, No. LXII, p. 298.

18 Consolidated text Journal of Laws of 2018, item 108.

19 Consolidated text Journal of Laws of 2018, item 155.

20 It should be emphasised, however, that L. Petrażycki states at some point, unfortunately without any justification, that "in general, the humanitarian and charitable release of certain parts of property from execution is unjustified in the case of a remuneration claim (…)" - cf. L. Petrażycki, *Polityka prawa cywilnego…*, p. 261.

21 What Petrażycki, being also an expert in Roman law, drew their attention to many times (*Ibidem*, pp. 57, 73). Even in the context of labour law, he wrote: "Roman slavery is to blame for the fact that the project contains a large gap as regards the regulation of rights within the scope of various types of freedom to work (obtaining income from work). Had it not been for slavery in Rome, had the various types of employment contracts in Rome been of approximately as great social significance as they are today, then Roman

locatio conductio operarum, disregarding the marginal nature of such a contract in ancient economic transactions[22], was not protected by the state and there were even provisions laying down a maximum limit of its amount, the crossing of which was punishable with the death penalty[23].

Secondly, "capitalists, by using a credit, can usually prevent the detrimental effects of a situation where their claims are not paid in due time and this detrimental for their households; but those who live from their work do not have any credits at their disposal (or have to pledge the necessary items)"[24].

It is astonishing that the above argument, uttered at the end of the 19th century, remains valid until this day, and even more so than in the past, seems to justify the increased protection of remuneration claims. On the one hand, it is based on the aforementioned general assumption of the maintenance function of remuneration for work. On the other hand, however, it refers to a broader perspective, because it compares the possibilities for the employee and the employer to obtain, in a short time, some alternative money from another (substitute) source. On the employees' side, there are basically no new ways of obtaining free cash in the market within a short time, apart from a credit or a loan, which additionally require meeting of different income criteria or agreeing to pay very high interest on the debt incurred. On the other hand, on the employer's side, in addition to the above-mentioned possibilities, there are also a number of other solutions, which, in the past, either did not exist, such as factoring or insurance of receivables, or, admittedly, existed, but were strongly limited in their availability or effectiveness (benefits for the employer), e.g. acquisition of an external investor, issue of securities, legal collection of receivables by an external company. Taking the above observations into account, it appears that the difference in treatment, by the legislator, of employees' and employers' claims, due to Petrażycki's argument under consideration, is now more justified than in the past.

Thirdly, L. Petrażycki states: "As the employer is, on average, economically and mentally stronger than the worker, there is no reason to fear that these rights

---

lawyers would certainly have shaped the extensive and detailed labour law, just as they created the extensive and decent law concerning slaves. Then, definitely, the project would also be different".

22 F. Zoll, *Prawo pracy w biegu wieków…*, p. 4.

23 The Diocletian's Tariffs are meant here, the justification of which was, among others, consumer protection at the expense of employee protection (see more in A. Kowalczyk, *Ochrona wynagrodzenia za pracę. Prawo rzymskie a współczesne regulacje prawa pracy*, Zeszyty Naukowe Uniwersytetu Rzeszowskiego 2014, No. 82, p. 71).

24 L. Petrażycki, *Polityka prawa cywilnego…*, p. 256.

can be used successfully for the exploitation and oppression of the employer in the event of recognition of a sharp protective weapon in favour of the remuneration claim. On the contrary, if properly implemented, these rights can mitigate the doubtful consequences of the employer's advantage for the economic and moral well-being of the nation"[25].

Apart from the validity of the above argument within the scope related to the impossibility of exploitation of the employer, one should pay attention to the fact that, in its centre, there is an observation about the actual inequality of the parties to the legal relationship in which the employee and the employer remain. This is an absolutely fundamental remark for the creation of labour law, in which almost all protective legislative mechanisms (including the semi-imperative nature of legal norms, which is common in this area[26]) are justified by such optics. For, it is the employers who have, at their disposal, the commodity, i.e. labour, which is limited in the market. The result is that the demand for it exceeds the supply. As a consequence, it is the employer who dictates the terms and conditions of the transaction, the subject of which is labour. This phenomenon is further enhanced by the fact that the employer has an informational advantage over the employee, which, in negotiations, is one of the most important factors determining the victory of one party over the other. It is the employers who know how much they can pay an individual employee and how much they pay other employees, what time possibilities they have in the work process, what is the actual degree of complexity of certain activities, what is the risk of failure or accident, what is the specificity of the industry in which the work is to be performed, what are the prospects for its development and development of the company, etc. The employees usually learn all this after concluding the contract and, beforehand, are forced to rely on the information provided by the employers, if any. On top of all this, of course, there is the economic advantage of the employer over the employee, about which L. Petrażycki wrote this way: "account must be taken of the fact that, for the employer, the demand for remuneration due usually appears to be a relatively small sum, which can easily be obtained without a significant shock to the employer's household"[27].

25 *Ibidem*, pp. 256–257.

26 The semi-imperative nature of labour law norms is currently considered to be one of the specific features of this field of law - see e.g. Goździewicz G., *Szczególne właściwości norm prawa pracy*, Toruń 1988, *passim*; W. Szubert, *Szczególne właściwości prawa pracy*, Studia Prawno-Ekonomiczne 1970, vol. IV, p. 53 ff.

27 L. Petrażycki, *Polityka prawa cywilnego…*, p. 257.

The argumentation presented above led L. Petrażycki to a more general conclusion that a different treatment of "capitalist obligation relationships and the remuneration claim" should prevail in the entire civil law, triggering its dualism in terms of, inter alia, "freedom of contract, the nature of equivalence, fulfilment of the contract, compensation, *mora debitoris* and *creditoris*, compensation of damages and the pledge right"[28].

The postulate that should be considered particularly interesting for further development of labour law is that of a different regulation of the freedom of contract, the nature of equivalence and compensation of damages. At the time when our thinker pronounced these words, the European legal systems, apart from fragmented, axiologically inconsistent and rather chaotic regulations protecting workers, were not guided by any coherent policy of protecting the working people. It seems that the reason for this state of affairs was precisely the excessive glorification, based on the French Revolution ideology, of the freedom to contract (based on the assumption of formal equivalence of the parties, while rejecting the empirical experience of the actual inequality of the employee and the employer), the absolutisation of individual freedom (disregarding the phenomenon of the employee's dependence on the employer) and the still too widespread belief that work is a commodity.

L. Petrażycki's views go against the current of this type of reasoning and their validity has been proven by the history of the development of labour law. At present, due to the prevalence of semi-imperative norms in labour law, almost the main point of this area of law is to restrict the parties' freedom of contracting, in order to guarantee employees, as the weaker parties to the contract, a certain minimum of legal and social protection, which they themselves, being dependent on the employer, are not able to guarantee through negotiations. In turn, writing about the nature of equivalence, L. Petrażycki probably meant that the legal system should, once and for all, abandon thinking about labour in terms of a commodity, which was officially and universally articulated at the legislative level only in the Philadelphia Declaration of 10 May 1944 concerning the objectives and tasks of the International Labour Organisation[29]. Finally, it is also appropriate for labour law to limit employees' liability for damages caused to

28 *Ibidem*, p. 258.

29 See Evju S., *Labour is Not a Commodity: Reappraising the Origins of the Maxim*, European Labour Law Journal 2013, No. 4, p. 222 ff. Previously, such a conviction was presented on the international arena mainly by representatives of Christian philosophy and social science of the Roman Catholic Church – see in particular the *Rerum novarum* encyclical of Pope Leo XIII of 1891.

the employer in the course of work or even to a third party (e.g. a customer or another employee of the same establishment)[30].

The views of L. Petrażycki on the dualism of civil law in the procedural dimension are also noteworthy. In addition to the above arguments, the following reasons for differentiated treatment of workers in this area are, in his opinion, to be taken into account.

First of all, since labour is the primary source of income for the worker, then: "If the trial threatens to take up many days of work (…), workers are much more likely to give up their good rights than to be sued. They are often afraid of being dismissed from their present jobs if they neglect work because of the proceedings"[31].

Secondly, "court costs are of a respectively different significance for a worker, who is often paid very little, and for people who have capital and credit at their disposal"[32].

Thirdly, court cases often require "professional litigation and survival without a significant loss of time" while waiting for the outcome of the case, which can be a non-transversal barrier for an employee[33].

As a consequence, L. Petrażycki reaches the conclusion that: "It is necessary to create a process for demanding remuneration, so that, instead of feeling (partly unaware, partly instinctual, but well-founded) fears and reluctance to assert their rights in court, workers could be sure that, without particular difficulties and waste of time, they can request a judge for help with a certain and rapid effect". To this end, according to Petrażycki, "not only the issue of court costs, proceedings, enforcement, but also the organisation of the court from the point of view of labour law should be reviewed in particular". As regards the latter issue,

30 In the Polish legal system, there are various limitations of employees' liability for damages, such as limiting the amount of compensation to three times the remuneration for work or limiting the liability for damages only to *damnum emergens* (when the damage was caused by unintentional fault). There is also the provision of Art. 120 of the Labour Code, according to which full liability for damages caused by an employee to any third party (i.e. other than the employer) is, first and foremost, borne by the employer, provided that it occurred during the performance of employee's duties. Only in the second place does the employer who has repaired the damage have the possibility to claim reimbursement of the costs incurred in this respect from the employee, but taking into account, among other things, the rules presented above limiting the employee's liability for the damage caused to the employer.

31 L. Petrażycki, *Polityka prawa cywilnego…*, p. 259.

32 *Ibidem*, p. 260.

33 *Ibidem*.

Petrażycki even went so far as to propose a specific solution, which would be to place the adjudicating judges in each smaller area of the city (e.g. a district), who would order, in an abbreviated mode, what is necessary in an individual dispute between an employer and an employee, with the possibility of appealing against such a judge's decision to an ordinary court.[34]

It seems that the proposal to introduce a single judge in individual small territorial districts, with the right of appeal by the parties to a normal court and consideration of the case in normal proceedings, should be considered ineffective (it is almost certain that employers would appeal massively against such decisions only because they would postpone the execution of a judgement favourable for the employee, which would further increase the length of the proceedings). However, the fact remains that other, more general comments on civil procedural law are fully relevant and have been reflected in the specific rules of many European legal systems. In Poland, cases related to labour law and social insurance fall within the material competence of specialised judicial units – labour and social security courts – and are examined on the basis of different procedural regulations, which are more protective and more convenient for an employee (Art. 459 of the Code of Civil Procedure et seq.)[35]

It is worth noting here, however, that, despite his clearly pro-employee views, L. Petrażycki also set a clear caesura for the legislator in creating protective legal regulations for employees. In his opinion, such regulations should not lead to a simple privilege for representatives of the world of labour, because the privileges "are in general contrary to modern folk (commonsense) psychology" and their introduction "is harmful for the law and morality in general, when it reduces respect for the law, harms the sense of justice, brings the sense of conflict of interests, hatred and jealousy closer".[36] Nevertheless, since "the representatives of capital in the current legal order enjoy a highly privileged position in relation to the representatives of the world of labour, which is still increasingly felt to be unjustified", the differentiation of workers' and capitalists' rights made above should rather be seen as a compensation for the unfair disproportions within the scope of rights and duties[37]. Furthermore, according to Petrażycki, the special treatment of labour in civil law and trial would be "free from the dark sides of privileges because it is not accidental and undeserved (for example, dependent

34 *Ibidem*, pp. 260–261.

35 A lot on the subject is written by M. Mędrala, *Funkcja ochronna cywilnego postępowania sądowego w sprawach z zakresu prawa pracy*, Warsaw 2011, *passim*.

36 L. Petrażycki, *Polityka prawa cywilnego…*, p. 262.

37 *Ibidem*.

only on birth) favouritism of one class, but will be the participation of everyone who enters into the relevant legal relations available to all" and, in addition, such concern of the legislator and labour law "would support and strengthen the respective moral views of the nation on labour"[38].

Regardless of the above, L. Petrażycki claimed that the legislator should, first of all, take into account the general public good. For this reason, "it is necessary to verify on a case-by-case basis whether the general good requires any specific regulation of labour relations"[39]. In consequence, he argued, for example, that, like other creditors, employees should not be granted an entirely free right of withdrawal from the agreement or the right to refuse to fulfil a contractual obligation because of a significant deterioration in the assets of the other party (employer), since this would promote the selfish and socially undesirable attitudes of the parties to the contract, without any objective justification[40] (the BGB project, on the other hand, granted this possibility to every creditor). He stated, however, that such a right could be enjoyed by employees when work for a particular employer would be their only source of subsistence and, consequently, not exercising such a right, they would risk falling into real misery[41].

3 Detailed Aspects of Petrażycki's Thought and Labour Law

Apart from the above mentioned views, which are mostly of a general or systemic nature, it is worth noting four more detailed issues contained in the works of L. Petrażycki, which seem useful for the development and evolution of labour law.

Firstly, the principle of *dies interpellat pro homine* adopted in the BGB project, essentially criticised by Petrażycki on the basis of classical civil law relations, should, in his opinion, be fully applied to "remuneration claims" because "the dependent and subordinate position of a worker in relation to the employer makes the reminder mentally impossible in an average case"[42]. Thus, in his opinion, "remuneration claims" should be immediately due, by virtue of law, without the need to call on the debtor (in this case the employer) to pay the amount due (remuneration for work).

38 *Ibidem*, p. 263.
39 *Ibidem*, p. 258.
40 *Ibidem*, pp. 258–259.
41 *Ibidem*, p. 259.
42 *Ibidem*.

Currently, it is generally accepted that claims with a clearly indicated time limit for their settlement (in a contract, act, collective agreement, etc.) are due without any additional call on the debtor to fulfil them (i.e. on the date when they may legitimately be demanded to be fulfilled). Under labour law, e.g. due to the adoption of the ILO Convention No. 95 concerning wage protection in 1952 (cf. Art. 12(1)), national legislation most frequently indicates at least the latest moment of payment of remuneration for work by the employer (in Poland this issue is regulated, e.g. by Art. 85 of the Labour Code). As a consequence, the enforceability of wage claims is realised under the labour law by virtue of the law itself. However, in practice, such a solution is weakened by the emergence, in the judicature, of the concept of abuse of the right to sue, which involves verification of whether, in specific circumstances, the creditor attempted to persuade the debtor to voluntarily perform the obligation before the decision to start the machinery of justice. As a rule, such circumstances are examined by the court as a result of an appeal against the costs of the proceedings filed by the debtor who has lost the case and is particularly justified when the parties have been in a permanent legal relationship with each other, where greater mutual loyalty is required (and the employment relationship certainly belongs to such relationships). If the debtor is not requested to make the payment, the court may consider as justified, for example, the mutual abolition of the costs of court proceedings, which will lead to a situation where the winning creditor bears the costs associated with bringing of an action (e.g. when the court concludes that the debtor would have performed the obligation even without instituting a trial)[43].

Secondly, L. Petrażycki postulated that the Act (by way of mandatory norms) should explicitly provide for situations which would be regarded as employee's justified failure to appear at work, without leading to consequences in the form of e.g. dismissal from work. He justified this, among other things, with the fact that "the morals and hygiene of a nation would have to suffer when workers, as a

43 This issue is of particular importance in countries such as Poland, where labour courts are overburdened with cases and proceedings have been going on for many years (even for discrimination, mobbing or sexual harassment). The theory of abuse of the right to sue, once present only in judicature, became particularly important in Poland after the amendment of the provisions of the Code of Civil Procedure in 2016, in particular Art. 187(1) indicating the formal requirements of the petition. As a result of the amendment, these requirements have also been supplemented with the information on "whether the parties have attempted to mediate or otherwise resolve the dispute out of court and, if no such attempt has been made, an explanation of the reasons for not doing so".

result of uncertainty and doubts about the possibility of justifying their absence (…), in order to avoid the risk of losing their wages or their jobs, would neglect their own or their relatives' ethical, civic and hygienic needs"[44].

Currently, all European countries guarantee employees, by virtue of applicable laws, regulations or collective agreements, the right to refrain from performing of work for reasons considered justified in these acts, while retaining the right to remuneration or social security benefits (usually due to illness, parental responsibilities or unexpected risks to the health or life of employees at work). These rights are of a social nature, as they lead to the release of one party to the contract (employees) from the obligation to perform the service (work) to which they have committed themselves in the contract, contrary to the generally accepted principle of *pacta sunt servanda*, while maintaining the obligation to perform the service (remuneration) of the other party to the contract (employers), or taking over the obligation to perform the service by the state budget. At present, it is believed that it is the multitude of such solutions in labour law that determines its specific character in comparison to other areas of law[45].

Thirdly, as a member of the Russian Constitutional-Democratic Party, L. Petrażycki, repeatedly and in various ways, emphasised the need to grant greater rights to women. This attitude was expressed, among others, in his speech delivered on 6 June 1906 in the Russian Duma, which was later published under the title "On rights for women" (Lviv 1919). First and foremost, he called for women to be given political rights, but also referred to the area of civil law (especially inheritance law) as well as inequalities and injustices in terms of access to the labour market and education. He argued, among other things, that prohibitions or restrictions on women existing in this field lead to wasting of the enormous intellectual and moral potential of the female part of the nation, which slows down social development, opposes the conscience and the ideal of the common good, and, as a result, demoralises the law[46]. L. Petrażycki believed that equal rights for women are a clear matter for all people "with a developed

44 *Ibidem*, pp. 259–260.

45 A. Sobczyk, *Prawo pracy w świetle Konstytucji RP. VOL. I. Teoria publicznego i prywatnego indywidualnego prawa pracy*, Warsaw 2013, pp. 105–137, From older literature, see L. Florek, *Ochrona praw i interesów pracownika*, Warsaw 1990, pp. 22–25; M. Skąpski, *Ochronna funkcja prawa pracy w gospodarce rynkowej*, Krakow 2006, pp. 56–105.

46 L. Petrażycki, *O prawa dla kobiet*, [in:] L. Petrażycki, O nauce, prawie i moralności…, p. 380

and cultural conscience, and those who are not mature enough need upbringing and not evidence"[47].

Today, the subject of women's equal rights is one of the leading issues of labour law, because, despite the passage of time, it is still a very current topic. As a side note, it can be mentioned that interdisciplinary and international work (more than 40 scientists from all over the world, representing various scientific disciplines) is now in progress on a new model of counteracting discrimination based on sex, within the framework of the PIUNA 2016–2019 project, the participants of which include countries such as Spain (*Universidad de Valencia, Universidad de Navarra, Universidad Internacional de la Rioja*), Italy (*Università degli Studi di Napoli Federico II, Università di Tor Vergata*), Poland (*University of Szczecin*), Argentina (*Universidad Austral de Buenos Aires*), Belgium (*Institute Dialogue Dynamics*), Columbia (*Universidad de La Sabana*), Mexico (*Universidad Panamericana*), Peru (*Universidad Santo Toribio de Mogrovejo*), Chile (*Pontificia Universidad Católica de Chile*) and even South Africa (*University of the Witwatersrand, Johannesburg*). The aim of this research is to base the prevention of gender discrimination on an intermediate model between the former patriarchal approach (based on the conviction that gender determines the functions or roles that a person should perform in society and not perceiving gender, cultural and social stereotypes, which, in spite of even the most equal rights, may lead to actual gender discrimination) and the radical-egalitarian trend of *gender feminism* (which, in turn, completely ignores the natural biological differences between the sexes, particularly in terms of psychological differences, claiming that they are mainly or exclusively the result of social interaction rather than biological or innate). While constructing the model studied within the PIUNA project, the arguments of all representatives of the previous anti-discrimination trends (also those not mentioned above) are taken into account and attempts are made to create a new flawless model of gender equality, sometimes referred to as a complementary model (equality in diversity)[48].

Finally, the fourth thing is that L. Petrażycki was opposed to the freedom to choose the form of a legal act in the case of certain contracts, such as a surety

47 *Ibidem*, p. 379.

48 More on the subject, see especially *Estudios sobre género y derecho. Hacia un modelo de género de la igualdad en la diferencia*, ed. A. Aparisi Miralles, Navarra (Pamplona) 2016. The subject matter is also discussed extensively in *Diritti umani e genere. Fondamenti scientifici, antropologici, storici e filosofico-giuridici del modello dell'uguaglianza nella differenza – Stelle inquiete. Interventi e confronti*, ed. A.C. Amato Mangiameli, Turin 2017

agreement or an interest agreement. Although he did not explicitly mention the employment contract among them, having become acquainted with his arguments, there is no doubt that they are fully applicable in the employee-employer relationship and are even strengthened in it. *Primo*, he emphasised that it is very easy to take advantage of the inexperience, credulity or recklessness of the economically weaker party in such contracts, which does not have to be fully aware of what it has committed itself to and under what conditions[49]. *Secundo*, in the event of a possible dispute between the parties over the detailed contractual terms, in 99 % of cases, sooner or later, the economically and mentally weaker party will resign[50]. Thus, the lack of the requirement of a written form for such contracts weakens the already weaker position of the party, which usually submits itself to the other and, as a consequence, leads to injustice in the distribution of goods in the economy[51] (the stronger gain economically at the expense of the weaker ones, without resolving about the final rightness of the parties to the existing dispute). *Tertio*, the economically and mentally weaker party, by giving up its arguments in the face of difficulties of proof, becomes even more dependent on the stronger party[52], which results in its being unable to fully benefit from its formal autonomy.

As part of a short commentary to the above views, which, as already mentioned, can be successfully adopted into labour law, it is worth emphasising that the requirement of a written employment contract or at least a one-sided written confirmation of the terms and conditions of employment by the employer is a standard throughout the European Union[53]. In Poland, this issue is regulated by Art. 29(2) of the Labour Code, according to which an employment contract is concluded in writing and, if it has not been concluded in writing, the employer shall confirm in writing the arrangements as to the parties to the contract, the type of contract and its conditions before allowing the employee to work. The employer's failure to comply with this obligation is subject to penal responsibility in the form of a fine from PLN 1,000 to 30,000 (Art. 281(2) of the Code of Criminal Procedure).

49 L. Petrażycki, *Polityka prawa cywilnego…*, p. 53.

50 *Ibidem*, p. 55.

51 *Ibidem*.

52 *Ibidem*.

53 See Council Directive of 14 October 1991 on an employer's obligation to inform employees of the conditions applicable to the contract or employment relationship (91/533/EEC).

4 Conclusion

The views of L. Petrażycki presented in this study and related to the present day, give rise to the formulation of many conclusions, four of which come to the fore.

First of all, Petrażycki's thought should be attributed a pioneering character in relation to many protective regulations or institutions of labour law, which are now widely recognised as obvious and natural for this area of law.

Secondly, many of the arguments put forward by L. Petrażycki in favour of increased standards of worker protection remain valid to this day and are even being strengthened in a globalised, technological and increasingly morally and materially stratified society.

Thirdly, L. Petrażycki's approach to legislative issues, characterised by a deep insight into legal problems from the moral, customary and social side, should be a model to follow for contemporary legislators, in particular those dealing with labour law, the highest value (meta-value) of which is the human dignity. This issue is currently gaining particular importance in Poland, due to the fact that we are on the eve of a new and extensive codification of labour law in this country[54].

Fourthly, taking into account the above conclusions, it should be considered that further study and analysis of L. Petrażycki's works, especially from the point of view of the "social ideal" in legal policy and the concept of "revival of natural law", mentioned only in the introduction, may prove useful for labour law specialists, contributing to a better understanding not only of the axiological mechanisms underlying labour law, but also of the social phenomena currently taking place in the labour market.

54 The Labour Law Codification Commission, composed of government, employers and employees' representatives, is to prepare two Labour Codes - individual and collective labour law, to be presented to the public in the first half of 2018.

K. Nizioł

Regulatory Impact Assessment in Poland as an Example of the Economization of Law – Evolution, Problems, Development Perspectives

1 Introductory Note

The research objective of this paper is to analyse Regulatory Impact Assessment (RIA) in Poland as one of the aspects of the broadly understood economization of law. This requires analysing the evolution of RIA which occurred in Poland under the influence of the solutions applied in the European Union (EU) and the Organisation for Economic Co-operation and Development (OECD). It is also important to analyse the current regulations regarding RIA in Poland, which will allow to assess them as well as to indicate further development perspectives. The aim of this study is to analyse one of the aspects of economization of law that is the so-called regulatory impact assessment (hereinafter: RIA) which is characteristic for the economic analysis of law *("law and economics")*. Economic analysis of law concentrates, i.a., on the effects of the applied legal solutions, costs and benefits of the legal entities subject to the given regulations, proportions between costs and associated benefits. RIA, in turn, includes examining the social and economic impact of the proposed or binding regulations[1].

The concept of economization of law also appearing in the literature [2] deals with the issues broader than those associated with the economic analysis of law. Economization of law concerns all associations between economics and law, thus also the economic formulations used in the regulations, including economic

1 W. Rogowski, W. Szpringer, *Problemy metodologiczne oceny skutków regulacji w Polsce – czy powstają nowe perspektywy ekonomicznej analizy prawa?* [in:] *Ocena skutków regulacji – poradnik OSR, doświadczenia, perspektywy*, eds. W. Szpringer, W. Rogowski, Warszawa 2007, p. 11.

2 Cf. e.g.: P. Bougette, M. Deschamps, F. Marty, *When Economics Met Antitrust: The Second Chicago School and the Economization of Antitrust Law*, GREDEG Working Papers 2014, No. 23, p. 2 et seq.; K. Nizioł, *Ekonomizacja prawa finansowego – nowy trend w polskim i unijnym prawie finansowym* [in:] *Prawo finansowe wobec wyzwań XXI wieku*, red. J. Gliniecka, A. Drywa, E. Juchniewicz, T. Sowiński, Warszawa 2015Warszawa 2015, p. 535 et seq.

processes (e.g. inflation, unemployment), as well as the use of economic methods and techniques for the analysis of regulations and, finally, for the recognition of economic objectives of the established and applied regulations.

Regulatory impact assessment is a method of improving the law which is currently commonly used worldwide. This is evidenced, for example, by the fact that many countries have developed documents concerning RIA[3]. RIA has also been implemented in Poland as an element of a legislative process or the stage of assessment of an already binding act in the law.

Therefore, the research objective of this paper is the analysis of RIA in Poland as one of the aspects of the broadly understood economization of law. This requires analysing the evolution of RIA which took place in Poland under the influence of the solutions applied in the European Union and the Organisation for Economic Co-operation and Development. It is also important to analyse the current regulations regarding RIA in Poland, which will allow to assess them as well as to indicate further development perspectives.

2 Regulatory Impact Assessment as One of the Aspects of Economization of Law

In order to define the concept of "economization of law" we can refer to its lexical term *"economization"*, meaning: *"making something more economical, cost-effective"*[4]. Lexical concept of economization refers to understanding this concept on the ground of economic science, i.e. the intention to increase economic efficiency understood as economically rational activity.[5] Although the lexical concept of economization is related to rational, economical activity, it is not sufficient to explain the concept of economization of law. In order to understand its scope, it is necessary to refer to economic analysis of law. As it has already been mentioned, economic analysis of law focuses mainly on establishing focuses on determining the extent to which the applied, established and proposed regulations have economic impact on the real economy as well as on the entities to which they apply. RIA is also performed as part of the economic analysis of the law, i.e. the examination of economic and social effects of the proposed (binding) regulations. On

---

3 A list of countries and documents each of them prepared for the purposes of RIA is available on the World Bank website: http://rulemaking.worldbank.org/ria-documents [access 20.02.2018].

4 M. Szymczak (ed.), *Słownik języka polskiego,* vol. I, Warszawa 1978, p. 522.

5 Cf. A. Stabryła, J. Trzcieniecki (ed.), *Organizacja i zarządzanie. Zarys problematyki*, Kraków 1986, p. 37.

the other hand, the economization of law covers not only the subject of economic analysis of law (including the RIA), but also all manifestations of the application of economics, economic instruments and economic categories in law. Therefore, several forms of legal economization can be distinguished.

Firstly, economization of law is reflected in the construction of legal norms that directly use the economic category of macro- or microeconomics (e.g. inflation, gross domestic product, unemployment, public debt, budget deficit, costs, depreciation, monopoly, competition), but without providing its legal definition[6]. Such economic definitions are usually used in financial law, tax law or competition law, hence in such areas of law which are closely tied to economy.

Secondly, economization of law is also granting clear normative meaning to a given concept under which there is a given economic category (e.g. using economic concept in a legal definition). For example, the concept of relevant market existing in the competition law is an example of a normative definition of the market in economic terms[7]. The aim of such procedure is to specify the market where monopolistic practices occur and need to be tackled. This can be achieved by distinguishing a certain market segment in terms of homogeneous operating conditions (i.e. the relevant market)[8].

Thirdly, economization of law may manifest itself in the establishment and application of standards which take into account economic or social objectives, while striving to meet criteria of economic efficiency or equity. This aspect of economization is also subject of research of economic analysis of law (RIA within its framework). This is an inconclusive form of economization of law in such a sense that realization of certain economic goals by the law may be difficult due to, inter alia, different view on the economic problems presented by different economic theories, different criteria of economic effectiveness, prioritising the criterion of economic efficiency without taking the social objectives of regulations (or vice versa) into account[9].

---

6 The economic variable used may be either a resource (it represents the value of the economic quantity at a particular moment) or a stream (expresses the value of the economic quantity at particular time)., R. Milewski, E. Kwiatkowski (eds.), *Podstawy ekonomii*, Warszawa 2005, p. 21.

7 *Legal definition of the relevant market has been set out in Article 4 point 9 Act of February 16, 2007 on Competition and Consumer Protection* i.e. Journal of Laws of 2017 item 229, as amended.

8 S. Gronowski, *Polskie prawo antymonopolowe. Zarys wykładu*, Warszawa 1998, pp. 26–28.

9 The literature enumerates the following economic aims of law: law *"must safeguard the fundamental economic objectives of legal entities; it must define an economically efficient*

Finally, economization of law may consist in application of specific economic instruments in the form of various techniques and models, selected depending on the aim of particular regulation or verification of the effectiveness of its application. It must be emphasized that conducting such studies is not always possible as it is difficult *"and sometimes impossible to use the tools of economic analysis (apply quantity methods) for these studies"*[10].

It is only possible to notice the complexity of this issue after considering all these forms of economization of law. Considering all the above forms of legal economization, it can be defined as providing normative meaning to economic categories by including them in the content of legal norms, as well as taking into account – when establishing and applying norms – the economic or social objectives, while striving to meet the criteria of economic efficiency or fairness, which can be verified using economic instruments in the form of appropriate economic techniques and models.

Therefore, it can be assumed that RIA is one of the manifestations of the economization of law which mainly consists in determining economic results at the stage of design (RIA *ex ante*), implementation (RIA ex post) or application of regulations (in practice, performed mainly by courts).

3 General Characteristics of RIA in Poland Compared to the Solutions Applied in EU and OECD

To begin with, terminological discrepancies occurring with reference to the concept of RIA should be pointed out. Both Polish and OECD terminology use the concept of *regulatory impact assessment – RIA*. Regulatory impact assessment is the element of the so-called better regulation programme, aimed at – among others – deregulation (limiting legal barriers) in these areas of economy where it is possible and improvement of the quality of introduced regulations[11]. Thus, RIA is an important element of providing high quality law and its reforms in

system of allocation of goods; it must enable the resolution of economic conflicts which may arise between legal entities; finally, it must seek to enhance individual and social well-being (both material and intangible) "., J. Stelmach, B. Brożek, W. Załuski, *Dziesięć wykładów o ekonomii prawa,* Warszawa 2007, p. 12.

10 M. Jerzak, M. Kitala, *Prawo w gospodarce. Metodyka oddziaływania prawa na gospodarkę,*"Materiały i Studia NBP" 2012, no. 276, p. 5.

11 *Evaluation of Regulatory Impact Assessments Compendium Report 2004–05, Report by the Comptroller and Auditor General,* The National Audit Office, London 2005, p. 10.

OECD countries, including Poland, within the framework of regulatory policy[12]. Another term is used by the European Commission (hereinafter: EC), namely *impact assessment – IA*[13]. Both RIA and impact assessment (hereinafter: IA) appear in Polish regulations as well (which will be discussed further in this study).

Regulatory impact assessment is performed based on various criteria of economic effectiveness[14] and reasonableness of the legislator. The legislator is usually assumed to act rationally. It results from Article 22 of the Constitution of the Republic of Poland [15], which reads as follows: "*Restrictions on the freedom to conduct a business may only be imposed by law and only on grounds of important public interest.*" Public interest, in turn, is based on reasonableness. The legislator's unjustified reliance on the circumstances indicating the existence of a public interest results in the legislator refraining from acting[16].

Two terms are used in Polish regulations: RIA and IA (*impact assessment*).

First of them, namely RIA, is specified in the Rules of Procedure of the Council of Ministers of October 26, 2013[17] (hereinafter Rules of Procedure) as "*results of*

---

12 Cf. *Recommendation of the Council on Regulatory Policy*, OECD 2012, http://www.oecd.org/gov/regulatory-policy/49990817.pdf [access 12.02.2018], *passim.*

13 M. Kałużyńska, *Ocena wpływu legislacji unijnej i jej oddziaływanie na rozwiązania krajowe* [in:] W. Szpringer, W. Rogowski (red.), *Ocena skutków regulacji…*, p. 58.

14 In practice, determining the economic effectiveness of law may be difficult due to the methodology of determining economic efficiency (e.g. the idea of maximising social welfare, efficiency in Pareto understanding, efficiency in the understanding of Kaldor - Hicks, efficiency in the sense of marginal analysis)., J. Stelmach, B. Brożek, W. Załuski, *Dziesięć wykładów o ekonomii prawa…*, s. 17 et seq.; The most frequently used efficiency criterion is Pareto, which boils down to such allocation of resources in the economy where the Pareto optimum is achieved. It means that the situation of any entity cannot be improved without deterioration of the situation of any of the others., J. Walulik, *O relacjach regulacji ekonomicznej i ochrony konkurencji – próba podsumowania debaty,* [in:] *Wyzwania dla ochrony konkurencji i regulacji rynku. Księga Jubileuszowa dedykowana Profesorowi Tadeuszowi Skocznemu*, eds. M. Bernatt, A. Jurkowska-Gomułka, M. Namysłowska, A. Piszcz Warszawa 2017, p. 480.

15 *Konstytucja Rzeczypospolitej Polskiej z dnia 2 kwietnia 1997 r.*, Journal of Laws of 78 item 483, as amended - hereinafter: Konstytucja RP [Constitution of the Republic of Poland].

16 J. Chmielewski, W. Hoff, *Regulatory Impact Assessment (RIA) and Rationality of Law – Legal Aspects*,"Management and Business Administration. Central Europe" 2015, Vol. 23, No. 2, p. 95.

17 *Resolution no. 190 of the Council of Ministers of October 29, 2013, Work regulations of the Council of Ministers*, i.e. M.P. of 2016, item 1006 as amended - hereinafter: Regulamin RM [Rules of Procedure of the Council of Ministers].

the assessment of expected social and economic effects "and constitutes a separate part of the draft normative act (or the objectives of the draft act)"[18]. In the Polish literature, RIA is specified as *"analytical method supporting politicians in the process of law-making, as well as an auxiliary method in designing, implementing and monitoring the expected effects of the regulatory system, methodically formed to provide knowledge on the possible consequences of the proposed and actual effects of the existing regulation."*[19] Pursuant to other definition, RIA is "*an analytical procedure allowing to determine as precisely as possible all the consequences, in terms of both benefits and costs, of the planned state intervention.*"[20] The aim of the regulatory intervention of the state is, among others, protecting the consumers, employees, vulnerable groups against abuse, promoting the effective market operations, environmental protection and stable economic growth[21].

Other definition of RIA regarding acts or other legal instruments or government policies is specified as "*systematic, mandatory and coherent assessment of their social, economic and/or environmental impact - benefits and costs." Such assessment should focus on the impact on all spheres of life except the government (state)."*[22]

The example definitions of RIA included in the Polish literature indicate that RIA is an element of a state intervention which takes the form of a specific analytical procedure, aimed at supporting the politicians in the lawmaking process. Its framework specifies (through comparing costs and benefits) the consequences of the proposed or binding regulations. Thus, the literature definitions of RIA are more extensive than those in the Rules of Procedure.

---

18 Pursuant to § 24 section 3 Rules of Procedure of the Council of Ministers, prior to the commencement of work on the draft government document and the draft objectives of the draft act, the applicant authority provides the assessment of the expected social and economic effects. The assessment is conducted in accordance with the guidelines for its implementation, provided they have been established by the Council of Ministers or its subsidiary body.

19 R. Śliwa, R. Żaba-Nieroda, *Ocena skutków regulacji jako element procesu regulacyjnego*,"Rocznik Administracji Publicznej" 2017, no. 3, p. 370.

20 J. Osiecka-Chojnacka, *System oceny skutków regulacji w Polsce*, Biuro Analiz Sejmowych, Infos 24.01.2008, no. 2, p. 1.

21 *Better Regulation: Evaluation of Regulatory Impact Assessments Compendium Report 2004–05, Report by the Comptroller and Auditor General*, The National Audit Office, London 2001, p. 2.

22 This definition has been created for the purpose of the project European for Better Regulation (ENBR)., W. Rogowski, W. Szpringer, *Problemy metodologiczne oceny skutków…*, p. 8 et seq.

However, the Rules of Procedure contain certain exemplary elements of RIA such as, for example: identification of entities affected by the draft normative act; information on consultations conducted before the draft preparation and their scope; presentation of the results of the analysis of the impact of the draft normative act on the entities affected by IA and the effect of the draft on significant areas of impact[23]. Moreover, RIA is supposed to indicate the source of funding. RIA should also identify the problem being solved, specify the aim and nature of the intervention, as well as compare the solutions adopted in other countries[24].

The other term used in Polish regulations (i.e. impact assessment – IA) had been included in IA Guidelines adopted by the Council of Ministers in 2015, in the form of interactive document available in the Government Centre for Legislation (Rządowe Centrum Legislacji)[25] (hereinafter: IA guidelines). This document specifies impact assessment as ***"an analytical process to support decision-making on regulatory solutions by providing information as full as possible on the options to address a specific problem and on the potential impacts (costs and benefits) of implementing them."***[26] **The concept of IA has also been defined in the government programme "Better Regulations" for 2012–2015 as** "*a process of identifying and analysing the problem (including the identification of stakeholders), defining the objectives of public intervention, identifying possible options for achieving the objectives, analysing the costs and benefits of these options and evaluating the applicable legislation.*"[27] Impact assessment contains elements such as regulatory test (in the form of a document in a synthetic manner presenting the results of the impact assessment at the level of the draft of the assumptions of the draft legislative act), *ex ante* RIA (also a document presenting the results of the impact assessment of the draft of the legislative act), *ex post* RIA (a document presenting the results of the impact assessment on the

23 In the Regulations of the Council of Ministers, the significant areas of influence were considered to be as follows: in particular, the public finance sector, including the state budget and budgets of local government units, the labour market, the competitiveness of the economy and entrepreneurship, including the functioning of entrepreneurs.

24 Cf. § 29 et seq. Rules of Procedure of the Council of Ministers.

25 Guidelines for impact assessment and public consultation as part of the government's legislative process, interactive document available on the website of Rządowe Centrum Legislacji (Government Centre for Legislation) http://www.rcl.gov.pl/book/wytyczne [access 12.12.2018 r.].

26 OSR guidelines, http://www.rcl.gov.pl/book/121-definicja-oceny-wp%C5 %82ywu [access 12.12.2018].

27 "Better Regulations" Programme for 2012–2015, Ministry of Economy, Warszawa 2012, p. 6.

binding legislative act). What is important, the basis of impact assessment is evidence-based policy, i.e. taking informed political decisions based on analytical data [28].

The concepts of RIA and impact assessment appear in the EU and OECD documents.

For the purposes of the OECD, regulatory impact assessment (RIA) is defined as the process of systematic identification and assessment of the expected impacts of legislative proposals using consistent analytical methods, such as cost-benefit analyses. Thus, regulatory impact assessment is a process of assessment and comparison (using identical methods) of effectiveness and efficiency, achievement of the intended regulatory objectives, considering the various regulatory options likely to be used[29]. The regulation of a given area is only justified if the expected result is improvement in the economic and social wealth[30]. Such result will be achieved provided that the ultimate benefits of the regulations will exceed the total costs for all members of the society. The state usually uses regulations to intervene in the event of *market failures*[31]. Their occurrence means that the sole market competition may not be sufficient to guarantee the effective economic functioning of the market. Market failures are not the only reason for regulations. The regulation is sometimes necessary due to the need to improve the situation of certain social groups (e.g. the poor)[32]. The OECD Recommendation on Regulatory Policy stipulates that the *ex ante* RIA should, for example, clearly define the objectives of new regulations (e.g. the need to correct market failures) and the most effective and efficient way of their implementation as well as consider the costs and benefits (with a distinction who will benefit from them and how they will be incurred). The welfare implications of regulation should also be considered, together with specifying the economic, social and environmental consequences or the results of redistribution[33]. In turn,

28 "Better Regulations" Programme for -2015 Warszawa 2012–2015…, p. 6.

29 *Introductory Handbook for Undertaking Regulatory Impact Analysis (RIA)*, OECD, 2008, https://www.oecd.org/gov/regulatory-policy/44789472.pdf [access 12.02.2018], p. 3.

30 In the literature on economics, the economic results are assessed based on two criteria: *efficiency and equity*., cf: J. Stelmach, B. Brożek, W. Załuski, *Dziesięć…*, p. 26 et seq.

31 Market failures include the existence of public goods, externalities, monopolies, imperfect information., R.S., Sobell *Welfare Economics and Public Finance* [in:] *Handbook of Public Finance*, ed. J.G. Backhaus, R.W. Wagner, Boston 2005, p. 25 et seq.

32 *Introductory Handbook…*, p. 6.

33 Zob. *Recommendation of the Council on Regulatory Policy*, OECD 2012, http://www.oecd.org/gov/regulatory-policy/49990817.pdf [access 12.02.2018], p. 10.

the OECD guidebook specified that the assessment of the effects of the regulation should be made based on the analysis of benefits and costs. They may be considered either in terms of quantity or quality. The inclusion of benefits and costs in terms of money makes it easier to compare the impacts of different regulatory options. Therefore, whenever possible, such solution should be applied, however it is not always possible to consider costs and benefits in terms of quantity. Thus, quantitative approach should be supplemented by a qualitative approach[34]. Hence, impact assessment is an excellent instrument of scrutiny for a legislator, as it enables the socio-economic impact of legislation to be assessed as early as during the preparatory stage.[35] In developing countries, however, RIA is at an early stage of its development[36].

As of IA (a term used by EC), the guidebook on that issue specifies impact assessment as a process of preparing arguments for the legislator, related to the advantages and disadvantages of possible solutions through indicating their potential effects. IA should establish, inter alia, the nature and scale of the problem to be solved, collect stakeholders' opinions on possible ways to achieve the objective, determine the potential economic and social impacts of these solutions (in terms of effectiveness, efficiency, coherence).[37]. Impact assessment is considered to be an optimal instrument for comprehensive control and evaluation of decisions by comparing their economic, social and environmental costs and benefits[38].

The term IA is understood differently by lawyers and economists. Lawyers usually refer it to standard procedure which may be, i.a., a procedural requirement integrating and standardizing the regulatory process which supports the government in selecting one of the options[39]. Economists, in turn, treat IA

34 *Introductory Handbook….,* p. 9 et seq.

35 Cf. F. De Francesco, C. M. Radaelli, V. E. Troeger, *Implementing regulatory innovations in Europe: the case of impact assessment,*"Journal of European Public Policy" 2012, vol. 19, no. 4, p. 491 and subsequent.

36 Cf. C. Kirkpatrick, D. Parker, Y.F. Zhang, Regulatory *Impact Assessment in Developing and Transition Economies: A Survey of Current Practice,* Centre on Regulation and Competition, Working Papers 2004, no. 83, p. 2 and subsequent.

37 *Impact Assessment Guidelines,* European Commission, 15.01.2009, http://ec.europa.eu/smart-regulation/impact/commission_guidelines/docs/iag_2009_en.pdf [access 12.02.2018], p. 4.

38 *Communication from the Commission to the European Parliament, the Council, the European Economic and Social Committee and the Committee of Regions,* SWD (2012) 422 final, European Commission, Strasbourg, 12.12.2012, p. 5.

39 A. Renda, *Impact Assessment in the EU. The State of the Art and the Art of the State,* Brussels 2006, p. 134.

differently, depending on the economic direction. For example, mainstream economists consider IA to be a method of comparing the potential indirect and direct costs and benefits of the proposed regulations. Moreover, they treat IA as a clearly established regulatory option using one of the effective economy criteria.[40]

This concept is also inconclusive in the Polish literature. On the one hand, IA is considered a component of the stated objective of the act (the view of lawyers preparing draft acts). On the other hand, IA is to form part of an autonomous assessment of the draft legislation (the view of economists)[41].

In case of the Polish regulations, the analysis of both terms, i.e. impact assessment and RIA allows to **establish that RIA in Poland has a form of documents drawn within the framework of impact assessment. These documents are then annexed to the valid Act (or draft thereof), which, according to the definition of the RIA included in the Guidelines by the Council of Ministers, is the result of assessments of expected socio-economic impacts.**

4 Evolution and Analysis of Current Regulations Regarding the Regulatory Impact Assessment in Poland

In Poland, the issue of regulatory impact assessment emerged with access to OECD in 1996. In practice, it was only in 2001 that RIA system was implemented, but in the initial period (2002–2005) it functioned quite ineffectively as the socio-economic impact assessment was not very reliable and the regulatory assessment was usually of a general nature.[42]. The following shortcomings of the RIA system used in Poland in 2001–2006 have been identified: reduction of formal requirements at higher stages of the legislative process as compared to the requirements in force at earlier stages, lack of obligation to analyse the baseline scenario (i.e. the expected development of the situation in the case of not taking any legislative intervention) or lack of resources and time to conduct economic and legal analyses.[43]

---

40 A. Renda, *Impact Assessment in the EU. The State of the Art and the Art of the State*, Brussels 2006, p. 133, See also the examples of economic efficiency criteria. F. Parisi, J. Klick, *Functional Law and Economics: The Search for Value-Neutral Principles of Lawmaking*,"Chicago-Kent Law Review" 2004, no. 79, p. 431 et seq.

41 W. Brzęk, *Regulation Impact Assessment (RIA) at Poland and at some EU countries*, "Procedia - Social and Behavioral Sciences" 2014, no. 109, p. 46.

42 J. Osiecka-Chojnacka, *System oceny…*, p. 2.

43 R. Zubek, *Jak i dlaczego reformować ocenę skutków regulacji w Polsce?, Opracowanie przygotowane na zlecenie Rzecznika Praw Obywatelskich, (wersja ostateczna 26/01/2007)*, https://www.rpo.gov.pl/pliki/12180262910.pdf [access 20.02.2018], p. 7.

Starting from 2006, a number of programmes related to regulatory reform have been prepared. The first, written in 2006 by the Council of Ministers, adopted, with the *ex post RIA among others.*[44] However, despite the convergence of the Polish RIA system with almost every OECD and EU recommendation, Polish regulations on this matter were rather incomplete and inconsistent at that time.[45]

Since 2009, *ex post* RIA had been developed in the Ministry of Economy. In 2011 the so-called regulatory test was introduced, referring to – as a separate part of the objectives of the daft act – an initial economic, financial and social analysis (among others), including the assessment of regulatory burdens and a comparison with those in other countries[46].

The next programme was the Regulation Reform Programme 2010–2011 "Better Law", assuming implementation of the following objectives: changes in the lawmaking system, improvement of the RIA system, reduction of administrative burdens, simplification of the law[47].

The next was "Better Regulations" Programme for 2012–2015[48],where a comprehensive system of development and assessment of regulations in Poland was designed. Its main aim was implementing *"the systemic and organisational solutions, necessary for the creation and evaluation of law based on analytical evidence, aimed at solving the real social and economic problems, including reduction of costs of conducting business activity and increasing the competitiveness of the Polish economy".*[49] The comprehensive IA system implemented within the framework of the Programme is based on the *evidence-based policy making.* Three detailed objectives have been formulated: transparent lawmaking solving the real problems, constant improvement of the existing legal setting and improving the communication with the stakeholders. It may be pointed out as an example that the specific objective of transparent lawmaking effectively solving real problems is to be achieved through, inter alia, improvement of the lawmaking system and development of the impact assessment system.[50] The Programme

44 J. Osiecka-Chojnacka, *System oceny…*, p. 2 et seq.

45 J. Osiecka-Chojnacka, *System oceny…*, p. 4., see also: J.A. Stefanowcz, K. Szamałek, *Analiza skutków regulacji prawnych w obszarze prawa geologiczno-górniczego*,"Zeszyty Naukowe Instytutu Gospodarki Surowcami Mineralnymi i Energii PAN" 2010, no. 79, p. 46 et seq.

46 "Better Regulations" Programme for -2015 Warszawa 2012–2015…, p. 12.

47 Council of Ministers Work Programme, January–June 2010, Warszawa 2010, p. 2.

48 "Better Regulations" Programme for 2012–2015, Ministry of Economy, Warszawa 2012.

49 Ibidem, p. 2.

50 Ibidem, pp. 2–3.

also adopted a number of actions aimed at creating the system fostering creating the law which would prove effective in solving real problems (e.g. amending the Work Regulations of the Council of Ministers[51] in terms of formulating transparent procedures for developing, discussing and adopting draft normative acts, creating the state e-legislation system), development of IA system (development of guidelines for carrying out IA, implementation of an impact test on the SME sector, preparation of a standardized *ex post* RIA form), improvement of the effectiveness of the implementation of Community law (e.g. development of guidelines for the creation of a regulatory test at the stage of legislative work in the EU)[52]. Another element of the Programme is developing the actions aimed at reducing the barriers for business development, improving communication with the stakeholders, fostering the access to legal provisions and case law[53]. It can be pointed out as an example that the process of public consultations in Poland (concerning the provisions of law procedures in 2012) showed numerous shortcomings. They referred to, among others, consultation of draft acts only at the stage of a draft law (and not at an earlier stage), using only traditional methods of consultation (e.g. publishing a draft on the Ministry's Public Information Bulletin website), improper identification of stakeholders (too narrow or too broad), period planned for consultations being too short, occasional response of the government to the comments submitted to the draft legal act by the stakeholders.[54] This leads to a conclusion that the process of carrying out public consultations in Poland progresses properly *"when a specific requirement is clearly specified in documents applicable to officials, for example in the Work Regulations of the Council of Ministers, then it is actually applied (e.g. An attempt to define the stakeholders during the preparation of all the examined draft acts)."*[55] This confirms that RIA in Poland, especially in the introductory implementation phase (2001–2007), was carried out in a superficial manner, without any real reference of the results of the regulation in question to the economic

---

51 Regulamin RM [Rules of Procedure of the Council of Ministers].

52 "Better Regulations" Programme for -2015 Warszawa 2012–2015..., p. 21–31.

53 Ibidem, p. 32 et seq.

54 G. Kopińska, *Najważniejsze wnioski i rekomendacje* [in:] G. Kopińska, G. Makowski, P. Waglowski, M.M. Wiszowaty, *Tworzenie i konsultowanie rządowych projektów ustaw. Raport z badania nad sposobem prowadzenia konsultacji publicznych i tworzenia dokumentów towarzyszących rządowym projektom ustaw w 2012 roku*, http://www.batory.org.pl/upload/files/Programy%20operacyjne/Odpowiedzialne%20Panstwo/Tworzenie_i_konsultowanie.pdf[access 20.02.2018], p. 12 et seq.

55 Ibidem, p. 15.

operators, impact on financial sector, labour market, situation of the regions. For example, it has been observed with reference to the regulations in the scope of mining and geological law (e.g. system of remuneration for concession)[56].

A certain inconsistency can be noticed in the Polish RIA regulations regarding the use of the terms RIA and IA. RIA seems to be an element of the impact assessment, as there are three documents prepared as part of IA in Poland. The first document is a regulatory test where the IA results, among others, are presented in a synthetic manner at the stage of work on the assumptions of the draft law. It is carried out mandatorily in the case of draft assumptions of the draft law[57]. Terminology of the other two documents refers directly to RIA. The first of these documents is the RIA which includes the results of IA estimated at the stage of drafting a legal act, whereas the second is the RIA (*ex post*) which assesses the legal act *ex post*. Thus, it includes the impact assessment results at the stage of its application[58]. Model forms have been prepared for both documents on RIA[59].

5 RIA Development Perspectives in Poland as Exemplified by the New Regulations on the Development of Draft Normative Acts in Economic Law and Evaluation of their Functioning

The regulations of the draft act of 26 January 2018 Entrepreneurs Law, [60] with Chapter VI (Articles 66–71) entitled "*Principles of preparing draft normative acts in the field of commercial law and evaluation of their functioning*", may serve as an example of direction towards which RIA may be developing in Poland[61]. This chapter sets out the actual rules for carrying out ex ante and ex post RIA of the draft normative acts on certain matter, e.g. economic law. Statement of

56 J.A. Stefanowcz, K. Szamałek, *Analiza skutków regulacji…*, p. 54.

57 IA guidelines.

58 Ibidem.

59 Both model forms are available at Biuletyn Informacji Publicznej Kancelarii Prezesa Rady Ministrów website, https://bip.kprm.gov.pl/kpr/bip-rady-ministrow/ocena-wplywu/4156,Ocena-wplywu-w-rzadowym-procesie-legislacyjnym.html [access 20.02.2018].

60 The legislative works on the act have not been finished. The text is available on Sejm website: http://orka.sejm.gov.pl/opinie8.nsf/nazwa/2051_u/$file/2051_u.pdf [access 20.02.2018].

61 The principles set out in this chapter do not apply to the exercise of a legislative initiative by citizens as defined in Article 118 section 2 of the Constitution of the Republic of Poland.

reasons concerning the draft [62] indicates the aim of these regulations is *"ensuring favourable legal conditions for commencement, performance and termination of economic activity through the introduction into the system the universally binding legal norms of law-making the principles related to commencing, performance and termination of economic activity, including preparation of regulatory impact assessments."*[63] Hence, it is advisable to clarify RIA in relation to economic law, as it is necessary to take into account specificity of the entrepreneurs' activity influencing various market entities (both on a micro and macroeconomic scale). Thus, making economic law requires special care and diligence[64]. It is all the more important because – as demonstrated by earlier discussion and also indicated in the explanatory memorandum to the analysed act – *"The existing regulations in the field of law-making are dispersed and only partially implement the requirements of evidence-based law-making, including the regulatory impact assessment."*[65]

The draft law sets out that the following steps are taken in the case of ex ante RIA (i.e. before the commencement of works on developing draft normative act specifying the rules of commencement, execution or termination of business activity): analysis of the possibility of achieving the objective of this normative act with the use of other means, assessment of the expected social and economic effects, including the IA on micro-entrepreneurs, small and medium-sized enterprises and the analysis of the compliance of the draft regulations with the provisions of the Act. Their results are included in the substantiation of a legal act (or RIA which constitutes its part). In this approach – as pointed out before – *ex ante* RIA takes the form of a document constituting part of the substantiation of the draft law.

The principles of proportionality and adequacy included in the new act, which the legislator is supposed to rely on in *ex ante* RIA regarding the draft normative act regulating commencement, execution or termination of business activity, should be evaluated positively. Implementation of these principles is aimed at, among others, limiting the administrative obligations regarding entrepreneurs (or not imposing these obligations whatsoever), limiting information obligations or implementing them in a less onerous manner, e.g. electronic form.

---

62 *Substantiation of the Entrepreneurs' Law,* Sejm paper of the 8th term in office of Sejm, no. 2051, http://www.sejm.gov.pl/sejm8.nsf/druk.xsp?nr=2051 [access 20.02.2018].

63 Ibidem, p. 58.

64 Ibidem, p. 58 et seq.

65 Ibidem, p. 59.

This means a special treatment for micro-entrepreneurs, small and medium-sized enterprises, thus a group of entrepreneurs considered to have significant impact on stimulating economic development. The development of this group of entrepreneurs also denotes increase in competition and entrepreneurship[66]. Therefore, the new act introduces the so-called SME test related to facilitation of business activity of this group of entrepreneurs[67]. Since the draft legal act is going to affect SME, the proportional reduction of the administrative obligations towards these entrepreneurs is sought at the stage of developing such project, or the lack of applying such limitations justified (Article 68 Entrepreneurs Law).

The regulations regarding the *ex post* RIA of the already binding legal acts, specifying the rules of commencement, execution or termination of business activity, should also receive positive evaluation. If any significant differences in the interpretation of law occur, or there is a risk that the given normative act causes significant negative economic or social effects, it is possible to conduct an *ex post* RIA of this legal act. What is important, the entities participating in this procedure have been specified, as well as the obligation to either conduct *ex post* RIA by the obliged entity or to justify the pointlessness of preparation of such RIA. Such process may be initiated by the Representative of Micro, Small and Medium-Sized Enterprises, i.e. a newly established entity which is to guard the rights of this group of entrepreneurs[68].

Another regulation which may be evaluated positively is the duty of the ministers in charge of government administration departments to annually review the functioning of normative acts defining the principles of commencing, execution or termination of economic activity; therefore, to conduct a complex *ex ante* RIA of the legal acts referring to this matter. As a result of the review, information on the activities undertaken within the framework of the review carried out in the previous year (Article 70 of the Entrepreneurs Law) is submitted annually to the Council of Ministers (no later than 30 June).

The changes introduced to RIA refer in practice to enforcing the elements of legislative procedure so that it takes RIA results into account to a greater extent than before. There is a clear tendency to specify in more detail the certain

---

66 Cf. I. Szczepaniak, *Rola małych i średnich przedsiębiorstw w gospodarce (na przykładzie przemysłu spożywczego)*,"Equilibrium" 2009, no. 1, p. 71 et seq.

67 *Uzasadnienie…*., p. 62.

68 Cf. Act of January 26, 2018 on the Representative of Micro, Small and Medium-Sized Enterprises The legislative works on the act have not been finished. The text available on Sejm website http://orka.sejm.gov.pl/proc8.nsf/ustawy/2052_u.htm [access 20.02.2018].

elements of RIA, entities obliged to carry out specific activities within the RIA, or the principles which they are to be guided by.

6 Final Conclusions

Regulatory impact assessment is one of the aspects of economization of law. Practically, it is the most often used instrument for the improvement of regulation quality. It is a result of – among others – regulatory policy implemented within the OECD, UE, as well as in Poland, where IA system is used and RIA takes the form of **documents prepared under the aforementioned impact assessment[69]. In practice, however, both these terms appear in literature and government documents (sometimes interchangeably), which unfortunately results in terminological incoherence.**

In the introductory implementation phase, the RIA system in Poland did not function efficiently, as evidenced, i.a., by the fact that RIA was usually of very general nature. Subsequent state programmes aimed at improving the law – including the last one of 2012–2015 – gradually facilitate the improvement of the functioning of the Polish RIA. They are aimed at changes in the lawmaking system, improvement of the RIA system, reduction of administrative burdens, simplification of the law. Currently, RIA is prepared based on the analysis of benefits and costs of a given regulation.

The development of the RIA in Poland will probably be aimed at more detailed regulation and clarification of its particular stages, greater transparency of competence of entities responsible for particular activities, more realistic and reliable assessment of the costs and benefits of a given regulation. Such approach is supported by the analysis of the regulations concerning economic law RIA, included in the new act. They clearly define, for example, the need to carry out an *ex ante* RIA before commencing works on a draft normative act, or the obligation to carry out an ex post RIA in certain situations. The solutions proposed in the

69 **Defining RIA and ex post RIA as the documents prepared within the framework of IA would favour adopting such approach. Assessment of the functioning of the Act (*ex-post* RIA) is** a document prepared within the framework of IA and presenting the knowledge of the functioning of a legal act hitherto in a structured manner. In turn, regulatory impact assessment **(RIA) has been specified as a document** made under IA, constituting development, specification and update of the regulatory test (which is also a document prepared under IA and presenting the results of previous analyses); see also the definitions of "functional assessment of the Act (ex post RIA)" and "regulatory impact assessment (RIA)", "regulatory test (RT)" included in the glossary to the IA Guidelines., http://www.rcl.gov.pl/book/31-s%C5%82owniczek, [access 20.02.2018].

new act should be assessed positively, as they foster removing the deficiencies of the RIA system in Poland, present in the initial period of its creation. Currently, the RIA system in Poland can indeed support the legislator in selecting the most economically and socially optimal regulation option.

K. Burdziak

Article 31 Section 3 of the Polish Constitution and Leon Petrażycki's Concept of the Policy of Law

1 Objective

In line with the title of the monograph for which this paper has been subjected (to recall, the title is *The Concepts of Modern Law. Central European Traditions*), each chapter it comprises should, firstly, refer to the modernist image and vision of the world that could be described using terms such as determinism, universalism, scientism, objective and methodological naturalism; secondly, to confront the said image or vision with the current state of contemporary Polish law (or, in a broader sense, the Central European law), and lastly, to identify the sources of modernist solutions in the Polish law (or, in a broader sense, the Central European law) by referring to, primarily, Polish authors, or in a broader approach, to authors of the Central European region. Thus one could determine in general the objective of this paper. The general objective of the paper, however, always takes a more detailed approach; we should then indicate, on a point of order, that the specific objective of this paper is, in the following order: 1) to provide a (brief, of course) analysis of a proposal of a scientific policy if law developed by Leon Petrażycki[1], 2) to prove the modernist character of this proposal and 3) to prove that it is correlated with the currently binding Article 31 Section 3 of the Polish Constitution.[2] In other words, the aim is to determine,

---

1 For more information on Petrażycki and his views see: A. Biernat, *Poglądy filozoficzne Leona Petrażyckiego i ich interpretacje*, Toruń 2002, p. 188; D. Gil, Ł. Pikuła (eds.), *Prawo i nauka w poglądach Leona Petrażyckiego*, Lublin 2013, p. 197; A. Habrat, *Ideał człowieka i społeczeństwa w teorii Leona Petrażyckiego*, Rzeszów 2006, p. 123; A. Kojder, *Godność i siła prawa,* Warsaw 2001, pp. 57–188; A. Kojder, *Idee społeczno-prawne Leona Petrażyckiego i ich współczesne kontynuacje*, in: Klasyczna socjologia polska i jej współczesna recepcja, J. Mucha, W. Wincławski (eds.) Toruń 2006, pp. 57–90; K. Motyka, *Wpływ Leona Petrażyckiego na polską teorię i socjologię prawa*, Lublin 1993, p. 230; J. Woleński, *Leon Petrażycki o prawie i moralności*, Rocznik Polskiej Akademii Umiejętności. Year 2016/2017, Kraków 2017, pp. 171–182.

2 The Polish Constitution of 2nd April 1997 (Journal of Laws no. 78, item 483, as amended).

as follows: 1) the source (at least the potential source) of modernist solutions in the Polish law, 2) the realness of the modernist character of the said source and 3) the refection of these modernist solutions in the currently binding Polish law.

2 Method

The conclusions arrived at in this paper were made: 1) in the course of an analysis of selected Petrażycki's publications; 2) in the course of an analysis of normative material referring to the examined issue, more specifically, in the course of an analysis of Article 31 Section 3 of the Polish Constitution; and also 3) in the course of an analysis of views presented in Polish literature and Polish caselaw.

3 The Scientific Policy of Law Developed by Leon Petrażycki[3]

The presentation of the scientific policy of law developed by Petrażycki will be made based on two fundamental text of this author, specifically, based on the paper 1) *O ideale społecznym i odrodzeniu prawa naturalnego*[4] and 2) *Wstęp do nauki polityki prawa*[5], in which Petrażycki clearly indicated that the objective he set out for himself and to the fulfilment of which he strived throughout his life was to justify the capacity and to prepare a scientific policy of law based on experimental-psychological examination of law and its causal properties (causal action).[6] In other words, the purpose Petrażycki set out for himself was to build

3 On Petrażycki's scientific policy of law see in particular: H. Leszczyna, *Petrażycki*, Warsaw 1974, pp. 69–89. Also see: S. Czepita, *Metodologiczna charakterystyka ewolucji koncepcji polityki prawa Leona Petrażyckiego*, Zeszyty Naukowe. Vol. 27. Prace Studium Administracyjnego. Vol. 1, Szczecin 1978, pp. 99–120.

4 L. Petrażycki, *O ideale społecznym i odrodzeniu prawa naturalnego*, in: L. Petrażycki, *O nauce, prawie i moralności. Pisma wybrane*, Warsaw 1985, pp. 153–166.

5 L. Petrażycki, Wstęp do nauki polityki prawa, in: L. Petrażycki, O nauce, prawie i moralności. Pisma wybrane, Warsaw 1985, pp. 331–367.

6 See L. Petrażycki, *O ideale*, p. 153. According to Petrażycki, law is a class of imperative-attributive emotions; emotions that consist in simultaneous experiencing of an obligation and a right. These emotions, in the view of the said author, are characterised by their ability to easily become popularised and their value lies in their enormous motivational force. Hence, Petrażycki's strong belief that there was a need for a policy of law to be created that would indicate how motivation could be used for reaching the social ideal (which will be discussed further on). See J. Woleński, *Marian Smoluchowski i Leon Petrażycki*, in: J. Skoczyński, J. Woleński (eds.) *Historia filozofii polskiej*, Kraków 2010, p. 347.

a special science that would aim to foresee outcomes (both good and bad) of specific legal provisions, whose efficiency would depend on a theory being created for it that would determine causal links between law and other social phenomena.[7]

The above-indicated experimental-psychological study of law and its causal properties was intended by Petrażycki (and rightly so, as it seems) as a sine qua non condition for conscious and rational use of law. However, it is difficult to imagine setting specific goals before law and expecting it to fulfil them in a situation where one does not even know what law is and how does it affect an individual and society.[8]

According to Petrażycki, "to know and understand what causal effects could be reached by means of law, what tasks could be put forward and solved in law-making and in legal creation in general, hence, what ideals could be put forward here not as utopian but as reachable, one must know the nature and causal properties of law as a specific causal factor in the social-psychical life."[9] Elsewhere, the said author indicates that "having examined (…) the essence and the ideal of law on the one hand and the area and measures of its action, i.e. the psyche of an individual and that of society, on the other, we will be able to consciously and reasonably direct the law-making process, we will be able to give a reasonable answer to legislators' questions, specify what law should be like, how should it be modified, what to preserve and what to complement so that it can be effective and compliant with its elevated and rational task."[10]

Given the above, it does not come as a surprise that Petrażycki complained on the contemporary lack of proper interest of jurisprudence in the above-indicated problem. He claimed, "if jurisprudence reached even a hundred or two hundred years ago, the experimental-psychological knowledge of law and the psychological study of its various complex effects on the individual and mass human psyche, its deep complex and various causal effects, as a factor that motivates action and creation, development and gradual transformation of human character, it would have a natural and scientific policy of law, i.e. consciously rational use of a proper theoretical scientific light for the good of mankind, to achieve the desired social conduct and social education. And if highly respected and conscientious researchers could claim that the popularised science would assume a

7 See J. Woleński, *Marian Smoluchowski i Leon Petrażycki*, p. 346.
8 See L. Petrażycki, *O ideale*, p. 153.
9 L. petrażycki, *O ideale*, p. 153.
10 L. Petrażycki, *Wstęp*, p. 339.

prophetic gift, it is explained in that there has not been a proper theoretical light as yet, i.e. an experimental cognition of law and its effect on psyche; for if we had the light, we could foresee the causal effects of these or other legal reforms without a prophetic gift."[11]

Here, it should be stressed that according to Petrażycki, law constitutes a psychic factor of social life and has a psychic effect. This effect consists in: 1) motivational influence or impulsive influence, i.e. evoking or suppressing reasons to various actions or omissions and 2) pedagogical effect, i.e. strengthening or weakening certain tendencies and traits of human character, shaping the psyche of a nation in the right direction.[12]

At the same time, Petrażycki points that law (as an entirety, but also as a single legal provision) triggers numerous causal effects that have practical importance. And thus, on the one hand, it acts as a motivating factor for individual and mass action (evokes specific individual actions and mass proceedings), where, firstly, in various categories of people it evokes different motives and, secondly, by modifying actions of some people, it triggers modification of actions taken by subsequent individuals. On the other hand, it alters the psyche of those who are subject to its effect with the very same decision in the very same people resulting in various educational outcomes, similarly as it may cause various numerous educational outcomes in various categories of people. Hence, in Petrażycki's belief, the 'double-purpose' understood as the necessity to take into account two types of the causal effect of law and two purposes: the social-motivating one and the social-educational one, should be given the rank of a general management principle. The 'double-purpose' should be understood not as the existence of only two purposes but as a "double-class nature of purposes".[13] At the same time, Petrażycki stressed that "the double-purpose nature should be indicated solely for management principles and not to formulate legal provisions: here, one more sentence related to the specific nature of law: multiple purposes to the power of three."[14]

---

11 L. Petrażycki, *O ideale*, p. 154.

12 See L. Petrażycki, *O ideale*, p. 157.

13 See L. Petrażycki, *Prawo jako czynnik wywołujący mnóstwo praktycznie relewantnych efektów*, in: L. Petrażycki, *O nauce, prawie i moralności. Pisma wybrane*, Warsaw 1985, pp. 424–426.

14 L. Petrażycki, *Prawo*, p. 426.

Considering the above, the policy of law faced two tasks (according to Petrażycki): first, to manage individual and mass proceedings rationally using proper legal motivation,[15] and second, to perfect human psyche (to relieve it of malicious antisocial tendencies).[16]

According to Petrażycki, "It comes down to gradual shaping of a certain ideal composition of emotional psyche, gradual eradication of egoistic malicious dispositions and hence, the very mental ability to act properly, to kill others, even those with the justified name of 'enemies', vicious wounding and hurting of any form, instilling, developing and reinforcing creative emotional dispositions and thus creating a mental necessity for acting in a good, merciful, gracious way."[17] Petrażycki assumed that in the future, the so-called ideal of love will be achieved. This very ideal was to be the fundamental and final objective of criminal law and the ideal of criminal policy, and not a struggle with these or other harmful actions of citizens.[18]

The method that should be used for implementing the above-indicated tasks should be psychological deduction – "inference based on proper psychological premises[19] regarding the mental, be it motivational or pedagogical, implications that should be obtained as a result of certain legal principles and institutions, or

---

15 S. Czepita rightly points that "One should note Petrażycki's remarks on the 'indirect' motivational effect of legal experiences. The 'indirect' motivational effect occurs in a situation where experiences of recipients of legal norms are too weak to make them engage in the action ordered by law and it consists in using non-ethical emotions of recipients of legal norms to ensure that the said norms are respected, e.g. by indicating positive or negative outcomes related to observance and violation of law, respectively. A specific type of 'indirect' motivation is the so-called 'free' motivation; it is evoked by creating a legal situation where a person intends to fulfil a state of affairs desired by the legislator despite this fulfilment not being ordered" (S. Czepita, *Koncepcja polityki prawa Leona Petrażyckiego a koncepcje współczesne*, Państwo i Prawo 1977, Vol. 7, p. 51).

16 See L. Petrażycki, *O ideale*, p. 157.

17 L. Petrażycki, *O ideale*, p. 159.

18 See L. Petrażycki, *Wstęp*, pp. 331–332. Petrażycki considered the ideal of love to be an axiom of practical thinking that requires no evidence and cannot be proved. However, two other fundamental theorems must be proved: first, that moral growth among specific nations and humanity as a whole is possible and historically confirmed; second, that law can and does affect the development of collective ethics in a way that reasonable policy of law creates or accelerates moral growth (see L. Petrażycki, *Wstęp*, pp. 331–332).

19 L. Petrażycki distinguished three fields of legal psychology, with the first one (science of motives) was to examine 1) traits of human nature that can be used by law to evoke

regarding legislative measures that can evoke certain desired motivational and educational effects on the psyche."[20]

Nonetheless, it seems that the ultimate goal of the policy of law should be to achieve a complete eradication of law (including or possibly most of all, criminal law). Petrażycki claimed that law exists only as a result of the fact that human psyche has not been yet sufficiently adjusted to the needs of social life; hence, its task is to make oneself redundant and to disappear.[21] The said author claims that "over time and for other people, as it has already taken place with regard to monarchs, penalty law and criminal law in general as well as national law will be abolished; and if and when the completely proper and social education, the psyche of love in our broad sense, and so on, will be achieved, then law will have no sense at all and its existence will even become mentally impossible (which of course does not exclude making common plans of action and eager fulfilment of such plans without any mental stress)."[22]

4 Petrażycki's Scientific Policy of Law and Modernism

Modernism (the notion of modernism) can be referred to two things, as Morawski rightly indicates. First, to the stage of development of contemporary societies, and second, to the theoretical attitude/though tendency that began to shape in the post-modern era; the latter shall be discussed here.[23]

And so, the modernist image and vision of the world can be described, as already mentioned, using terms such as 1) determinism (natural and social worlds ruled by objective causal relations); 2) universalism (rules of science that describe causal relations that rule the world - with a universal range; the universal range is also characteristic of rationally justified moral norms); 3) scientism (reason, science and technology determine universal models of assessment of our actions and institutions; only that which is compliant with science

---

specific motives triggering one to take specific actions or omission, 2) the character, occurrence and meaning of motives themselves, which are used by law to make an impact and 3) mutual effect of various motives, whereas the second one (science of legal education) was to examine the way in which character is shaped under the influence of law, whereas the third one was to be the science of regularities of the shaping of the obtained improvement in social education in the form of objective views, principles and tools, coexistence rules (see L. Petrażycki, *Wstęp*, pp. 337–339).

20 L. Petrażycki, *O ideale*, p. 158.

21 See L. Petrażycki, *O ideale*, p. 165.

22 L. Petrażycki, *O ideale*, p. 165.

23 See L. Morawski, *Filozofia prawa*, Toruń 2014, p. 339.

is rational); 4) objective naturalism (the purpose of all sciences is to discover regularities, causal links or functional links between phenomena in nature and society); 5) methodological naturalism (methods applied in all sciences are the same; social sciences should be modelled on methods used in natural sciences).[24]

The above views seem to be shared also by Petrażycki. It suffices to indicate the following words of the said author: 1) "if jurisprudence reached even a hundred or two hundred years ago, the experimental-psychological knowledge of law and the psychological study of its various complex effects on the individual and mass human psyche, its deep complex and various causal effects, as a factor that motivates action and creation, development and gradual transformation of human character, it would have a natural and scientific policy of law, i.e. consciously rational use of a proper theoretical scientific light for the good of mankind, to achieve the desired social conduct and social education"[25]; 2) "the policy of law is a psychological science. The theoretical basis of the policy of law should be a general psychological familiarity with factors and processes that motivate human action and the shaping of human character, as well a special knowledge of nature and the causative properties of law, particularly the knowledge of legal motivation and legal education. The basic method of legal-political thinking is psychological inference, making conclusions based on proper psychological premises regarding the psychical (…) implications that should be obtained as a result of certain legal rules and institutions acting"[26]; 3) "It comes down to gradual shaping of a certain ideal composition of emotional psyche, gradual eradication of egoistic malicious dispositions and hence, the very mental ability to act properly, to kill others, even those with the justified name of 'enemies', vicious wounding and hurting of any form, instilling, developing and reinforcing creative emotional dispositions and thus creating a mental necessity for acting in a good, merciful, gracious way. Thus, in view of psychology, there will be an inevitable change in countless ways and in countless directions not only of peoples' attitude towards other people and humanity, but also the attitude of *Homo sapiens* to other animals and suffering creatures"[27]; 4) "The greatest good we should pursue in general politics and in policy of law in particular is the moral growth of a human being, prevalence of high reasonable ethics among people, the so-called ideal of love. (…) moral progress among specific nations

24 See L. Morawski, *Filozofia*, pp. 335–342.
25 L. Petrażycki, *O ideale*, p. 154.
26 L. Petrażycki, *O ideale*, p. 158.
27 L. Petrażycki, *O ideale*, p. 159.

and humanity as a whole is possible and historically confirmed. (…) law can and does affect the development of collective ethics in a way that reasonable policy of law creates or accelerates moral growth; reasonable law is a school of morality, an educational institution for the nation and entire humanity"[28].

Thus, as can be seen, Petrażycki wanted to base the policy of law on scientific grounds; in his view, only then would rational management of an individual/society and his/her/its growth be possible (management by means of law, naturally). This reasonable management would not be possible without the knowledge of the nature of law and causal links that exist between it and specific social phenomena; the nature and links that, we can add here, are universal and described in universal laws of science, that are to be reached by means of applying methods characteristic of natural sciences. The aim of Petrażycki's policy of law was (in assumption) to reach the ideal of love, to create the psychical necessity of a proper good, merciful, gracious conduct among the entire humanity (a universal moral attitude). Hence, one cannot fail to notice the modernist character of postulates related to Petrażycki's concept of the policy of law. This was indicated by Morawski, who noted that "modernist influences are visible in many theoretical-legal concepts that usually refer to the tradition of the Enlightenment, legal positivism and liberalism (…). One should also notice that this train of modernist thought is focused not on projects that would rationally explain the surrounding reality but on projects that aim to transform it in a rational way. We could call these two types of modernism theoretical modernism and practical modernism, respectively. Legal realism with the project of social engineering (…), the idea of Petrażycki's policy of law unknown in most western states (…) are the most spectacular examples of practically oriented legal modernism."[29]

5 Article 31 Section 3 of the Polish Constitution

Article 31 Section 3 of the Polish Constitution states, "Any limitation upon the exercise of constitutional freedoms and rights may be imposed only by statute, and only when necessary in a democratic state for the protection of its security or public order, or to protect the natural environment, health or public morals, or the freedoms and rights of other persons. Such limitations shall not violate the essence of freedoms and rights."

28 L. Petrażycki, *Wstęp*, pp. 331–332.
29 L. Morawski, *Filozofia*, p. 345.

In accordance with Article 31 Section 3 of the Polish Constitution, the fundamental requirement for implementing restrictions regarding the use of rights and freedoms a man enjoys is the requirement that they are set in a statutory act (formal premise).[30] This gives rise to two obligations: first – an obligation to set a restriction in the act, and second – an obligation to set the restriction in a way that the postulate of the completeness of statutory legislation is met.

The meaning of the above-indicated requirement seems obvious. Suffices to point that it ensures that the parliament takes part in the shaping of an individual's legal situation and, hence, ensures transparency of the decision-making process, safeguards hasty and reckless moves and also allows governmental legislative activity to be kept in check.[31]

Restrictions regarding the use of constitutional human rights and freedoms can take place only in a situation where it is necessary for ensuring safety of the state or public order, safeguarding the environment, health or public morality, or freedoms and rights of others. In other words, interference with an individual's rights and freedoms is possible only when supported by a significant public interest. However, Wojtyczek rightly points that "the highly general and vague way in which these premises are specified (under Article 31 Section 3 of the Polish Constitution – the Author's note) does not significantly obstruct (…) the legislator's freedom to act and allows in practice for ensuring observance of criminal law with respect to nearly all constitutional values."[32]

However, although determining the link between restricting human freedoms (or rights) and protecting one of the values indicated in the Polish Constitution is undoubtedly a necessary condition for considering such restriction acceptable, it is not the only condition. Such a restriction also has to satisfy proportionality principle (Article 31 Section 3, sentence 1 of the Polish Constitution), and moreover it cannot breach the essence of individual freedoms or rights (Article 31 Section 3 sentence 2 of the Polish Constitution).[33] To simplify, the proportionality principle boils down to a claim that the legislator cannot excessively interfere with the freedoms and liberties of an individual, while verification whether in a given case such an excessive interference does not take place calls

---

30 See L. Garlicki, *Przesłanki ograniczania konstytucyjnych praw i wolności (na tle orzecznictwa Trybunału Konstytucyjnego)*, Państwo i Prawo 2001, Vol. 10, p. 10.

31 See J. Zakolska, *Zasada proporcjonalności w orzecznictwie Trybunału Konstytucyjnego*, Warsaw 2008, p. 118.

32 K. Wojtyczek, *Zasada proporcjonalności jako granica prawa karania*, Czasopismo Prawa Karnego i Nauk Penalnych 1999, Vol. 2, p. 41.

33 See L. Garlicki, *Przesłanki*, p. 18.

for answering three questions: 1) can the introduced provision bring about the outcome it envisages (principle of usefulness); 2) is that provision necessary for safeguarding the public interest it is related to (principle of necessity); 3) do the effects of the introduced provision remain proportionate to the weight it puts on the citizen (principle of proportionality in the strict sense).[34]

6 Article 31 Section 3 of the Polish Constitution and Leon Petrażycki's Policy of Law

With due account of the above-indicated characteristics of Article 31 Section 3 of the Polish Constitution, one cannot fail to notice an analogy between the wording and the content of the said provision and (modernist) postulated regarding the policy of law proposed by Petrażycki.

Let us remind that for Petrażycki one of the tasks to be fulfilled by the policy of law (and even its main task) should be to perfect human psyche, to relieve it of malicious antisocial tendencies, to reach the so-called ideal of love (which is universal for the world and the entire humanity). Nonetheless, the above fact is also mentioned by the constitutional legislator in Article 31 Section 3 of the Polish Constitution. After all, every statutory restriction imposed on human freedoms and rights should be made with the aim to ensure the security of the state and public order, environment, health and public morality or freedoms and rights of others. Therefore, by means of setting accurate legal provisions the legislator should strive to ensure that the above-mentioned values protected by the

34 See the Constitutional Court's decision of 26th April 1995, K 11/94, LEX no. 25538. Importantly, in Article 31 Section 3 of the Polish Constitution the problem of "the necessity to restrict" is referred to the notion of a "democratic state". Consequently, in the event of a question whether a given restriction is necessary, useful and proportionate, it is imperative that one takes into account legal consequences of standards of democracy (see J. Zakolska, *Zasada*, p. 125; L. Garlicki, *Przesłanki*, p. 21). It is also worth to note that "using the proportionality principle in the strict sense always requires one to 'weigh goods' (…). In the most general approach, one has to take into account two elements: the weight of contradictory values and the degree of their implementation. The higher the value violated by a given interference and the higher the degree to which it is violated, the greater the value to be protected by the interference and the higher degree of implementation of the other value. The fact that a given value in the abstract hierarchy of values takes a higher place than the other does not mean that in certain situations it cannot be sacrificed – to some extent – for the sake of realising the value that takes a lover position in the hierarchy." (K. Wojtyczek, *Zasada*, p. 42).

law are not violated (this aim cannot be achieved otherwise than by evoking or suppressing motivation to various actions or omission in individuals, as Petrażycki recalled). Alternatively, once they are violated, the society should be showed that this violation is not only an undesired act but also unprofitable for the one who commits it. Hence, the legislator should strive to shape an individual and society in a way that ensures peaceful existence for all values significant for an individual, other individuals, as well as for society.

In the context of the Polish criminal law, Pohl rightly indicates that "the safeguarding function of criminal law is realised in many dimensions. First of all, one should notice that by legal norms included in the provision of that law, which indicate which behaviour is forbidden under penalty, by suggestively influencing the will of recipients of these norms, that law stimulated these people to observe them (…). The discussed dimension of the safeguarding function of criminal law is directly related to the general preventive role of criminal law which, as future-oriented, is intended to deter recipients of sanctioned criminal law norms from violating them. Internalisation of the axiological system adopted by the legislator is also achieved by the safeguarding function of criminal law fulfilled in the process of applying measures of criminal law response to a prohibited act towards the perpetrator of the said punishable act. This is because the penalty imposed on the offender is not considered in the modern model of criminal law response to a specific violation of a sanctioned criminal law norm to be embedded in the past and thus regarded as a primitively defined 'an eye for an eye' principle but primarily serves as a measure of prospective (since re-educational) influence on the intellectual-mental structure of the convict aiming to shaping in that person a socially desired axiological system that would increase the probability of that individual being effectively discouraged from committing punishable acts in the future. What is also important, this individual-preventive dimension in which the safeguard function is fulfilled is not currently limited only to the indicated influence. This is because a measure of criminal law response to an offence applied in a specific criminal case should evoke a social resonance every time, meaning that the said measure (hence, an imposed measure and not only a threatening measure) should be used for fulfilling grand general preventive needs aimed at stopping other members of society from committing punishable acts."[35]

We would also like to recall that Article 31 Section 3 of the Polish Constitution requires us to determine whether the implemented provision can bring about

35 Ł. Pohl, *Prawo karne. Wykład części ogólnej*, Warsaw 2015, pp. 26–27.

the outcomes it envisages (the principle of usefulness). Making such conclusions is difficult without knowing or previously examining the essence of law (while the constitutional legislator probably wants to force this type of studies on the legislator by introducing necessary studies of the usefulness of a given legal provision) and how does it impact an individual and society. For example, it is difficult to determine whether introduction of a criminal law prohibition of taking one's own life supported by a sanction of, e.g. imprisonment (a prohibition of this kind would not be anything new in the history of global criminal law, obviously) could force a person to stay alive or not in a situation where in fact one does not know, first of all, how to affect another human's psyche and, secondly, whether the criminal law prohibition of this sort (of this particular shape) could have any meaning in this respect. Meanwhile, as it was previously indicated, an experimental-psychological study of law and its causal properties was intended by Petrażyński as a sine qua non condition for conscious and rational use of law. To recall, he claimed that "if jurisprudence reached even a hundred or two hundred years ago, the experimental-psychological knowledge of law and the psychological study of its various complex effects on the individual and mass human psyche, its deep complex and various causal effects, as a factor that motivates action and creation, development and gradual transformation of human character, it would have a natural and scientific policy of law, i.e. consciously rational use of a proper theoretical scientific light for the good of mankind, to achieve the desired social conduct and social education."[36]

Introduction of a given legal provision requires at the same time (pursuant to Article 31 Section 3 of the Polish Constitution) previous decision whether a given provision is necessary for securing the public interest it is related to (principle of necessity). In other words, one has to determine whether a given provision is in fact necessary for achieving a given goal, *a contrario* – if it is not essential for achieving that goal or not anymore essential for achieving it, it should be abandoned and replaced with other measures that interfere with human freedoms and rights to a lesser extent, or all measures should be abandoned altogether.

The above is in line with Petrażycki's statement that law strives to self-annihilation and previous adjustment of law (the 'stress' it creates) to the degree to which individuals fail to observe conduct desired by society. "All mental legal stress (Petrażycki claimed – the Author's note) aimed at a certain conduct assumes specific inadaptability of human psyche; on the grounds of unconsciously successful social mental adaptation, the stronger inadaptability and the

36 L. Petrażycki, *O ideale*, p. 154.

inherited emotional drive to engage in a different, malicious conduct, etc. and the lesser or weaker motives for engaging in socially necessary conduct, it is even stronger; accordingly, stress in the history of law weakens with gradually achieved educational effects; it gradually weakens and subsides; law is a law of upstream progression of motivational stress – with zero stress, i.e. disappearance of proper law, ultimately."[37]

In conclusion, it should be stated that like Petrażycki, the constitutional legislator notices causal links between law and specific social phenomena and the possibility to use law to effectively influence psyche of both an individual and an entire society. What is more, like Petrażycki, he seeks to base legislative actions on scientific foundations, study of law and its causal properties and thus introduced universal and objective scientific law (it would be difficult to interpret the requirement of studying usefulness of a given legal provision otherwise).

Lastly, like Petrażycki, the constitutional legislator notices the systematic development of law and the growth of specific communities and their mutual adaptation to each another as part of historical development (cf. principle of necessity), and also notices the necessity to perfect human psyche and to relieve it from malicious antisocial tendencies, achieving something that remind of the so-called ideal of love; the ideal, it should be added, that is universal and objective, for Article 31 Section 3 of the Polish Constitution seeks to ensure proper safeguard for all values that are significant for individuals and it is difficult to imagine that such an attitude is not commonly accepted and, in an objective view, commonly desired.

7 Conclusions

Given the above, it should be stated that Petrażycki's modernist postulates on creating scientific policy of law from the turn of the 20th century are reflected in the Polish Constitution of 1997. Obviously, claiming that it was the said author's view that served as the ground for introducing the analysed provision to the Polish Constitution would not be true. For "the concept of proportionality requirement for interfering in constitutional rights of an individual as a safeguard against violation of these rights stems from the German law system, just like the prohibition to violate the essence of rights. The origin of the proportionality principle (…) reaches back to the late 19th century with its source in the case law of the Prussian Higher Administrative Court (…). Under the

37 L. Petrażycki, *O ideale*, pp. 163–164.

influence of the German model, the proportionality principle was adopted in constitutional orders of many countries, in the EU law, and also in European and international human rights systems."[38]

Nonetheless, it should be stressed that Petrażycki showed us an appropriate way forward analogous to the present one, that in any moment could become an alternative source for introducing a relevant provision (such as Article 31 Section 3 of the Polish Constitution analysed in this paper) to the Polish legal order. The above shows clearly that Petrażycki's views are universal and timeless, and that "R. Pound (…) was right when he claimed that Petrażycki's concept was ahead of the time when it was formulated."[39]

---

38 A. Niżnik-Mucha, *Zakaz naruszania konstytucyjnych wolności i praw w Konstytucji Rzeczypospolitej Polskiej*, Warsaw 2014, pp. 153–154.

39 H. Groszyk, A. Korybski, *O programie tworzenia nauki polityki prawa Leona Petrażyckiego*, Annales Universitatis Mariae-Curie Skłodowska. Sectio G 1981, Vol. XXVIII, s. 2.

M. Kowalewska-Łukuć, M. Nawrocki

From the Psychologism of Leon Petrazycki to the Model of Subjective Criminal Liability in the Polish Law

1 Introduction

The contemporary model of criminal liability in the Polish law is the outcome of the clash of various outlooks, approaches or even the whole concepts – legal, psychological and sociological. The position of Poland on the map of Europe is also important, as well as the associated historic turmoil. The modern Polish criminal law has evolved under the influence of the occupant law (German, Russian and Austria from the turn of the 19th and 20th century), as well as the views of the legal scholars of that time, with the German scholars having the biggest impact on the Polish legal system. It is also worth noting that Polish criminal law remained under the influence of the Soviet thought for decades, which also left its mark on some modern normative solutions. Currently, in the age of globalisation, the Polish legal system – criminal law included – remains under the influence of various trends, not necessarily associated with particular nationality, quite often originating in the international (supranational) entities (organisations) like the Council of Europe or the European Union. As a result, the modern system of Polish criminal law is very varied in terms of the sources of solutions adopted therein.

It is worth emphasising that the system of Polish criminal law is very dynamic, as it is undergoing constant transformations. Some problems disappear, to be replaced by other. In this regard, it is worth noting – in the last several years in Polish science of criminal law, and to some extent also in Polish case law (mainly the judgments of the Supreme Court) – the extraordinary popularity of the concept of objective attribution of effect as a structure designed to provide a simple answer to whom and when to assign liability for a consequence resulting from human conduct, and which was thus supposed to be easy to apply in criminal proceedings on committing material crimes (understood as crimes with significant consequences). This publication, however, is not devoted to this concept, although it was necessary to mention it in order to introduce an alternative – or even complementary – concept, i.e. a construct (model) of subjective attribution of criminal liability. This concept has been chosen as the main subject of this publication in order to show that in the modern efforts to develop almost entirely objective criteria of criminal liability there is also a tendency to address these criteria from the subjective point of view. In the recent years, the model of subjective attribution of criminal liability has been developed by J. Giezek. It can be stated that the grounds for this concept had been formulated much earlier as they can be traced back to the legal thought of Leon Petrazycki, believed to be a founder of the psychological theory of law.

Thus, it can be clearly pointed out that the aim of this publication is to show relations between Leon Petrazycki's psychologism and the contemporary model of criminal liability, with plenty of room for subjective elements.

2 Psychological Theory of Law by Leon Petrazycki

Leon Petrazycki, more than any other representative of the theory of law at that time, acknowledged the importance and necessity of basing all reflections on law on the solid theoretical and methodological foundations. It seems that it is justified to claim that all scientific works of Leon Petrazycki assumed that the science of law must be based on a proper scientific methodology, proper methods of reasoning and research.[1] In his quest to find the right method, Petrazycki focused mainly on the science of psychology of that time[2]. The so-called emotional psychology became the main focus of his deliberations and Petrazycki based his subjective concept of law as a psychological phenomenon on this psychology[3]. According to Petrazycki, it is indispensable to establish how human motivation functions in order to understand the essence of morality and law. In his opinion, this motivation is not based on the Bentham's utilitarism at all[4]. When carrying out the critical analysis of the existing psychological knowledge, Leon Petrazycki concluded that the trichotomic division of the internal states into cognition,

1 L. Petrażycki, *O nauce, prawie i moralności. Pisma wybrane*, Warszawa 1985, p. 199.

2 Ibidem, p. 200.

3 J. Helios, *Metody psychologiczne w prawie. Szkic problemu*,"Wrocławskie Studia Erazmiańskie" 2014, no. 8, p. 202 i L. Matraszek, *Socjologiczne pierwiastki teorii prawa Leona Petrażyckiego*,"Ruch Prawniczy, Ekonomiczny i Socjologiczny" 1975, z. 3, pp. 227.

4 A. Kojder, *Idee społeczno-prawne Leona Petrażyckiego i ich współczesne kontynuacje*, http://www2.wpia.uw.edu.pl/files/Idee_spoleczno-prawne_LP.pdf?short=, access 20.02.2018.

feelings and will is erroneous. He paid special attention to the role of emotions in human functioning and clearly distinguished them from feelings[5].

When characterising the psychological theory of law by Leon Petrazycki, it should be pointed out in the first place that it was a reply to the objections he had towards the achievements in the psychology of his times. He questioned the existence of experience with only one direction of impact, where cognition and feelings are unilaterally passive and the will is unilaterally active. He pointed out the existence of another type of psychic experience, defined as emotions or impulses, which were of mixed nature, i.e. active-passive (sensational-impulsive)[6]. According to Leon Petrazycki, "emotions govern physical life, movements and countless other physiological processes, as well as the psychic life of the creatures endowed with consciousness. It is the emotions that causatively determine the direction and energy of attention and the course of associations in thought and thinking; the strength, vividness and character of the perceptions and traces left by cognitive processes (memory) depends on them; causal feelings of satisfaction and dissatisfaction come with them; they also direct the will, removing the opposite aspirations of will and evoking the resolutions of will corresponding to their demands, provided that such resolutions occur in certain cases (usually when the action is postponed for the future) and trigger will-based actions instead of the usual impulsive, directly emotional actions."[7].

According to Petrazycki, emotions are not the psychic creations only, but also play important role on the grounds of morality and law, as he assumed that morality and law have no subjective sense (reference). There is no separate ethical experience or the subject it refers to. According to Leon Petrazycki, the legal and moral emotions, as well as everything we refer to as law and morality on daily basis, constitute the ontologically inseparable unity[8]. It should be emphasised that Leon Petrazycki held the view that morality, as unilaterally imperative ethics, is a perfect precedent of law. Moreover, the social progress occurs through transition from unilateral, imperative emotions to bilateral, imperative-attributive emotions – law among them[9].

5 L. Petrażycki, *O pobudkach postępowania i o istocie moralności i prawa*, Warszawa 2002, p. 5 and 14 and idem, *O nauce…*, p. 203.

6 L. Petrażycki, *Wstęp do nauki prawa i moralności*, Warszawa 1959, p. 401; idem, *O pobudkach postępowania…*, p. 14.

7 L. Petrażycki, *Wstęp do nauki prawa…*., p. 475.

8 P.J. Smoczyński, *Oceny i normy postępowania w psychologistycznej koncepcji prawa i moralności Leona Petrażyckiego*,"Etyka" 1984, no. 21, p. 76.

9 L. Matraszek, *Socjologiczne pierwiastki…*, p. 234.

Leon Petrazycki's psychological theory of law assumes that emotions play essential role in the process of lawmaking. Pursuant to the assumptions of this theory, a normative fact is anything that an entity can link their or other persons' rights and duties to[10]. Normative facts, regardless of the experiencing entity, have no binding effect and may not even be considered the rules of procedure, as the latter occur only at the moment of ethical experience, evoked by perception or image of a normative fact. This perception or image may originate in the psyche of a person experiencing a legal or moral emotion. If the entity links certain legal effects (understood as rights and duties) or moral effects (duties only) with a particular normative fact, a proper rule of procedure – understood as a dynamic emotional state – is established. Thus, a norm-setting fact would be any item which humans can perceive or imagine and in which the entity locates their own or other people's rights and duties – legal or moral – at a particular moment[11].

Since law is a psychological experience, but also a regulator of social life, the question arises as how to observe and study it. In that regard, Leon Petrazycki has indicated a common mistake in the perception of law. "The content of the science of law, the way it is presented and the attempt to solve its problems are under the influence of an optical illusion, consisting in the fact that science does not see legal phenomena where they actually occur, but seeks them where they cannot be found and investigated, namely in the world external to the entity who is experiencing legal phenomena."[12]. Leon Petrazycki emphasised that these phenomena occur much closer, namely within ourselves, our consciousness or the consciousness of a person experiencing similar thoughts at that time[13]. Consequently, he considered self-monitoring method, called introspection (internal observation, inward perception of what is happening in one's own psyche), as the only correct and possible way of observing legal phenomena, allowing to understand their nature[14]. However, he did not exclude the use of the method of external monitoring, with a reservation that it only makes sense to use it if it is an element of a joint internal-external observation as an auxiliary way and means of stepping outside own legal psyche of a researcher[15].

In the context of the above deliberations it should not be overlooked that although Leon Petrazycki puts a lot of emphasis – within the psychological

---

10 P.J. Smoczyński, *Oceny i normy…*, p. 78.
11 L. Petrażycki, *Wstęp do nauki prawa…*., p. 51; P.J. Smoczyński, *Oceny i normy…*, p. 80.
12 L. Petrażycki, *Wstęp do nauki prawa…*., p. 51.
13 Ibidem, p. 59.
14 Ibidem, p. 61.
15 Ibidem, pp. 70–71.

theory of law he formulated – on the own experience of an individual, the psychologism based on such assumption is not an extremely subjective construct. As underlined in the literature, it is only the legal experience that is of subjective nature in Petrazycki's concept – perceived as something that one entity experiences as their rights or obligations. It exists only in the consciousness of one person, regardless the similar or different experiences of other entities. Law, on the other hand, comprises the norms experienced by different entities and is of at least intersubjective – if not objective – nature. This is because law exists in our consciousness, in such sense that we are aware when other people experience it. The operation of law, in turn, contrary to the subjective nature of the experience and the intersubjective nature of law, would be objective in nature by including social impacts in the form of changes in social behaviour[16].

The framework of this article, however, does not allow for a more thorough and holistic analysis of the psychological theory of law by Leon Petrazycki. Undoubtedly, his works in which he was trying to contain the essence of law psychological categories may still be an inspiration for further quest of the theory and method of law[17]. It also seems that psychology, which constituted a starting point for the deliberations and analyses by Leon Petrazycki, may not only bring certain answers to the question of the theory of law as such, but might also be useful in the analysis of the detailed issues from different branches of law. Narrowing down to criminal law only, the works of W. Wolter[18], K. Daszkiewicz[19] or M. Król-Bogomilska are worth mentioning[20]. These authors directly referred to the research results and findings in the field of contemporary psychology. However, it is J. Giezek who seems to be a criminal law scholar drawing the most from the area of psychology nowadays.

3 The Model of Subjective Attribution of Criminal Liability

It should be remembered when attempting to describe the model (models) of attribution of criminal liability that there is no unified catalogue of criteria of distinguishing them and a particularly lively discussion regarding its (their)

---

16 L. Matraszek, *Socjologiczne pierwiastki…*, p. 235.

17 A. Kojder, *Idee…*, p. 29.

18 W. Wolter, *Czynnik psychiczny w istocie przestępstwa*, Kraków 1924.

19 K. Daszkiewicz, *Przestępstwa z afektu w polskim prawie karnym*, Warszawa 1982, eadem, *Przestępstwo z premedytacją*, Warszawa 1968.

20 M. Król-Bogomilska, *„Formy winy" w prawie karnym w świetle psychologii*, Warszawa 1991.

functionality on the grounds of criminal law has been continuing for years without any prospect for any change in this respect, which relates mainly to the construct of the objective attribution of the effect.

When constructing any model of criminal liability, it should not be overlooked that the reality evaluated within its framework – to which the model is supposed to relate – is complex, as human conduct, constituting the element of the reality that we hold our interest in, includes both what is external (understood as objective) and internal (therefore subjective). Crime, being a "subcategory" of human conduct, must therefore consist of both external (objective) and internal (subjective) elements.[21]

Both ontological and normative foundations of subjective attribution of criminal liability for committing prohibited act should be taken into consideration in outlining its essence. Such consideration – as emphasised by J. Giezek – assumes that the subjective party may not be narrowed down to psychic processes only, since the criminal and political evaluation also determines its occurrence. Ontological criterion of subjective attribution is thus related to the state of consciousness of the perpetrator, while the normative criterion is situated on the so-called volitional area, where intention and inadvertence play the main roles[22].

It is worth remembering that attribution of criminal liability is a dynamic and complex process. This is due to the fact that human conduct is not, by its nature, a criminal offence, but only becomes an offence in connection with a multidimensional evaluation procedure. First of all, apart from the entity named the perpetrator, to whom the liability (act, effect, illegality, fault) is attributed, there must be – secondly – an entity, usually a judge, who attributes such liability and – thirdly – there are also other indispensable instruments or tools (called criteria) whose application may result in desirable standardization of the whole procedure. In other words, a person is liable not only due to their specific conduct, but becomes liable because a person of authority (the court embodied by a judge) perceives their conduct as deserving criminal liability[23].

From the perspective of the addressed problem, the model of subjective attribution of criminal liability should be sought primarily where psychological elements occur, namely in the ontological foundation of this type (model) of

---

21 J. Giezek, *Świadomość sprawcy czynu zabronionego*, Warszawa 2013, p. 270.

22 Ibidem, p. 257.

23 J. Giezek, P. Kardas, *O kryteriach obiektywnego oraz subiektywnego przypisania z punktu widzenia podstaw odpowiedzialności karnej - uwagi wprowadzające* [in:] *Obiektywne oraz subiektywne przypisanie odpowiedzialności karnej*, eds. J. Giezek, P. Kardas, Warszawa 2016, p. 17.

attribution, narrowed down to reconstruction of the perpetrator's state of consciousness, carried out as part of criminal procedure. It should be emphasised here that the causative explanation of the existing state of affairs constitutes the ontological basis in the "competitive" model of objective attribution. Although there is indeed a significant difference between the indicated models on the grounds of ontological foundations, an important element – the factitive experience which every entity (usually a judge) who decides on such attribution is equipped with – should not be overlooked in both cases. As J. Giezek points out, taking such experience into account would allow to notice a parallel between diagnosing and prognosing reality (within the framework of subjective attribution) and causative explanation (in the case of objective attribution). It will then turn out that the reconstruction of the perpetrator's prediction follows the same pattern which is applied in the case of causative explanation. The grounds of such reconstruction are the factitive regularities which the entity carrying out the reconstruction refers to[24]. However, a certain subtleness should be noted. The fact of the matter is that "for one fundamental reason, it seems to be easier to find the answer as to why the effect which is an element of the outside world has occurred, than to determine why a specific image of the surrounding reality has arisen in the consciousness of the perpetrator. This is due to the fact that we are asking about the reason for the state of affairs which occurred objectively in the first case, whereas in the second case it was visibly subjective, and only subject to the process of intersubjectivisation. If we were to use an example illustrating the difference indicated herein, we would say that a death of a person as a result of external conduct is a state of affairs that is much easier to confirm than establishing that the image of such death actually occurred in the perpetrator's consciousness. (…) the effect as the object of objective attribution is simply stated, while the state of consciousness of the perpetrator, as a subject of subjective attribution, is reconstructed *ex post*"[25].

4 Subjectivity – Then and Now

Following the brief characteristics of the psychological theory of law by Leon Petrazycki and the model of subjective attribution of criminal liability by Jacek Giezek, it is time to draw and present conclusions.

---

24 J. Giezek, *Świadomość sprawcy…*, p. 259.

25 Ibidem, 261. See also: J. Giezek, *Strona podmiotowa czynu zabronionego a model i kryteria subiektywnego przypisania* [in:] *Obiektywne oraz subiektywne przypisanie odpowiedzialności karnej*, eds. J. Giezek, P. Kardas, Warszawa 2016, pp. 109–110.

First of all, it should be pointed out what concept of subjectivity has been used in this paper, as this term should be understood as the commonly recognised manifestation of subjectivism, namely "being guided in their actions and in the evaluation of facts and phenomena by personal beliefs and preferences only"[26]. Consequently, "subjective" means subordinate to individual judgements, tastes, interests, dependent on individual experiences,[27] tinged with individual views, and thus dependent on the experiencing entity[28].

Undoubtedly, Leon Petrazycki's psychological theory of law may be considered a subjective theory due to the fact that – as it has already been underlined – it puts significant emphasis on own experience of the individuals which, in the form of emotions, becomes the driving force of human conduct. It is important from the point of view of the title of this publication that the legal experiences, understood as the rights or duties an individual is aware of, are subjective in nature. Such experience exists only in the consciousness of one person, regardless of the similar or different experiences of other entities. Law, as a certain set, comprises the norms experienced by different entities and is at least intersubjective – if not objective – in nature. It is because law exists in our consciousness, in such sense that we are aware when other people experience it.

In Jacek Giezek's approach, subjectivity focuses on considering criminal liability using not only the objective criteria. To a very large extent, such liability is conditioned by the perpetrator's awareness of what they have committed (being aware of the fact that the behaviour of a given entity executes prohibition). In this approach, the driving force behind human conduct is the conscious knowledge of reality (things, phenomena, cause and effect). The fact particularly deserving to be emphasised is that subjectivity is in a way qualified by the fact that the evaluation of the perpetrator's experience (evaluation of the state of their consciousness) is carried out by external subject, i.e. usually the judge who – due to own level of knowledge and experience – may (however does not have to) evaluate in a very different way the perpetrator's state of consciousness when committing criminal act.

Therefore, as much as Leon Petrazycki recognised the great significance of emotions in the functioning of a human being and in the sole essence of law, the studies of Jacek Giezek, acknowledging the science of psychology, focus mainly on the role of consciousness. It must be pointed out again that the considerations

26 E. Dereń, E. Polański, *Wielki słownik języka polskiego*, Kraków 2015, p. 788.
27 Ibidem.
28 L. Drabik, E. Sobol, *Słownik języka polskiego PWN*, Warszawa 2007, p. 598.

of Jacek Giezek focus only on criminal law, specifically the subjective foundations of criminal responsibility. However, it seems that indeed in the case of criminal law and examining the grounds for criminal liability, the psychological findings should be obligatorily considered. Since we claim that the modern criminal law has already evolved from purely objective to subjective liability, it becomes necessary to clarify what we actually consider subjectivism in criminal law. It seems justified to claim that the subjective element of criminal responsibility should include the perpetrator – their individual abilities and psyche. Thus, on the ground of criminal law, it is necessary to consider the perpetrator's state of consciousness, but also their emotions, motivations, decision-making processes, volitional processes and the degree of perpetrator's freedom in the course of these processes, often defined as opportunity for reasonable self-determination.

It is not hard to see that the aforementioned elements constitute the subject of the offence and the nature of fault attributed to the perpetrator. Needless to say, there is no need to cite a broad argumentation in favour of the thesis that psychology is the science which may provide most information on consciousness, emotions, motives, will or reason of human beings. If so, the psychological determinations regarding the aforementioned phenomena should be of scientific interest for the criminal law scholars.

Jacek Giezek, as previously mentioned, focused primarily on the role of the perpetrator's awareness. It was years ago when Leon Petrazycki, while considering the law in general, emphasised the role of emotions very clearly. However, he also noticed their function directly on the ground of criminal law[29]. The awareness and emotions do not exhaust psychological phenomena building the subjectivity of criminal liability. Therefore, the influence of the perpetrator's motivation, volitional and decision-making processes and the degree of their freedom on the existence and scope of criminal liability certainly requires research and analysis.

Moreover, it is quite obvious that the perpetrator's consciousness, emotions, will or motivation are closely interdependent and various mental processes are parallel and cannot be clearly separated from each other. Therefore, new areas of science, situated on the border of psychology and other sciences, can prove all the more useful in the examination of the above in the context of criminal responsibility. It applies especially to neuroscience, the findings of which are becoming increasingly apparent in the area of criminal law deliberations.[30]

29 L. Petrażycki, *O pobudkach postępowania…*, p. 25.

30 A. Barczak-Oplustil, *Zasada koincydencji winy i czynu w Kodeksie karnym*, Kraków 2016, p. 182.

Hence, there is a great need, as well as possibility, to continue the psychological trend in criminal law. The significance of findings which might result in the process is immense. As these findings may translate primarily into the subject of the offence and perpetrator's guilt, they may also affect the foundations of criminal liability. It should be noted here that the Polish science of criminal law still lacks unanimity regarding the issue of particular forms of the subject of the offence. For example, the enormous problems with grasping the essence of the intention of possible or unaware inadvertence can be indicated here. Defining the essence of guilt and indicating its consistent theory is no less problematic.

To sum up the above deliberations, it should be indicated that both in the concept of the psychological theory of law by Leon Petrazycki and the model of subjective attribution of criminal liability by Jacek Giezek, subjectivity is inherently related to the object pivotal to each of these concepts – a human being. For both authors, the decisive element is the individual and his or her individual qualities which influence the perception and experience (awareness) of their surroundings. A human being is never fully objective, as the perception and experience always depend on their own experience, views, preferences, level of knowledge, intellectual abilities. Emphasising the subjective element, regardless of its definition, always results in certain difficulties, as psychological processes are very complex and difficult to conclude, therefore cognizable to a very little extent[31]. This does not mean, however, that it is sufficient (and proper) to apply only the objective attribution criteria to criminal liability. Subjectivity – even if more demanding, as it takes into account certain individualities – is indispensable. As nearly every aspect of social life is subject to generalisation, typologization and unification in the modern world, it is important to stress individualism leading to subjectivisation. It is due to the fact that not all aspects of social life can be categorised and catalogued, which is especially noticeable in case of criminal liability, where such liability (in its strict sense), as well as any possible onerousness, is determined by individual elements (the question of abolition or limitation of sanity when assessing the grounds for criminal liability or taking into account the characteristics and personal conditions of the perpetrator and the way of life before and after committing the offence when imposing the sentence).

31 I. Andrejew, *Zagadnienia typizacji przestępstw*,"Studia Iuridica" 1981, vol. 10, pp. 30–31.

Ł. Pohl

Scope of Moral Evaluation of a Man's Act as a Co-creating Element of Intuitive Law and Positive Law as regards the Model Structure of a Sanctioned Norm in Criminal Law (A Contribution to the Possible Impact of Leon Petrażycki's Theory of Criminal Law)

One of the best-known concepts in Leon Petrażycki's theory of law is his concept of law[1] in which the so-called intuitive law and positive law[2] are distinguished. To recall, the former is said to comprise individual imperative-attributive experiences of a person who acts reasonably, hence, thoughts about the obligation to behave in a given way in a given situation (the imperative element) – thoughts correlated with a thought of the external requirement to fulfil the said obligation (the attributive element). In turn, the latter is said to be affected by the so-called normative facts which under the discussed concept take the form of various messages about law from a positive legislator, an institution that applies law or an entity that provides a scientific reflection on law; for Petrażycki emphasised that the dividing line between intuitive law and positive law runs along the criterion of becoming aware of the existence of a normative fact.[3]

1 See L. Petrażycki, *O pobudkach postępowania i o istocie moralności i prawa*, Warsaw 2002, *idem*: *Teoria prawa i państwa w związku z teorią moralności*, Vol. 1, Warsaw 1959, *Teoria prawa i państwa w związku z teorią moralności*, Vol. 1, Warsaw 1960.

2 For more information on the said division, see in particular S. Tkacz, *O „pozytywności" i „oficjalności" w teorii prawa Leona Petrażyckiego*, Ruch Prawniczy, Ekonomiczny i Socjologiczny, 2005 Vol. 1, p. 80 and subsequent ones, as well as A. Kojder, *Idee społeczno-prawne Leona Petrażyckiego i ich współczesne kontynuacje* (in:) J. Mucha, W. Wincławski (eds.), *Klasyczna socjologia polska i jej współczesna recepcja*, Toruń 2006, p. 57 and subsequent ones (this text is available also in an electronic version – see https://andrzejkojder.weebly.com/uploads/4/7/2/7/47279911/idee_spoleczno-prawne_lp.pdf, p. 35).

3 See L. Petrażycki, *Teoria* …, Vol. 2, p. 246.

In such a relation in which positive law is largely based on intuitive law[4], for the latter is clearly primary with respect to positive law[5] – it gives rise to

4 The degree of this measure is undoubtedly debatable. Anyway, one can also allow an interpretation of the discussed Petrażycki's concept where intuitive law is considered the sole determinant of positive law, as well as one where intuitive law is only a basis for positive law, hence, a basis that is subjected in the subsequent phase of the positive law construction process to transformations stemming from, for instance, agreements made by intuitive law entities regarding the perception of the content of intuitive law norms or the scope to which it should be incorporated into positive law. The fact that positive law is based on intuitive law is clearly stated by S. Tkacz, who stressed that "(…) intuitive law and positive law are not isolated from each other, since beyond the area of exclusive influence of positive law and that of intuitive law there is also a field where the scope of influence of the two mentioned types of law overlap, namely, the field of attribution of goods and weights" – S. Tkacz, *O „pozytywności"* …, p. 81. The shaping function of intuitive law is also stressed by A. Kojder, who claims that the purpose of positive law is to incorporate intuitive law norms that individuals of a higher ethical level are aware of – A. Kojder, *Idee* …, pp. 8–9. At the same time, the author draws attention to the fact that "Petrażycki acknowledged the primary of law both with regard to the state and morality. He pointed that compared to morality, legal experiences have a stronger effect on a man's psyche and behaviour. Morality is passive, as it shapes primarily a sense of duty, an awareness that certain rules should be obeyed. In turn, law allows a sense of one's own rights to develop, creating a man-citizen who is aware of his or her own dignity, who values his or her freedom and seeks to enforce what he or she righteously deserves. Law is hence more valuable in social life than morality and plays a more important role in the shaping of people's attitudes and behaviours on a mass scale, strengthens habits, traits of character and social tendencies more effectively than morality does" – A. Kojder, *Idee* …, pp. 10–11. The above conclusion does not naturally undermine in any way the idea of the shaping of intuitive law and, consequently, positive law forced herein by referring to moral norms. On the contrary, it provides another example that supports it. For more information on the relation between intuitive law and positive law in Petrażycki's approach also see J. Nowacki, *O stosunku prawa intuicyjnego do prawa pozytywnego w teorii Leona Petrażyckiego* (in:) K. Opałek (ed.), *Z zagadnień teorii prawa i teorii nauki Leona Petrażyckiego, Studia opracowane dla upamiętnienia stulecia urodzin*, Warsaw 1969, p. 89 and subsequent ones.

5 This is evidenced by, e.g. the so-called axioms of intuitive law – for more information on this subject, see L. Petrażycki, *Teoria* …, Vol. 2, p. 452 and subsequent ones. After all, it should be stressed that Petrażycki clearly emphasised the role of intuitive law in the shaping of positive law by claiming that positive law stems from principles of co-existence as axioms and complements them – see L. Petrażycki, *Teoria* …, Vol. 2, p. 454. For more information on this issue, also see, i.a. S. Tkacz, *O „pozytywności"* …, p. 89. Nonetheless, in the discussed context another Petrażycki's statement is highly

a question on decisive factors that determine the shape of intuitive law. When taking a closer look at Petrażycki's statements one can notice that in his view, one of such factors – and probably the fundamental one, at the same time – is morality.[6] This is due to the fact that in the depicted concept, morality has an imperative character that determines only the obligation to perform a given behaviour. Let us recall again that in the case of Petrażycki's approach to law, law is characterised by its attributive nature based on a previously determined scope of compulsory behaviours. In short, the indicated characteristic of law entitles us to put forward an idea that law is secondary to morality (moral law norms).[7]

In this respect, limiting the scheme to the discussed correlation, the law-making process including criminal law we are interested in would take on the following form: morality > intuitive law > positive law. One could risk here a statement that the indicated process follows a top-down formula on every stage[8], hence, the so-called topical order is rejected in favour of a systematic order.[9] Stages of this process allow hence to put forward a bold idea that a moral norm structure serves as a basis for a positive law norm structure, including the structure of a norm sanctioned under criminal law.[10] Therefore, in this discussion we shall address the possible impact of the former structure on the latter.

In the presented system, the starting point would then take the form of the concept of a moral norm[11] as the one the observance of which would make a man

significant, specifically that "(…) intuitive law exerts pressure on the positive law interpretation and application towards settlements compliant with requirements of the intuitive-legal conscience or at least those that are least noncompliant with respect to these requirements" – L. Petrażycki, *Teoria …*, Vol. 2, p. 273.

6 See A. Kojder, *Idee …*, pp. 10–11 and also (and most of all) J. Nowacki, *O rozróżnieniu prawa i moralności w teorii Leona Petrażyckiego*, Studia Filozoficzne, 1981 Vol. 5, p. 51 and subsequent ones.

7 Obviously, this does not mean that law is limited to a certain annex to moral law, for not every moral law norm deserves the status of a positive law norm.

8 Obviously, in the sense that not everything immoral is prohibited by law.

9 For more information on this formula, see for instance Z. Jędrzejewski, *Bezprawność jako element przestępności czynu. Studium na temat struktury przestępstwa*, Warsaw 2009, p. 24 and other references provided therein, particularly I. Kant, *Krytyka czystego rozumu. Tom II*, Warsaw 1986, PWN, p. 577 and subsequent ones.

10 After all, this is justified by Petrażycki's view o the role of law. In line with his policy of law, the target role of law is to attain the ideal socialisation of all individuals conditioned by their high level of morality.

11 Therefore, I do not share this approach (which, I must add, has been arbitrarily adopted in my view) on intuitive law as law whose provisions "(…) loosely adapt to specific

experience a sense of duty (necessity) to engage in a given behaviour.[12] Let us see then how the indicated norm is approached in the literature.

According to Ślipko, moral evaluation of a human act is a resulting evaluation of numerous factors.[13] The said author stressed that this evaluation concerns not only factors of objective nature but also those subjective. In Ślipko's view, "This evaluation is thus determined in the first place by the quality of the very act committed by the entity. Suffices to compare two acts such as helping a sick person and robbing that person to know that they are subjected to different evaluation. However, awareness tells us that aside from the quality of an act also motives and intentions of a given entity come in play, which are the purpose a given act was performed for (whether it is selfless assistance or with a certain advantage in mind), the wide variety of outcomes that may result from a given act, and lastly, a vast number of yet different factors that allow one to formulate a conclusion on the moral qualification of a human act only when considered as a whole."[14] The fact that moral evaluation of a man's act is done also with account of subjective factors was subjectively discussed by Pope John Paul II, who stressed that when formulating rational criteria of a right moral decision one should take into consideration both (although not exclusively) the intent and the consequences of a given behaviour.[15] This stance was also adopted by, i.a. Znamierowski, who pointed that limiting the subject of moral evaluation to sole physical event results in an incomplete evaluation that has a purely utilitarian character.[16]

---

individual circumstances of a given case, a specific system of relations in life (...)"– S. Tkacz, *O „pozytywności"* ..., p. 80.

12 Here, one should notice that such a system is fully compliant with the *leges sine moribus vanae* principle, which states that law that has no grounds in morality is helpless. For more information on this principle, see in particular Z. Ziembiński, *Zarys zagadnień etyki*, Poznań-Toruń 1994, p. 13 and subsequent ones, in which the author suggests that "(...) the evaluation system does not act in a way that is 'mechanical' based on algorithms but with due account of evaluation adopted in the legal environment or in the entire society, particularly moral evaluation" – Z. Ziembiński, *Zarys* ..., p. 109. The quoted author states directly that "moral approval of legal institutions and specific legal norms, which should be the purpose of civil education, is a significant factor that determines its efficiency" – Z. Ziembiński, *Zarys* ..., p. 109. I would like to add that I fully approve of this point of view – see Ł. Pohl, *Struktura normy sankcjonowanej w prawie karnym. Zagadnienia ogólne*, Poznań 2007, pp. 114–115.

13 See T. Ślipko, *Zarys etyki ogólnej*, Kraków 2004, p. 166.

14 T. Ślipko, *Zarys* ..., p. 166.

15 See Jan Paweł II, *Veritatis splendor* (in:) *Encykliki Ojca Świętego Jana Pawła II*, Kraków 1997, p. 792 and subsequent.

16 See C. Znamierowski, *Oceny i normy*, Warsaw 1957, p. 384.

The above consideration takes on significance given that moral qualification (evaluation) of a man's deed is determined by whether a moral norm was violated.[17] This is particularly emphasised by Wojtyła, who claimed, "A man's deeds make him morally good or morally bad, depending on what these deeds are. The quality of deeds, which is determined by a moral norm and, ultimately, by conscience, is transferred onto the man – the perpetrator. Perpetration in itself is not the condition for becoming a man who is morally good or bad – this is determined by an attitude towards what we refer to as a moral norm (…)."[18] In turn, a moral norm itself is considered, to quote Wojtyła again, to be "(…) what somehow produces moral value and is in a way directly present at its birth (…)".[19]

Obviously, the last of the quoted views gives rise to a question on the validity of the formulated moral norm. To not investigate this exceptionally complicated issue in more detail, suffices to say that a concern whether a moral norm indeed produces moral values, as Wojtyła claims, is well-grounded, for in that case we would have to seek the validity of the discussed norm outside the said value, which would undoubtedly hinder the attainment of a justification for a moral norm that would refer to a purely objectively rational criterion. However, this does not appear to be thoroughly true; it is not true that a moral norm produces moral value, as Wojtyła stated, but a violation of such a norm allows one only to qualify the behaviour that allegedly caused the violation as immoral.[20] Such an approach would not force through the thesis about a moral norm being an expression that creates moral value. This is because it seems that a moral norm is secondary to this value (most probably based on the initial criteria of good and evil) and it is this value serves as the foundation of this norm. The above conclusions regarding a moral norm, given the assumption that a moral norm serves as a basis for a positive law norm, which is attributed to Petrażycki (morality > intuitive law > positive law) – seems to give rise to two significant implications regarding the structure of the model of a sanctioned criminal law norm, which shall be addressed in further remarks.

---

17 I therefore reject the stance that moral evaluation of a man's behaviour serves as the basis for shaping a moral norm – see Ł. Pohl, *Struktura …*, p. 115.

18 K. Wojtyła, *Osoba i czyn*, Lublin 2000, p. 147.

19 K. Wojtyła, *O metafizycznej i fenomenologicznej podstawie normy moralnej. Na podstawie koncepcji św. Tomasza z Akwinu i Maxa Schelera* (in:) K. Wojtyła, *Zagadnienia podmiotu moralności*, Lublin 2001, pp. 245–246.

20 Given this approach, one can completely agree with Wojtyła's view that a man becomes either morally good or morally bad by means of his deeds, depending on what these deeds are – see footnote no. 10.

The former pertains to the subject of a norm (the scope in which it is set out in legal provisions).[21] It is beyond any doubt that the key element of the scope to which a moral norm is set out in legal provisions, i.e. (obviously) a man's behaviour, is approached under this scope in a utterly non-ancillary manner. This approach is best evidenced in the already mentioned Wojtyła's quote, in which the author states that "A man's deeds make him either morally good or morally bad (…)."[22] If this is due to his own deeds than not due someone else's – one could logically sum up. As a result of this approach, given the assumption that of its faithful transposition on the structure of a sanctioned norm of criminal law, violation of the said sanctioned norm would be determined solely by behaviour of its recipient. Thus, no effect on violation of the norm would be exerted by other factors, including another entity's behaviour.

I already have had the opportunity to write about such an "non-anancillary" approach being fully accurate also in the case of a sanctioned norm in criminal law[23], although at the time, I based my reasoning in this regard primarily on the argument that refers to the scheme of a legal norm, in which – as we know – the variable 'C' can be replaced only with one type of behaviour.[24]

---

21 To recall, the scope of norm standardisation covers most of all the class of factors standardised by it. For more information on how this scope is perceived see in particular Z. Ziembiński, *Logiczne podstawy prawoznawstwa*, Warsaw 1966, p. 72; idem, *Metodologiczne zagadnienia prawoznawstwa*, Warsaw 1974, p. 128, and also Ł. Pohl., *Struktura …*, p. 62 and subsequent.

22 K. Wojtyła, *Osoba …*, p. 147.

23 See in particular Ł. Pohl, *Struktura …*, p. 136 and subsequent; also, idem, *Obiektywna istota sprawstwa w ujęciu polskiego prawa karnego (Uwagi na marginesie lektury pracy P. Kardasa „Teoretyczne podstawy odpowiedzialności karnej za przestępne współdziałanie")*, Ruch Prawniczy, Ekonomiczny i Socjologiczny, 2004 Vol. 2, p. 287 and subsequent, *Zawartość normatywna przepisu art. 18 § 1 k.k.*, Prokuratura i Prawo, 2006 Vol. 2, p. 19 and subsequent, *O kulturze prowadzenia dyskusji i jej meritum słów kilka – uwagi na marginesie artykułu Piotra Kardasa „Sprawstwo kierownicze i polecające – wykonawcze czy niewykonawcze postaci sprawstwa?"*, Przegląd Sądowy, 2006 Vol. 11–12, p. 262 and subsequent., *Prawo karne. Wykład cześci ogólnej*, Warsaw 2015, p. 150 and subsequent, *O znaczeniu refleksji naukowej Profesora Tomasza Kaczmarka*, Państwo i Prawo, 2017 Vol. 12, p. 91.

24 To recall, this scheme has the form of the following expression– (on the example of a normy zakazującej): "Entity X is forbidden to engage in act C in a situation S" – for more information on this issue see in particular W. Patryas, *Zaniechanie. Próba analizy metodologicznej*, Poznań 1993, p. 55 and subsequent., idem, *„Norma sankcjonowana w prawie karnym (…) – kilka uwag do artykułu Łukasza Pohla*, Ruch Prawniczy, Ekonomiczny i Socjologiczny, 2006 Vol. 1, p. 66; idem, *Na polemikę dra Łukasza*

However, it should be honestly pointed out that despite the emphasised accurate views, different solutions are very often still forced through, the best example of which is the stance of a vast majority of Polish criminal law experts regarding interpretation of provisions that specify non-executive forms of causative participation.[25] To recall, it is assumed under the said stance that they are completed, i.e. the moment when a command perpetration and the moment when a perpetration by order are committed, upon fulfilment of a prohibited act, hence, its criteria are satisfied by the entity whose actions were commanded in the case of a command perpetration or an entity who was ordered to commit a prohibited act in the case of a perpetration by order. Importantly, the indicated interpretation of law disregards the terminology of the provision that typifies the said forms[26], for it gives no basis that would allow them to be considered ancillary, conditioned by a prohibited act being performed by the perpetrator. It is hence an expression of theoretical beliefs the strongest general theoretical grounds for which were provided by Kardas in the form of an extensive approach of one sanctioned norm for all forms of causative participation (which prohibits a prohibited act from being performed) with a condition that the prohibited act must be done by the perpetrator that is essential for its violation.[27] When it comes to the essence of this basis the author claimed that "considering a sanctioned norm

---

Pohla – odpowiedź, Ruch Prawniczy, Ekonomiczny i Socjologiczny, 2006 Vol. 4, p. 178; idem, *Jeszcze w sprawie normy sankcjonowanej w prawie karnym*, Ruch Prawniczy, Ekonomiczny i Socjologiczny, 2006 Vol. 4, p. 188. On the scheme of a legal nirm see also in particular C. Znamierowski, *Z rozmyślań teoretyka prawa*, Ruch Prawniczy, Ekonomiczny i Socjologiczny, 1929 Vol. 2, p. 178; Z. Ziembiński, *Logiczne …*, p. 70 and subsequent; W. Patryas, *Rozważania o normach prawnych*, Poznań 2001, p. 53 and subsequent.

25 Nonetheless, surprisingly, Polish criminal law science adopts a thoroughly different position on sanctioned norms prohibiting incitement and accessory. This is surprising because, analogously to command perpetration and perpetration by order, incitement and accessory are behaviours that cannot serve as means for committing a prohibited act.

26 To remind, pursuant to Article 18 Section 1 of the Criminal Code, it is not only the person who commits a prohibited act by himself or in collaboration or in agreement with another person who is liable for perpetration, but also he who commands the implementation of a prohibited act by another person or who employs another person's dependence on himself orders that person to execute such an act.

27 See P. Kardas, *Teoretyczne podstawy odpowiedzialności karnej za przestępne współdziałanie*, Kraków 2001, various pages, for instance, pp. 434–435, 461, 497, 544–545.

(which determines unlawfulness) all forms of perpetration listed in Article 18 Section 1 of the Criminal Code are characterised by an identical wording of the prohibiting/ordering norm. This norm is in all cases decoded from the provision of a specific part that determines a given type of a prohibited act. Every form of perpetration is grounded in a violation of a prohibition/order of identical content. The provisions of Article 19 Section 1 of the Criminal Code do not constitute the basis for any modifications of a sanctioned norm. A legislative approach on three 'extended' types of perpetration (i.e. participation, command perpetration and perpetration by order) serves a constitutive role for unlawfulness That boils down to expressing legislative criteria for attributing violation of the norm by another person including those who did not do it themselves or did not do that completely."[28] According to Kardas, "the difference between particular types of perpetration lies exclusively in ways in how a prohibited act can be done considered acceptable by the legislator. In this context, a certain regularity might be notices. Individual perpetration is a term related to features of a prohibited acts determined by provisions of the specific part. This link is determined by a phrase 'performs a prohibited act by himself' which seems a repetition at first (*superfluum*). All other types of perpetration ale also characterised by performance of a prohibited act with the exception that it takes place in a somewhat different manner than in the case of individual perpetration. This also means that other types of perpetration described under Article 18 Section 1 of the Criminal Code are focused on types of prohibited acts described in the specific part and ultimately consist in all features being manifested in one of the ways listed under Article 18 Section 1 of the Criminal Code. In other words, types of perpetration defined under Article 18 Section 1 of the Criminal Code perceived in the context of features of a type of prohibited act determined by the provision of the specific part is nothing else than technical means for manifesting these features."[29]

As I have already repeatedly mentioned, I do not agree with this concept in this particular approach.[30] In this regard, I somewhat primarily focused on the fact that the nature of behaviour that consists in commanding the performance of a prohibited act and ordering another person to commit such an act makes them unable to violate a norm that prohibits performance of a prohibited act. Here, I stress that introduction of the condition of performing a prohibited act in the case of norms prohibiting common perpetration and norms prohibiting

---

28 P. Kardas, *Teoretyczne* ..., pp. 544–545.

29 Ibidem.

30 See footnote no. 23.

perpetration by order is inaccurate, since then such a condition would have to be situated in the scope of application of these norms, and such a solution would be absurd and beyond the suggestive function of a norm; however, one should note that in this approach, which situates performance of a prohibited act among conditions determining violation of the discussed norms, command perpetration and perpetration by order, hence, behaviours that unquestionably precede perpetration of the prohibited act, would become prohibited penalised behaviours only when the perpetrator would commit the prohibited act, thus, in the moment following the performance of the act, which would remain in grave conflict with the function of how a norm influences behaviour of its recipient before the performance.

It all resulted in a competitive approach being formulated, under which a model was proposed with separate sanctioned norms (otherwise than in the common model) for each form of criminal participation that can be violated only with a behaviour that is specified therein in the form of a prohibition. Therefore, it was adopted that, among others, a different form of a sanctioned norm prohibits common perpetration, another prohibits perpetration by order, yet another prohibits engaging in individual perpetration and yet another prohibits executive perpetration implemented as participation.

Given the above, conclusions drawn from the shaping of the moral norm provide another argument for the 'non-ancillary' approach to a sanctioned norm in criminal law I am forcing through. This is because it rejects the model in which violation of a norm could be determined by another entity's behaviour that is not a subject of this norm. Petrażycki's concept of positive law, given the assumption that this law was shaped based on moral law, as adopted herein, seems then scientifically productive also on the grounds of the criminal law theory, since it enriches this theory by significantly extending the number of arguments in the dispute on the adequate approach to the sanctioned norm in criminal law – obviously for the benefit of the stance that violation of such norm is determined solely by the behaviour of its recipient that is standardised by that norm.

The presented Petrażycki's interpretation of the concept of positive law by means of referring to its fundamental element of moral norm gives another argument for a subjective element being included into the structure of a sanctioned norm in criminal law, specified in criminal law theory by the perpetrator of an act prohibited under penalty.[31] This is because the above-mentioned opinions

31 Elementary information on the perpetrator of a penalised prohibited act is provided in almost every general criminal law handbook – see, for instance, W. Wróbel, A. Zoll,

clearly prejudge the necessity to take this element into consideration in the process of morally evaluating a man's deed.[32]

The transposition of this approach onto the sanctioned norm in criminal law obviously gives rise to a question on the where the indicated subjective element should be positioned in the said norm. It seems that the best position would be the scope of the indicated norm which would be in this case situated by the standardised behaviour located within the scope of norm. This is because such a situation allows one to effectively refute possible allegations of this approach being methodologically incorrect, for these would be completely correct in the case where the subjective element is situated in a variable determining the standardised behaviour, since then one could claim that this element is a constituent of the said behaviour and such a resolution would render explanation of that behaviour under the so-called humanist interpretation impossible, though it assumes a methodologically justified separation of the explained behaviour from its intellectual-volitional causes, i.e. its determinants.[33] Let me briefly remind that the humanist interpretation is a procedure aimed at explaining human behaviour that is implemented in two distinct phases.[34] In the first one, the state of affairs produced by the entity is identified, thus, it pertains only to the entity's deed with regard to its effect, whereas in the other, "(…) explaining the fact of a given act being committed by the perpetrator consists in determining the rationality of the said perpetrator, recreating (a fragment of) its knowledge and preferences, determining the situation which the given perpetrator was in, and proving that description of all these elements provides a logical conclusion

---

Polskie prawo karne. Część ogólna, Kraków 2010, p. 203 and subsequent, and also Ł. Pohl, *Prawo …*, p. 133 and subsequent.

32 I have already adopted a stance that includes subjective features into the structure and content of a sanctioned criminal law norm – see, among others, *Podmiotowe znamiona czynu zabronionego w strukturze przestępstwa*, Państwo i Prawo 2006 Vol. 2, p. 62 and subsequent, *Norma …*, p. 62 and subsequent, *W odpowiedzi …*, p. 174 and subsequent, *Uwagi …*, p. 183 and subsequent, *Struktura …*, p. 110 and subsequent.

33 For more information on this issue see in particular Ł. Pohl, *Struktura …*, p. 120 and subsequent.

34 The concept of humanist interpretation was developed by J. Kmita, a science methodologist and culture theorist from Poznan – see J. Kmita, *Z metodologicznych problemów interpretacji humanistycznej*, Warsaw 1971, and regarding criminal law theory, it was significantly developed also by W. Patryas, a science methodologis and culture theorist from Poznan– see W. Patryas, *Interpretacja karnistyczna. Studium metodologiczne*, Poznań 1988.

that the perpetrator of the explained act indeed performed it."[35] Here, it should be added that in the version of the depicted concept developed by Patryas and adopted to the needs of criminal law, called by him a criminal law interpretation, the aim of the described procedure is to determine whether the perpetrator is guilty of the act he committed and if so, in what form.[36] Obviously, given the findings of contemporary criminal law theory, we know that thus set objective is not fully accurate, since the chronology of considerations adopted by Patryas is incorrect. This is because it is not the foundation of determining the forms of the perpetrator of the prohibited act to be blamed, as evidenced by normative approaches to guilt (comprehensive and clear), developed as a scientific answer to numerous shortcomings of the psychological approach on guilt that limits it to the perpetrator's intellectual-volitional relation to the act he commits.

The above considerations on the use of humanist interpretation in criminal law has also another meaning, namely, it brings to light the methodological incorrectness of final approaches on an act. This is because these approaches attempt at situating the subjective element in the perpetrator's behaviour[37], which, as indicated above, due to the lack of methodologically desired separatedness of the subjective element and the act in a causal approach makes explaining the perpetrator's behaviour by means of the indicated procedure of humanist explanation impossible. Hence, it proves that by applying the said procedure, one can be an advocate of the approach that situates the intellectual-volitional element in the structure of a sanctioned norm in criminal law without supporting the final understanding of the central element of the subject of such a norm, i.e. its recipient's behaviour.

Naturally, in the subject literature one can come across various stances on the approach that situates the subject feature in the structure of a sanctioned norm. Some express their scepticism in this regard, strongly supporting the position that this feature should be situated only in a sanctioned norm.[38] In contrast,

---

35 W. Patryas, *Interpretacja …*, p. 21.

36 See W. Patryas, *Interpretacja …*, p. 5.

37 For more information on this issue see in particular Ł. Pohl, *Struktura …*, p. 126, and also papers of W. Mącior's *O finalizmie w prawie karnym*, Państwo i Prawo, 1971 Vol. 6, *W związku z dyskusją na temat finalizmu*, Państwo i Prawo, 1972 Vol. 5 quoted and analysed therein.

38 As in, i.a. A. Zoll, *O normie prawnej z punktu widzenia prawa karnego*, Krakowskie Studia Prawnicze, 1990 year XXIII, p. 69 and subsequent.

others maintain that such a location of the discussed feature is correct.[39] The mentioned Zoll, when taking part in this dispute, argues that "the source of a negative evaluation hence stems from both the objective actual state resulting from a man's behaviour and the behaviour itself. These two elements are constitutive for the negative evaluation contained in the norm and their presence determines that a behaviour is considered noncompliant with a norm. Here, there is only an apparent congruence of the presented concept on elements that form a negative evaluation of behaviour with the concept of subject-oriented unlawfulness created by finalists. The concept of subject unlawfulness assumes that the negative value of behaviour is determined by a negative value of outcome (Erfolgsunwelt) and a negative value of the act (Handlungswert). The difference between the concepts lies in the negative value of the act itself. While advocates of the subject-oriented concept of unlawfulness link the negative value of an act with the attitude of the perpetrator, his or her intent, in the concept presented in this paper the negative value of an act is justified by the very violation of a rule of conduct with a given good. However, this difference pertains only to evaluations related to violation of a sanctioned norm, hence, significant for determining the unlawfulness of behaviour. The subject-oriented approach of the perpetrator can play a decisive role in determining criminality of a given conduct, hence, under conditions determining actualisation of a sanctioning norm. (…) I have already adopted a stance that the negative value of an act is determined by violation of good (alternatively, the threat of it being violated) and violation of the rule of handling good. In fact, these elements are objective and do not require an analysis of the perpetrator's mental experience regarding the act he commits for determining them. (…) Assuming that the axiological structure of a sanctioned norm structure presented here is correct, one has to approve of the claim that intentionality or unintentionality of a violation or a threat of a legal good being violated or a rule of conduct with a given good have no effect on the very occurrence of a negative evaluation of an act. Intentionality or unintentionality are hence not features that characterise behaviour incongruent with a sanctioned norm (unlawful behaviour). Intentionality and unintentionality are features that determine only its penalisation, as they constitute features characterising a type of a prohibited act. (…). Intentionality and unintentionality are features that

39 As in, i.a. Z. Jedrzejewski, *Uwagi o pojęciu przestępstwa w projekcie kodeksu karnego*, Państwo i Prawo, 1993 Vol. 10, p. 93 and subsequent, and also Ł. Pohl, *Struktura …*, p. 110 and subsequent.

determine the rate of social threat, however, they do not determine in any way the negative evaluation of an act itself."[40]

In thus polarised dispute an argument that provides a reference to the assumption on identical structure of a moral norm and a sanctioned norm in criminal law is most valuable, as it strengthens (and, additionally, to a great degree) the position of one of the sides in the dispute. Its value also manifests in the fact that it is a theoretical argument, hence, completely independent of any legislative resolution.

Instead of a conclusion: Restraining from the desire to make a self-evaluation of the reinterpretative ideas presented in this paper, one can claim that the only certain thing is that the above-depicted proposed consequences of the bold idea presented herein regarding the transference of the structure of a moral norm on the structure of a sanctioned norm in criminal law undoubtedly proves the great potential of Leon Petrażycki's scientific legacy, including its grave impact on the analytically oriented criminal law theory. I have no doubt that further and more in-depth studies on this matter would provide numerous other findings of great value to this theory, which (as I am highly convinced) would most likely allow one to analyse general and more specific problems of contemporary criminal law theory in a more appropriate manner.

40 A. Zoll, *O normie* ..., p. 80 and subsequent.

S. Słotwiński

Sensus Spiritualis of Polish Civil Law – A Few Words on the Autonomy of the Will

The discussion of the role and significance of the autonomy of the will in the doctrine of civil law does not bring about much controversy in this branch of law.[1] It is universally accepted that in the light of the autonomy of the will participants in civil law transactions may, within the boundaries of the law, freely shape their legal situation.[2] Whereas the main, though not the only, tool allowing turning the postulates resulting from this principle into reality, that is the possibility of creating legal relationships binding on the parties, is a legal act.[3] Usually, the autonomy of the will rises to the rank of a civil law pillar, and is mostly conceived as one of the fundamental principles of this branch of law. Unfortunately, rarely are normative arguments confirming this phenomenon pointed to. One may get the impression that *communis opinio doctorum* it is an issue so obvious that it does not require any reasoning. Anywhere the consensus of the parties is necessary to bring about legal effects, naturally the autonomy of shaping this legal relationship also occurs. Despite such profound significance of

---

1 A. Wolter, J. Ignatowicz, K. Stefaniuk, *Prawo cywilne*, Warszawa 1998, p. 33: characterize the principle of the autonomy of the will pointing out that a person "may by their own power shape their legal relationships, naturally within the limits of the law (…). A basic instrument serving the realization of private autonomy is legal acts". P. Grzybowski, [in:] P. Grzybowski (ed.), *System prawa cywilnego. Cześć ogólna. Vol. 1*, Wrocław-Warszawa-Kraków-Gdańsk 1974, pp. 51–52, stresses that "the parties' autonomy of the will remains a principle regardless of how extremely it is limited"; A. Stelmachowski, *Zarys teorii prawa cywilnego*, Warszawa 1998, p. 83, assuming that "parties' autonomy, including especially its fundamental link, namely the freedom of contract (freedom of parties' will), is undoubtedly one of the leading principles of modern civil law", at the same time explains that the freedom of contract means "state transferring its regulation-making competences to the parties themselves, in other words – state's resignation from the sovereign regulating of parties' mutual relations" (p. 89); recently, most broadly M. Safjan, [in:] M. Safjan (ed.), *System Prawa Prywatnego. Prawo cywilne – część ogólna,. Vol. 1*, Warszawa 2012, p. 329 ff.

2 After many, see M. Safjan, [in:] M. Safjan (ed.), *System Prawa Prywatnego. Prawo cywilne – część ogólna. Vol.* 1, Warszawa 2012, p. 329 ff.

3 M. Niedośpiał, *Autonomia woli w części ogólnej prawa cywilnego*,"Państwo i Prawo" 1984, No. 12; idem, *Swoboda czynności prawnych*, Bielsko-Biała 2004, pp. 26–31.

this institution in mutual relations between civil law entities, the legislator did not express it directly in any provision of the Civil Code – contrary to the principle of freedom of contract, which has been explicitly pronounced in Article 353^1 CC since 1990. For these reasons, one needs to ponder whether in the current legal state one should talk about legal autonomy as a principle of the law, or perhaps a conclusion about a solely axiological basis of the current civil law which is a logical consequence of the historical development of the law and the philosophical reasoning for the sources of rules for procedures binding on legal entities is more well-founded.

Our reflections should begin by stressing clearly that the autonomy of the will, contrary to the freedom of contract (Article 353^1 CC), is not limited to the said institution of civil law, or especially to a specific field of this branch of law[4]. Wherever a civil law entity shapes their legal situation by their own (autonomous) behaviour, they enjoy the freedom afforded to them, which has been continuously expanding from the moment of first transformations of social and economic structures in the 19th century and is still in place today. This is proven even by today's discussion relating to categories of personality rights that the legal entity may dispose of, which in the first instance leads to a question about the scope of freedom of disposal thereof[5]. Already at this stage of reflections a generalization is possible that assumes that autonomy in deciding about oneself is indeed the source of the autonomy of the will. Yet, in order to fully reflect the way the autonomy of the will is rooted in private and legal regulations, it is necessary to refer to a concept created in the 1980s by A. Stelmachowski which analyses this construction on the structural and functional plane[6].

The structural plane of the autonomy of the will refers to a normative basis shaped by the system, and more precisely to conditions that allow civil law

---

4 After many, see A. Stelmachowski, *Wstęp do teorii prawa cywilnego*, 1st edition, Warszawa 1969, p. 40.

5 On the consent of the injured party see M. Sośniak, *Znaczenie zgody uprawnionego w zakresie cywilnej odpowiedzialności odszkodowawczej*, „Zeszyty Naukowe Uniwersytetu Jagiellońskiego. Prace prawnicze" 1959, z. 6, p. 136; Z. Banaszczyk, in: K. Pietrzykowski, *Kodeks cywilny. Komentarz. Art. 1–449^{11}, Vol. I*, Warszawa 2013, p. 1168 and A. Olejniczak, in: A. Kidyba, *Kodeks cywilny. Komentarz. Art. 1–449^{11}, Vol. III*, Warszawa 2014, p. 420, M. Zelek, [in:] M. Gutowski (ed.), *Kodeks cywilny. Komentarz. Art. 1–449^{11}, Vol. I*, Warszawa 2016.

6 See A. Stelmachowski, *Wstęp do teorii prawa cywilnego*, 2nd edition, Warszawa 1984, p. 99. When describing the structural plane the author focused solely on the then controversial concept of legal persons' being persons before the law and the legal capacity they were entitled to.

entities to shape legal relationships in a binding way. On account of that, first, a personal issue emerges as only addressees specified by the content of civil law norms, thus civil law entities, may decide on legal relationships. Apart from norm addressees, it also concerns persons that are beneficiaries of the behaviour of the norm's addressee and also persons whose actions update the obligation of the norm's addressee.[7] Based on Article 1 in conjunction with Article 33^1 CC, it does not raise greater doubt that participants of legal transactions include natural persons, legal persons and organizational units with no legal personality but which are granted legal capacity under the law.[8] However, legal personality itself does not decide on the significance of the autonomy of the will, even though this status makes it possible for specified entities to act as parties to legal relationships.[9]

However, a key issue is the legislator conferring upon civil law entities attributes that are to make it possible for them to use the scope of freedom in the fullest possible way. To present the significance of the structural approach, it is necessary to outline globally the scale in which the legislator decides in Polish legislation about the scope of freedom in deciding on one's legal situation. The basic attribute of any natural person, legal person and aforementioned organizational units is legal capacity. It is universally defined as the possibility of being an entity that has rights and obligations under civil law[10]. It is worth noting a conclusion that legal capacity is not equal to the capability of acquiring rights and obligations by one's actions.[11] Therefore, it is a normative category of a dualistic nature. On the one hand, legal capacity has a passive implication, on the other, it is an abstract value. The described legal attribute is not differentiated by civil law

7 P. Machnikowski, [in:] E. Gniewek, P. Machnikowski (ed.), *Kodeks cywilny. Komentarz, do art. 1 nb. 4*, Legalis (access: 14.02.2018).

8 After many, see Z. Radwański, *Podmioty prawa cywilnego w świetle zmian Kodeksu cywilnego przeprowadzonych ustawą z 14 lutego 2003*,"Prawo Spółek" 2003, no. 7–8, p. 11 ff. Up until the amendment of the Civil Code in 2003, separating a category other than natural and legal persons was a disputable issue. See M. Pazdan, *Podmioty bez osobowości prawnej po nowelizacji Kodeksu cywilnego z 2003 roku*, [in:] *W kręgu teoretycznych i praktycznych aspektów prawoznawstwa. Księga jubileuszowa Profesora Bronisława Ziemianina*, ed. M. Zieliński, Szczecin–Poznań 2005, p. 91 ff.

9 Differentiating between legal entities and parties in a legal relationship, see A. Klein, *Elementy zobowiązaniowego stosunku prawnego*, Wrocław 2005, p. 34 ff.

10 M. Pazdan [in:] M. Safjan (ed.), *System Prawa Prywatnego. Prawo cywilne - część ogólna*, Vol. 1, Warszawa 2012, p. 1022 ff.

11 After many, see B. Ziemianin, Z. Kuniewicz, *Prawo cywilne- część ogólna*, Poznań 2007, p. 32 ff.

provisions, which does not, however, exclude the possibility of the system of law making the admissibility of acquiring certain rights and obligations dependent on defined qualifications of the legal entity. Limiting legal capacity will therefore affect the scope of the entity's freedom itself[12]. One needs to highlight here that scopes of legal capacity of natural persons and legal persons do not overlap, which naturally affects the possibility of making use of the afforded freedom. Currently, their scope in not specified, in the sense that the legislator does not speculate what categories of rights and obligations are concerned, or which rights or obligation are not included in legal capacity.[13] The beginning of natural persons' legal capacity occurs the moment a live human being is born.[14] This issue seems to be more problematic with legal person as the Civil Code does not offer a provision which would expressly confer such capacity on them. The literature stresses that this does not pose much of a problem as recognizing an organizational unit as a person is equalled with conferring legal capacity upon them.[15] The legislator, however, prejudges when we can recognize a given organizational unit as a legal person at all, thus as an entity actively participating in civil law transactions. Pursuant to Article 37 CC, only with the moment of entry in an appropriate register does the acquisition of legal personality occur. However, it is not the only way to bring about such an effect.[16]

---

12 M. Pazdan, [in:] M. Safjan (ed.), *System Prawa Prywatnego. Prawo cywilne - część ogólna. Vol.* 1, Warszawa 2012, p. 1023 ff.

13 The legislator used to adopt a different solution as regards legal persons before Article 36 CC was repealed in 1990. This provision expressed a concept of the so-called special legal capacity of legal persons, that is legal capacity in a positively specified way. More on this subject, cf. J. Wiszniewski, *Specjalna zdolność prawna osób prawnych*,"Studia Prawnicze" 1970, No. 26–27, p. 326 ff.; J. Mojak, A. Kidyba, *Zdolność prawna przedsiębiorstw państwowych w świetle ustawy z dn. 25 września 1981 o przedsiębiorstwach państwowych*,"Annales Universitatis Mariae Curie-Skłodowska. Ius" 1982, Vol. XXIX, p. 254 ff; M. Pazdan, *Specjalna zdolność prawna osób prawnych (uwagi de lege lata i de lege ferenda)*, [in:] *Prace cywilistyczne. Księga ku czci prof. Jana J. Winiarza*, ed. P. Wójcik, Warszawa 1990, p. 201 ff.

14 In light of Article 8 section 1 CC every human being has legal capacity from the moment of birth.

15 J. Frąckowiak [in:] M. Safjan (ed.), *System Prawa Prywatnego. Prawo cywilne - część ogólna, Vol. 1,* Warszawa 2012, p. 1142

16 E.g. a university or a local government unit acquire legal personality by statute. See Article 12 of the act of 27 July 2005. Law on higher education (Dz. U. of 2012 item 572) or Article 2 section 2 of the commune self-government act of 8 March 1990 (Dz. U. of 2013 item 594).

Apart from passive capacity, the legislator equipped civil law entities in active capacity, i.e. the capacity to perform legal acts. When analysing this attribute of being persons before the law one needs to unequivocally prejudge, that realization of the autonomy of the will depends indeed on this competence of legal entities. One cannot talk about the autonomy of the will if one cannot effectively create one's own legal situation by one's own actions. The capacity to perform legal acts is the characteristic that allows bringing about specific results in the sphere of civil law. However, without taking up the subject matter of locating this qualification of legal entities one needs to point out that it is an excerpt of a broader category, namely capacity to take legal action.[17] An argument substantiating the above thesis is the legislator regulating this issue, who only used the structure of capacity to perform legal acts.[18]

The capacity to perform legal acts allows a civil law entity to bring about such events with which civil law links the establishment, change or termination of a legal relationship. In other words, the action of a legal entity leads to the acquisition of a right or to the undertaking of an obligation by a legal act, thanks to which they create their own legal situation. In order to maintain the validity and effectiveness of consequences of performed legal acts, the conditions for the existence of this attribute must be met, which in turn is a gradable category not only with reference to the scope of this institution, but also to the categories of entities. The entitlement to and scope of this attribute will be evaluated differently for natural persons and legal persons, including organizational units pursuant to Article 33[1] CC.

An analysis of civil code provisions shows that with natural persons – due to their age or certain medical prerequisites [19] – we can distinguish three situations. First, a natural person may have no capacity for legal acts at all.[20] Second, they may have limited capacity for legal acts.[21] And last, they may be afforded full capacity for legal acts.[22] An optimal state for full realization of the autonomy

17 M. Pazdan [in:] M. Safjan (ed.), *System Prawa Prywatnego. Prawo cywilne - część ogólna. Vol. 1*, Warszawa 2012, p. 1032

18 See Articles 11–22 of the Civil Code.

19 E.g., in light of Article 13 CC, due to mental illness, mental retardation or other mental disorder, in particular alcoholism or drug addiction.

20 Pursuant to Article 12 CC individuals who have not attained thirteen years of age and persons fully legally incapacitated do not have capacity for legal acts.

21 Pursuant to Article 15 minors who have attained thirteen years of age and persons partially legally incapacitated have limited capacity for legal acts.

22 Pursuant to Article 11 CC full capacity for legal acts is acquired at the moment of becoming an adult.

of the will is full capacity for legal acts. On this basis a natural person performs legal acts in their own name, as a result of their own action, independent of other participants in transactions and for his own account. Removing the effectiveness of a performed legal act depends solely on objectively verifiable circumstances relating to this act being contrary to the law or the principles of community life[23] (Article 58 CC) or by the occurrences of defects in a declaration of intent, or other irregularities provided by the system of law.[24]

An issue of capacity for legal acts of a legal persons, and thus the scope of the autonomy of the will afforded to those organizational units is different in this framework. There is no use in looking in the Civil Code for the provision that, similar to natural persons, directly confers such a legal qualification. An essential clue is included in Article 38 CC, which states that a legal person acts through its bodies in the manner prescribed by the law and its articles of association based on that law. This means that a legal person is a legal construction where the body is the most important structural element.[25] As can already be seen, a special structure of such an abstract legal being is not free from influence on the manner of enjoying the capacity to create independently and freely one's own legal situation. However, the impossibility of this legal being expressing volitional processes dear to man means that the actions of its body (and more pointedly, the guardian of this body, who is always a natural person) need to be considered as actions of a legal person. As a result, thanks to constitutive rules in the legal system, the body's guardian's disposing of the decision-making freedom translates into the scope of the legal person's the autonomy of the will in the structures this natural person operates in. One cannot forget that natural persons who have the status of the body's guardian do lot lose their status of being persons before the law.[26] On this basis, a legal person may perform legal acts as well as undertake other actions, such as acts similar to declarations of intent, as well as acts prohibited

---

23 Article 58 CC, cardinal for civil law.

24 E.g. exploitation – Article 388 CC, abusive clauses – 385 CC.

25 See J. Frąckowiak, [in:] M. Safjan (ed.), *System Prawa Prywatnego. Prawo cywilne - część ogólna*. Vol. 1, Warszawa 2012, p. 1145. A legal person's body needs to be understood as a natural person or persons (body's guardians) who were formally appointed to carry out function in it, thanks to which their behaviour, under circumstances defined by law, will be treated as behaviour of the legal person itself.

26 The literature points out the circumstances that are to differentiate between situations where it is the legal person's body who acts and where its representative acts. See J. Frąckowiak, [in:] M. Safjan (ed.), *System Prawa Prywatnego. Prawo cywilne - część ogólna. Vol. 1*, Warszawa 2012, p. 1145.

and allowed by law.[27] This is why its bodies are so essential. It is them that make decision-making and then the expression of a legal person's will possible, which determines the possibility of making proper use of the applicable principle of the autonomy of the will.

Already at the outset it was pointed out that the main tool allowing the realization of postulates resulting from the autonomy of the will is a legal act. The attributes described above of being persons before the law, though key to the autonomy of the will, would not be able to fulfil their function if the legislator had not regulated the measure that makes their real use possible. A legal act allows the transformation of one's will into an event resulting in specified effects protected by law. Even though the Civil Code does not feature a normative definition of a legal act, the said definition has been recreated from the entirety of civil law regulation.[28] A legal act ought to be understood as an actual state (human action) whose indispensable element is at least one declaration of intent given in order to bring about legal effects, bringing about at least some legal effects intended by the person giving the declaration of intent.[29] One cannot talk about a legal act without its most important element, that is the declaration of intent. One can assume on this basis that it consists of internal will and an expression of this will. Consistency between the taken internal decision and its external expression is the postulated state.[30] Should this not be the case, in order to remove the inconsistency between them, the legislator regulated the institution of declarations of intent. In the Polish legal order, only an expression of internal will, thus its declaration, carries legal significance.[31] The legislator equipped civil law entities in necessary attributes and tools that allow them free and independent participation in legal transactions. Naturally, the security

27 After many, see Radwański, *Prawo cywilne*, 2005, p. 162.

28 Act of 18 July 1950. General provisions of civil law (Dz.U. No. 34 item 311) in Article 40 provided than an act, aiming to bring about a change in or dissolve a legal relationship (legal act) brings effects not only expressed in it, but also such that result from a statute or a custom.

29 See B. Ziemianin, Z. Kuniewicz, op., *op. cit.*, p. 65.

30 See Z. Radwański [in:] Z. Radwański (ed.), *System Prawa Prywatnego. Prawo cywilne – część ogólna. Vol. 2*, Warszawa 2008, p. 13 ff. The author presents main directions of understanding the concept of declaration of intent in Polish and world literature.

31 Ibidem, cf. judgment of the Supreme Court of 21 January 2003, case file no. III RN 6/02, Legalis "Whether in a given case we are dealing with a declaration of intent depends on the fact whether the intent is expressed and whether a given entity (its body) is aware of it and wants what he expresses to be treated as his declaration of intent which is to bring about certain effects in the sphere of civil law relations".

of legal transactions and the protection of interests of these persons required that their independent action should be limited in certain situations. However, the indicated limitations are usually of an objective nature and depend on the person's age and psychological state.

To sum up this part of reflections, the legislator has created a coherent structural regulation of the autonomy of civil law entities which fully meets the requirements of the economic regime. Mostly on account of the fact that civil law entities may independently create their own legal situation, and more so, enter into legal relationships corresponding to their current life need. Legal entities are more flexible in their behaviours and react to changes more quickly, which in the end allows complete satisfaction of their own needs. Nevertheless, before a declaration of intent may take place, which results in the establishment, change or dissolution of a specified legal relationship, the legal entity must first take an appropriate internal decision. This conclusion leads to further reflections addressing functional autonomy.

According to A. Stelmachowski, functional autonomy shows direction of using the tools outlined by the structural autonomy. The relation between these terms is as follows. The structural autonomy delineates the space of permitted enjoyment of the afforded freedom and independence of participating in civil law transactions. It focuses on who and with what means affects the course of private life. On the other hand, functional autonomy fills this space as it initiates activity of legal entities in shaping their legal situation as well as the way the rights afforded by the legislator are enjoyed. They are terms that permeate and condition each other. One cannot talk about functional autonomy without structural autonomy, and vice versa. Otherwise, they would just be empty postulates proving the illusory nature of the freedom of civil law transactions. The functional autonomy is a more complex term than the structural autonomy as it concerns not only the normative strata but also a philosophical approach to the sources of the idea of freedom and independence of shaping one's own situation in a meaning broader than legal.

For the sake of almost unlimited application of contracts in the course of trade, one may assume that the autonomy of the will has been entirely dominated by one of its manifestations (freedom of contract), which significantly reduces its value.[32] However, such a trend cannot be accepted. The main argument against

32 This trend is noticed by J. Kaczor, Zasada autonomii woli w świetle filozofii liberalnej, Ruch Prawniczy, Ekonomiczny i Socjologiczny 2001, issues 1–2, p. 2; Z. Radwański, *Teoria umów*, Warszawa, 1977, p. 96.

such a stand is the criterion of distinguishing civil law in the system of law through adopting a method of regulation other than the one in administrative law and criminal law.[33] The essence of private law is indeed the fact that the realization of one's own interest by way of civil law relations requires dialogue and *consensus*.[34] Reaching this state is not possible without maintaining an autonomous position towards one another by potential parties to civil law relations. The autonomy of the will is also expressed in the fact the addressees of civil law norms may shape the content of legal acts in a way deriving from the normative model.[35] It is necessary here to present briefly the philosophical ideology substantiating the power of man's act of will to create normatively binding legal relationships. It needs to be stated without doubt that the autonomy of the will is only an excerpt of the naturalistic concept of human autonomous nature at all. Hence, it is necessary to explain its origin since only by doing so will it be possible to establish the proper content of the autonomy of the will and to establish the boundary delimiting its influence over other rules of civil law relating to detailed solutions reflecting in a greater extent the nature of defined fields of civil law.

Reflections on the philosophical basis of the autonomy of the will need to begin with consensualism. This trend assumed that a man's act of will is an event creating legal effects binding on him. The first element of this concept can be already found in the Roman law. Unfortunately, the development of this system did not lead to the adoption of a general rule saying that consensus is "the most essential, indispensable element of each contractual obligation".[36] In the medieval era, the canonical law consolidated the view that appealable obligations may also arise from non-formal promises (*nudum pactum*).[37] The concept of consensualism was also taken up the secular trend of the law of nature. *H. Grotius* himself believed

33 Sz. Słotwiński, *Status prawny energii elektrycznej jako wyznacznik stosunków umownych w polskim prawie prywatnym*, Warszawa 2017, p. 29.

34 A. Stelmachowski, *Zarys teorii prawa cywilnego*, Warszawa 1998, pp. 36 and 40.

35 Judgment of the Supreme Court of 16 December 2003, case file no. II CK 335/02, Legalis, judgment of the Supreme Court of 16 December 2004, case file no. V CK 332/04, Legalis.

36 M. Sośniak, Rozwój historyczny konstrukcji umowy obligacyjnej, Katowice 1986 quoted after Z. Radwański [in:] Z. Radwański (ed.), *System Prawa Prywatnego. Prawo cywilne – część ogólna. Vol. 2*, Warszawa 2008, p. 2.

37 A. Ohanowicz, *Wolność umów w przyszłym polskim kodeksie cywilnym*,"Ruch Prawniczy, Ekonomiczny i Socjologiczny"1926, No. 3, p. 148 presents after Z. Radwański [in:] Z. Radwański (ed.), *System Prawa Prywatnego. Prawo cywilne – część ogólna. Vol. 2*, Warszawa 2008, p. 3.

that the consensus itself obligates – "*solus consensus obligat*".[38] Nevertheless, it was the liberalism's thought that shaped the current concept of the autonomy of the will by linking it with an individual's personal freedom.[39] It is worth recalling a thought expressed by J. Locke: "*we must consider, what state all men are naturally in, and that is, a state of perfect freedom to order their actions, and dispose of their possessions and persons, as they think fit, within the bounds of the law of nature, without asking leave, or depending upon the will of any other man*".[40] In order to ensure an individual's freedom they need to be guaranteed an opportunity to make decisions consistent with their values and preferences.[41] The above-mentioned concepts which fit the slowly emerging free market economy had an impact on 19th century's codifications, and thus influenced the shaping of the fundaments of the modern science of civil law. Main emphasis was placed on freedom, which was the best plane for the realization of needs and interests[42]. The essence of the autonomy of the will was most strongly expressed in Article 1134 of the Napoleonic Code. It was decided in this paper that a contract legally concluded is a law between those who entered into it. As a consequence, it means that in a country respecting individuals' free and independent action, in order to achieve an individual goal, negotiations and compromises need to be involved. The formulated premises allowed the assumption that the only limitation of an individual's freedom is his own will expressed in a contract.[43] However, a belief that human nature is the main source of binding legal relationships while the law only plays a side role protecting the formed laws was subject to criticism in the 20th century.

Currently there is a view that it is not the naturalistically understood individual's autonomy of the will, but the system of law that is the basis of the binding force of legal acts performed by participants in legal transactions.[44] In the Polish law, a legal act is one of legal events with which norms of law bind certain legal effects. Due to this, a legal norm, and not parties' act of will, creates a binding legal relationship.[45] According to Z. Radwański such a solution allows

38 Ibidem.

39 J. Kaczor, *Zasada autonomii…*, p. 7.

40 J. Locke, *Dwa traktaty o rządzie*,,Warszawa 1992.

41 See J. Kaczor, Zasada autonomii…., p. 7 together with literature quoted therein.

42 Ibidem, p. 18.

43 Z. Radwański, *Uwagi ogólne o autonomii woli* [in:] *II Kongres notariuszy Rzeczypospolitej Polskiej. Referaty i opracowania*, Poznań 1999, p. 258.

44 Z. Radwański [in:] Z. Radwański (ed.), *System Prawa Prywatnego. Prawo cywilne – część ogólna. vol. 2*, Warszawa 2008, p. 5.

45 Z. Radwański, *Uwagi….*, p. 261; A. Stelmachowski, *Zarys teorii prawa cywilnego…*, p. 88.

first, the protection against state coercion of only those legal relationships which correspond to the values realized by the legal system, and second, the assurance of axiological cohesion to all legal relationships.[46] The author concludes that the naturalistic theory of the autonomy of the will is based solely on respect for individual will, which in the modern legal system is not a superior value.[47] It is not difficult to imagine the consequences to the security of legal transactions if a legal entity's individual will, awarded the power of shaping legal relationships in a binding way, was the superior value of the system of law.

The issue presented above, and especially the naturalistic understanding of the will of an individual human entity, is inherently associated with the freedom afforded to them and allows the recreation of the content of the autonomy of the will in the modern understanding of this term. Without a doubt, one needs to conclude that the autonomy of the will, through its content, shows the plane in which legal entities may act based on the consequences of their own decisions. Due to the philosophical basis of the autonomy of the will which intertwines with the normative manifestation of this institution, one needs to point out the elements co-creating the content of the autonomy of the will giving it a practical implication. The doctrine of civil law has repeatedly presented a catalogue of attributes of the autonomy of the will.[48] However, there is no full agreement as to the final content scope of the autonomy of the will, but there are some features that appear in each approach. First, freedom of decisions on forming a civil law relation. A civil law entity has the opportunity to make a choice between performing and not performing a legal act. This feature deserves special attention from the point of view of the contracting obligation and its characteristics against civil law. Second, freedom of choice of the other party of a legal relationship. It is a consequence of the first above-mentioned attribute. Freedom of choice of the other party to a legal act is essential also due to the fact that only interpersonal relations are legally significant. Third, freedom of terminating a legal relationship. There is a sign of the autonomy of the will which is subject to the greatest legal regulation. Sometimes the dissolution of a legal relationship

46 Z. Radwański (ed.) (in:) *System*…., p. 6.

47 Ibidem.

48 Cf. M. Safjan, [in:] M. Safjan (ed.), *System…, Vol. 1*, p. 333; Z. Radwański, [in:] Z. Radwański (ed.), *System…, Vol. 2*, p. 10; J. Kaczor, *Zasada autonomii…*, p. 4; P. Grzybowski, [in:] P. Grzybowski (ed.), *System…, Vol. 1*, p. 52; Z. Radwański, [in:] Z. Radwański (ed.), *System Prawa Prywatnego. Prawo cywilne – część ogólna, vol. 2, Warszawa 2008*, pp. 10–11 together with literature quoted therein; J. Kaczor, *Zasada autonomii*…., p. 4.

will not be as easy as its establishment and all will depend on the specific nature of the created legal relations. Also, one cannot forget that the main attribute of civil law relations is equality of entities, thus the autonomy to dissolve a legal relationship is limited by the autonomy afforded to the other party. Due to this fact, independent realization of such a right without prior arrangements with the other party will not be possible. Otherwise, the party terminating the existence of a legal relationship may face claims for damages. Fourth, the freedom of shaping the content of a legal act. The greatest significance of this aspect is expressed in the contract law. This, however, does not mean that it has a marginal importance in other branches of civil law. The legislator is particularly interested also in this sphere of the autonomy of the will pointing to various sanctions in the case of determining contents in a way contrary to the law. Further, freedom of changing the content of a legal relationship. The specific nature of this aspect of the autonomy of the will allows independent influencing of the content of the shaped legal relationships by only one of the entities. Equality of legal entities towards each other makes sovereign deciding about the content of mutual relations impossible. And finally, freedom of choice of form for the legal relationship. It is an attribute which raises most controversies in legal literature on the ground of the principle of the autonomy of the will.[49]

In view of the fact that the autonomy of the will is present in each manifestation of civil law transactions, the indicated features are common to all legal acts[50], which, based on the rules of the system of the law, result in creating civil law relationships.

On this basis, we can move on to the last of the discussed problems, that is giving an answer to the question whether the autonomy of the will may be treated as a principle of law. The issues of principles of law are at the centre of interest of representatives of the theory of law, who developed a universally accepted concept in this issue.[51] S. Wronkowska, M. Zieliński and Z. Ziembiński distinguished principles of law in a prescriptive and descriptive approach. The first kind of principles of law means applicable norms of law. However, what is essential, it does not have to be a norm directly expressed in a legal act. It is sufficient that it can be interpreted out of legal norms by way of appropriate legal conclusions.

---

49 Z. Radwański (ed.), [in:] *System…*, pp. 11–13 refers to it critically. In turn, most legal literature admits this attribute.

50 It needs to be expressly highlighted, that a legal act is not only a contract, though it is this type that carries the greatest significance for transactions.

51 See P. Wronkowska, M. Zieliński, Z. Ziembiński, *Zasady prawa. Zagadnienia podstawowe*, Warszawa 1974.

Moreover, a principle of law in a prescriptive approach may be justified by a consistent opinion presented in legal literature, backed by arguments about common axiological reasons of a certain group of norms and lack of provisions excluding the validity of this principle.[52] In turn, a principle of law in a descriptive approach means a model of "shaping of a specified object of regulation"[53], constructed by functionally interrelated legal norms. The relationship between these two meanings is presented in such a way that a legal principle in a descriptive approach may have its expression in a principle conceived in a prescriptive way.[54] One of the attributes of a principle of law is the fact that it presents the state of affairs best preferred by the legislator, where said state should be realized in the broadest possible way.[55] Straight away one can notice some likeness between the doctrinal understanding of the "principle" of the autonomy of the will and the presented concept of a principle of law in the descriptive approach. The autonomy of legal entities is one of the pillars of civil law, which reflects its essence. Arguments in favour of this statement include the occurrence of dispositive norms which confirm that civil law entities do indeed enjoy the competence of establishing civil law relations and shaping their content.[56] The very occurrence of norms of a relatively obligatory nature does not prejudge the existence of the "principle" of the autonomy of the will in the prescriptive sense, whereas it only proves the existence of a certain model of shaping legal relationships of a private law nature.[57]

To sum up, the principle of the autonomy of the will is recognized in the literature and the case law as a fundamental pillar of civil law, which designates the content and form of instruments allowing the shaping of an individual's legal situation. Contrary to the principle of the freedom of contract, though, it has not been directly expressed in the form of a provision of law. Therefore, one can put forward a thesis that the way of regulating civil law issues proves the existence of the principle of the autonomy of the will in a descriptive approach, whereas the mere existence of the autonomy of the will affects this, not another, way of shaping civil law regulations. This leads to a simple conclusion that the autonomy

52 P. Wronkowska, M. Zieliński, Z. Ziembiński, *Zasady prawa. Zagadnienia…*, pp. 59–60.

53 Ibidem, pp. 28–48.

54 M. Zieliński, *Konstytucyjne zasady prawa*, [in:] Charakter i struktura norm konstytucji, ed. J. Trzciński, Warszawa 1997, p. 74

55 P. Wronkowska, M. Zieliński, Z. Ziembiński, *Zasady prawa. Zagadnienia…*, p. 114.

56 See M. Piotrowski, *Normy prawne imperatywne i dyspozytywne*, Warszawa 1990, p. 24.

57 J. Kaczor, *Zasada autonomii woli z perspektywy teorii prawa*," Acta Universitatis Wratislaviensis. Przegląd Prawa i Administracji" 2005, no. 69, p. 77.

of the will sees its source in the system of values preferred by the legislator. The said dependence is reinforced by the activity of civil law entities. The analysed principle allows a contract to be used as a flexible and effective instrument for shaping economic relationships.[58] Taking into account that the most important aspect of the autonomy of the will is the possibility of independent shaping of one's own legal situation (most profoundly defined in the case law as party's decision-making freedom), it will not be possible without this entity's legally guaranteed sphere of independence of other participants in legal transactions. If no entity can arbitrarily affect the situation of the other party, then this leads to a conclusion that persons participating in private law relationships must have an equal position. It is this attribute that is the main criterion for distinguishing civil law according to the method of regulating legal relationships. Only equality of entities, not only in their mutual relationships as future parties to an established legal relationship, but also in terms of legal measures they are entitled to, will allow an actual realization of the freedom afforded to them. One cannot talk about independent making of decisions about one's rights and obligations without the equality of autonomous civil law entities.[59] The autonomy of the will fully realizes elementary principles concerning mostly freedoms of man on every plane of his participation in legal transactions. On this basis the autonomy of the will is *sensus spiritualis* of civil law, which shaped appropriate instruments allowing the realization of the discussed principle of law.

58 A. Stelmachowski, *Wstęp do teorii prawa cywilnego*, Warszawa 1969, p. 18.
59 J. Kaczor, *Zasada autonomii…*., p. 79.

O. Bogucki

Values in the Interpretation of Law. (From the Traditional to the Contemporary Approach in the Polish Theory of Law)

1 Introduction

Interpreting the texts, or, more generally, linguistic expressions, has long been the subject of consideration in all the areas of humanities – from philosophy to linguistics or cultural anthropology. The general preconception that interpretation in way expresses the values and depends on them has probably been present in the humanities since their beginning, however it was the recent decades – particularly due to the theories such as hermeneutics, neopragmatism or the latest analytical philosophy – that this preconception has been specifically expressed. In view of this keen interest of the relation between the issue of interpretation and the questions of axiology, it is justified to talk about a certain ethical turning point in the humanities. [1]

In the legal sciences, there has also been a keen interest in the relationship between the legal interpretation and the values. It should be emphasized, however, that each legal culture explains the given problem in their own, to a certain extent separate, way. It is due to the fact that the manner of reflecting on the issue mentioned depends, to a significant degree, on the history, type of legal system it is based on, as well as on the legal tradition and the general philosophical, ethical and scientific tradition. There are certain differences between the reflection over the relationship between the interpretation and values in the American legal thought and the relevant reflection in the mid-European theory or philosophy of law. The aim of this paper is to outline the certain tradition of the issues mentioned and to present the contemporary normative model for inclusion of values in the interpretation of law proposed in the modern theory of law. The first part of the paper outlines the achievements of the Polish reflection over the judicial interpretation, whereas the second part contains the general characteristics of the model.

1 A. Szahaj, *Zwrot antypozytywistyczny dopełniony (zamiast wstępu)*, [in:] *Filozofia i etyka interpretacji*, eds. A. F. Kola, A. Szachaj, Kraków 2007, pp. 7–14.

2 Development of Reflection on the Role of Values in Legal Interpretation

2.1 Classic Theories of Legal Interpretation

The systematic reflection over the interpretation of law has its beginnings in the inter-war period. It formed on the grounds of a positivistic vision of law as a set of norms established by the state authorities (although significantly "interceded" by the legal tradition and the views of the legal scholars). Thus, in the aforementioned period the focus was mainly on the linguistic aspects of the interpretation of law. The significance of the non-linguistic issues had already been noticed at that time. E. Waśkowski, author of the first Polish theory of judicial interpretation, distinguished (including in this regard also the findings of the legal tradition) two stages of the interpretation: verbal and real [2]. In terms of the real interpretation, he distinguished, i.a., the element called the premise of the provision which may occur in several versions, particularly the following: (1) legal (when a more general norm is the premise for thema content of another norm), (2) theological (when the objective of the provision adopted at its making constitutes the premise), (3) psychological, (4) historical (taking into account the content of the previous provisions), (5) external (taking into account the actual, not declared, reasons for the introduction of certain legal regulations)[3].

It is worth adding that the inter-war period has also marked the beginning of the development of the modern Polish analytical philosophy (the philosophy of language, i.a.), practised at that time within the framework of the so-called Lvov-Warsaw School. Although it was not significantly affecting the theory of law at that time, certain symptoms of such effect had already appeared, exemplified by the works of the so-called Vilnius School in the theory of law. The structural theory of judicial interpretation presented by Sawa Frydman[4] originated within its scope, constituting an original concept which considered the judicial interpretation to be a structure of best practice and assigned this practice to the legal text.

After World War Two the political situation has changed considerably, which affected the Polish theory and philosophy of law. The communist system and law fostered the positivistic paradigm in reflecting on the law. Thus, the linguistic

2 E. Waśkowski, *Teoria prawa cywilnego*, Warszawa 1936, p. 47 et seq.

3 Ibid.

4 This theory has been presented mainly in the following work: S. Frydman, *Dogmatyka prawa w świetle socjologii*, [in:] *Ogólna nauka o prawie*, B. Wróblewski, Vilnius 1936.

interpretation still remained the centre of attention. The law was based on the "only proper" axiological foundations, hence the overly speculative and critical consideration of these issues might have turned out even dangerous.

Nevertheless, Polish theory of judicial interpretation was still evolving, while the impact of the Lvov-Warsaw School was becoming increasingly visible. It is clearly noticeable in the theory of judicial interpretation by Jerzy Wróblewski[5]. Due to the solid theoretical foundation and practical approach, this concept has significantly affected Polish theory of law and is an important point of reference in the reflections over judicial interpretation nowadays. Its importance also results from the fact that it has been treated as a normative concept[6].

What is significant from the point of view of this paper, is the fact that Jerzy Wróblewski introduced order to the terms related to the judicial interpretation, distinguishing its three types: linguistic, systemic and functional. Pursuant to this approach, the axiological issues lie within the scope of the functional interpretation. The author understood the functional interpretation as establishing the meaning of a legal text based on its functional context, i.e. the context of the genesis or the operation of the legal provision, comprising the complex economic, political and cultural phenomena[7]. According to the author, the functional context is quite complex as it comprises the economic, social and political system the legal norm applies to, the general culture of the society expressed in the assessments and norms adopted there, the social and political objectives formulated by the leading groups in the society, and, moreover, the specific civilizational phenomena requiring the regulation of the behaviour of the people in the society[8]. Jerzy Wróblewski has not considered this enumeration to be exhaustive – he assumed that actually all phenomena which do not constitute linguistic or systemic context of the interpreted provisions can be considered in this case. The author grouped the elements of the functional context into two sets of issues. The first refers to the role of the objective in the interpretation of law, whereas the other refers to the role of the assessments and rules which do not constitute legal norms adopted in the society. The author specified the interpretation based

5 J. Wróblewski, *Zagadnienia teorii wykładni prawa ludowego*, Warszawa 1959. A later version of this theory has been presented in: idem, *Rozumienie prawa i jego wykładnia*, Wrocław 1990.

6 It is worth adding that J. Wróblewski had not actually intended the clarification concept to be a normative concept - it only started to be considered as such later on.

7 J. Wróblewski, *Zagadnienia teorii wykładni prawa ludowego*, Warszawa 1959, p. 353 et seq.

8 Ibid.

on granting consideration to the objective of the legal regulations as the teleological interpretation[9]. Since the findings of Jerzy Wróblewski, the axiological issues of the interpretation of law has been traditionally linked to the concept of the functional interpretation, as well as the teleological interpretation within its framework. It should be added, however, that the modern literature sometimes also refers to the term of axiological interpretation, referring only to the axiological problems of interpretation of law.

Since the 1970s, the so-called derivative theory of interpreting a legal text has been developed in the Polish literature. The first version was developed in 1972 by Maciej Zieliński[10], whereas it was inspired by Zygmunt Ziembiński's differentiation between the legal provision as an editorial unit of a legal text and a legal norm as an expression unequivocally ordering the specific conduct of the specific addressee in certain circumstances[11]. Pursuant to the derivative theory, the interpretation of law consists in recreation of legal norms from legal provisions. The derivative theory is still being developed by Maciej Zieliński, as well as the other authors of the so-called Szczecin-Poznań School of legal theory. The importance of the derivative theory consists mainly in the fact that it contains an extensive set of rules of interpretation which is coherent and internally organized. Although many aspects of the derivative theory have been critical towards the earlier derivative theory (especially when it comes to specifying the beginning of interpretation), it is certainly similar in terms of axiological aspect of interpretation. The derivative theory has adopted the division into a linguistic, systemic and functional interpretation, whereas the axiological issues have been included within the framework of the latter one.

Both the clarifying and derivative theory have focused mainly on the linguistic (syntactic and semantical) issues of the interpretation of law. It is probably related to the fact that they originated under the positivistic paradigm and the influence of the Polish analytical philosophy. Focusing on the linguistic issues has resulted in the catalogue of rules of the functional interpretation being rather modest and their content very general, both in the clarification theory and in the earlier versions of the derivative concept. In the clarification theory, they

9 II, p. 378.

10 M. Zieliński, *Interpretacja jako proces dekodowania tekstu prawnego*, Poznań 1972. Contemporary version of this theory has been presented in the book *Wykładnia prawa. Zasady, reguły, wskazówki*, which had seven editions (first: Warszawa 2012, seventh: Warszawa 2017).

11 Z. Ziembiński, *Przepis prawny a norma prawna*, „Ruch Prawniczy, Ekonomiczny i Socjologiczny" 1960, no. 1, pp. 105–122.

required the compliance of the established meaning of the provision with the objective of the legislator, as well as with the other elements of the non-linguistic context. The earlier versions of the derivative theory assumed that the interpreter has to establish which meaning of the legal text is best justified in the light of the factual knowledge assigned to the rational lawmaker (i.e. leads to the most effective solution) and, moreover, which of the meanings is best justified in the light of the objective assigned to the rational lawmaker, also in view of other values (other than the objective). In the event of a discrepancy in the results, the interpreter must make a choice, giving priority to the results justifying the constitutional values[12].

2.2 Other Approaches

Despite their significance, the clarifying and derivative concepts are not the only theoretical approaches in the judicial interpretation presented in Polish literature. The significant achievement of the Polish literature in this regard should be emphasized here. Especially since the 1990s, there has been an increasing number of publications on theoretical and practical issues related to the interpretation of law, often presenting very different theoretical, philosophical-legal or general philosophical assumptions. It is worth adding that there has been an increasing degree of reference to the interpretative approaches which did not originate in the Polish theory and philosophy of law, as an attempt to "introduce" them into Polish ground.

Hence, Polish literature contains the views referring to the philosophical and legal hermeneutics,[13] legal argumentation theory[14] as well as the other theoretical approaches, such as interpretative holism[15], intentionalism[16], being just a trend in the Anglo-Saxon judicial theory.

---

12 M. Zieliński, *Wykładnia prawa. Zasady, reguły, wskazówki*, Warszawa 2017, pp. 340–343.

13 E.g. M. Zirk-Sadowski, *Hermeneutyka a problemy filozofii prawa*, "Studia Prawno-Ekonomiczne" 1982, vol. XXVIII; J. Stelmach, *Współczesna filozofia interpretacji prawniczej*, Kraków 1995; H. Leszczyna, *Hermeneutyka prawnicza – rozumienie* i *interpretacja tekstu prawnego*, Warszawa 1996; T. *Stawecki*, O *praktycznym zastosowaniu hermeneutyki* w *wykładni prawa*, [in:], Teoria i praktyka wykładni prawa, ed. P Winczorek, Warszawa 2005.

14 E.g. K. Płeszka, *Reguły preferencji w prawniczych rozumowaniach interpretacyjnych*, [in:] *Studia z filozofii prawa*, vol. 2 ed.: J. Stelmach, Kraków 2003; J. Stelmach, *Kodeks argumentacyjny dla prawników*, Kraków 2003; T. Spyra, *Granice wykładni prawa*, Kraków 2006; B. Brożek, *Rationality and Discourse: Towards a Normative Model of Applying Law*, Warszawa 2007.

15 M. Matczak, *Summa Iniuria. O błędzie formalizmu w stosowaniu prawa*, Warszawa 2007.

16 Z. Tobor, *W poszukiwaniu intencji prawodawcy*, Warszawa 2013.

The aforementioned views concentrate mainly on the general issues related to the judicial interpretation, such as the manner of understanding the interpretation, its epistemological status, argumentative nature, understanding the language or the role of interpretative community in establishing the meaning of the text. The importance of taking the values into consideration in the interpretation has been stressed within the framework of all the aforementioned approaches, although their source and the manner of this consideration is not uniformly perceived.

It should be emphasized that there has been a number of publications in the modern Polish literature which dealt with the axiological issues of the interpretation in various aspects[17]. Despite the significant analyses of the axiological conditions of the interpretation of law, the earlier approaches have been either related to a certain aspect of this issue or remained at some level of generality which did not offer any sequential, ordered, properly detailed, yet complex and comprehensive normative model of taking the values into consideration in the interpretation of law.

It is worth noticing that there is quite a potential for formulating the indicated normative model in the argumentative approach to judicial interpretation in a procedural version (a significant achievement in terms of reflection over the rationality of the discourse and communication ethics). The procedural approach as such is already positive – aimed at defining some "system" of legal argumentation which could contain certain arguments concerning functional interpretation. However, the main doubt related to this approach refers to the degree of conclusiveness of the possible model, which, in turn, is related to the fact that it is of "ponderative" nature. Understanding the arguments or interpretative directives (also in the scope of a functional interpretation) as principles within the meaning derived from Dvorkin and Alexy does not seem to facilitate the conclusiveness of the judicial interpretation. Evidence-based pondering of the interpretative directives (against the background of the case requiring a solution) may bring unequivocal conclusion in some situations; in many situations, however, it will not provide such a conclusion (without certain radical clarification of the ponderation procedure itself or specification of the relations between the arguments *in abstracto*). Therefore, the possibility to formulate properly detailed model of functional interpretation on the grounds of argumentative approach

17 E.g. M. Zirk-Sadowski, *Rozumienie ocen w języku prawnym*, Łódź 1984; M. Kordela, *Zasady prawa. Studium teoretycznoprawne*, Poznań 2012; M. Smolak, *Wykładnia celowościowa z perspektywy pragmatycznej*, S. Wojtczak, *O niewspółmierności wartości i jej konsekwencjach dla stosowania prawa*, Łódź 2010.

should not be negated in principle, however it may be concluded that such an approach should be the subject to significant clarification and particularization.

3 Holistic Model of Functional Interpretation

3.1 General Characteristics

Based on the achievements of the Polish reflection over the interpretation of law outlined above, I had a chance to present – first time in the Polish literature – a properly detailed, coherent and conclusive model specifying the manner in which the values and factual (non-legal) knowledge should be considered in the process of interpretation[18]. Traditionally, I have defined this consideration as functional interpretation. The model has been based on a derivative theory of interpretation of law as the most developed normative concept presented in the Polish literature. The reference to the derivative theory allowed to properly locate the functional interpretation in a coherent and complex interpretation model Formulating the interpretation model required much more elaboration and clarification of the derivative theory, as well as introducing certain modifications. It may be stated that the model described derives to some extent from the previously outlined robust achievements of the Polish reflection over the judicial interpretation. Its formulation, however, is the effect of the constructive criticism of legal culture. Legal culture is not an internally coherent creation, but rather a space for the "clash" of various elements This constructive criticism of the legal culture was intended to present a certain set of elements, as coherent as possible, together with a proposal to reject other elements.

The model discussed contains 109 directives (rules) of the functional interpretation[19]. They have been divided into general directives, the directives referring to recreation of the factual knowledge, directive referring to the recreation of the objective of the norm, directives regarding the recreation of other values and systemic organization of the global assessments and the directives referring to modifications of the linguistic meaning. These directives have been constructed in such a way as to solve not only the practical interpretative issues, but also the ones that may occur from theoretical point of view. Due to limited volume of this paper, it is not possible to discuss the whole model in detail. Thus, the outline of the model and its main features will be presented in the further part of the paper.

---

18 I have formulated this model in the following work: O. Bogucki, *Model wykładni funkcjonalnej w derywacyjnej koncepcji wykładni prawa*, Szczecin 2016.

19 Ibid., pp. 261–278.

3.2 Outline of the Model

The content of the terms used in the said model is a particularly important factor affecting its shape. Certainly, the sole concept of the functional interpretation is essential. It is understood as interpretative acts aimed at establishing factual knowledge and global assessment assigned to a rational legislator, followed by indicating such linguistic expressions that would have the strongest justification in view of the restored knowledge and assessment. In particular, the analyses of the concept of value, global assessment and the system of values had a very significant impact on the model.

The concept of value has been characterized in formal terms for the purpose of the model discussed. First of all, the concept of a simple value has been introduced, associated with the idealizing approach to metaxiology developed by L. Nowak[20]. A simple value is a set of states of affairs W = {Z(max),…, Z,…, Z(min)} having a maximum and minimum relationships organizing this family. The sets Z(max), …, Z(min) are the sets of equally valuable (equivalent) states of affairs. They have been organized by the relationship of general preference. A set of states of affairs Z is generally preferred before a set of states Z' when each state of affairs p belonging to Z is preferred over each state of affairs q belonging to Z'. These sets constitute the degrees of a certain value. There is a set of axiologically neutral states of affairs of Z(ind) between the most preferred set of Z(max) and the least preferred set of Z(min). The Z-sets preferred to the Z(ind) are called the degrees of good in the specified value, while the sets to which Z(ind) is preferred are defined as the degree of evil of this value.

The concept of the complex value and the global assessment is also significant in the model discussed. The global assessment of the state of affairs consists in the comparison of valuations of this state of affairs from the point of view of various values. A composite value is a specific order of global assessments labelled with a specific name. Therefore, a composite value is deemed to exist when there is a function that assigns a specific degree of good or evil from the point of view of all the components, or an indifference, to each global assessment in a composite value. Moreover, the existence of some substantive relationship between the component values justifying the attribution of a specific name to this value (as a certain 'bundle' of component values) is necessary in order to talk about a composite value. For example, the "child's best interest" will be a name of a value constituting the values such as: material security of the child's decent living

20 Ibid., pp. 64–67.

conditions, emotional bonds between the child and parents, safety of the child, emotional development and intellectual development of the child.

The concept of the system of values, used in the model discussed, is strictly related to the aforementioned concept. A system of values is considered a set of systemic orders of global assessments, i.e. the ones assigning a certain degree of good or evil to the global assessment from the point of view of values as a whole, which, in turn, allows to resolve the non-conformity of values when referring to their system.

One of the basic theoretical assumptions of the model discussed is the assumption of the isomorphy of the assessment and standards[21]. It may be expressed in the following manner: the content of the specific N norm (injunction, specifying the addressee, circumstances, conduct) corresponds to the content of the specific global assessment GA (covering the specific objective O pursued at grade 'n' as well as the other values 'W(1) to (W(n)' pursued at the relevant grades 'n'). Thus, the objective is understood as one of the values distinguished due to the content of the norm. Recreating the proper pair – the global assessment and the corresponding norm – may be the ultimate result of the functional interpretation. Therefore, the concept of interpretative structure is very important. All interpretative variants acceptable in view of the rules of the linguistic interpretation constitute the interpretative structure. Thus, it may be concluded that it is created by the potentially interpretable (in view of the linguistic interpretation) norms of conduct. Interpretative structure is a starting point of a functional interpretation, creating certain "space" where the interpreter moves.

It is worth noting that in the light of the discussed model both the knowledge and the global assessment are assigned to the rational legislator as a certain conceptual design, although sometimes they might be recreated from the sources not directly originating from the real legislator (e.g. the case law and the views of the legal scholars). It is worth noting that pursuant to the model described, recreating the knowledge assigned to the rational legislator is not an independent goal of the functional interpretation. Recreating the knowledge is to facilitate the proper recreation of the global assessment assigned to the rational legislator, thus provided for as the first in the chronological order.

Pursuant to the model described, recreating factual knowledge requires stating which states of affairs will result from implementation of the particular interpretative variants (potentially interpretable norms). First of all, it should be carried out based on the general knowledge in the given field and if that fails – as

21 O. Bogucki, *Model ...*, p. 278.

an alternative – by having recourse to the expertise of an expert in the field in question and – subsequently – to the common knowledge of an interpreter. The particular states of affair should be organized in the so-called explanation matrix, i.e. a compilation of general interpretative variants and the states of affairs their implementation leads to. Such explanation matrix is a point of recreation of the global assessment.

When it comes to the recreation of the global assessment, recreating the objective is envisaged as a matter of priority, followed by other values constituting the particular global assessment. The framework of the model includes detailed characteristics of the manner of recreating the global assessment from the legal text (considered the basic source of information in this regard), as well as, alternatively, the case law and the views of the legal scholars, legislative materials, as well as the interpretative presumptions.

It should be noted that it is important to differentiate the internal and external recreation of the objective in the model discussed. The internal (in relation to the specified interpretative structure) recreation of the objective occurs when the objective is recreated based on the comparison of the interpretative variants involved in a given case. In turn, the external (regarding the specified interpretative structure) recreation of the objective occurs when the objective is recreated based on the comparison of the interpretative variants with the legislator's statements on the objectives to be implemented by the given norms (e.g. contained in the preamble or the first Article of a given normative act). Pursuant to the model discussed, the external recovery of the objectives should be a priority and the internal recovery shall apply in the case where it is not possible to reach conclusions. Shall neither the external, nor the internal recreation of the objective from the legal text bring any conclusions, the case law and the views of the legal scholars should be referred to as an alternative. If that does not bring conclusions either, legislative materials should be referred to as an alternative, further followed by *in dubio pro libertate* presumption. The model specifies in detail the situations where the findings of the case law and the views of the legal scholars should be deemed conclusive.

The issue of non-conformity of values is very important in recreating the full global assessment. When recreating the global assessment, it is crucial to establish whether there is any inconsistency between one of the other values identified by the interpreter and the value constituting the objective of the norm within the framework of the reviewed interpretative structure; thus, whether adopting the interpretative variant (potentially interpretable norm) implementing the objective of the norm to the greatest degree does not cause decrease in implementing this other norm. The model discussed specified in detail how to solve the potential non-conformity of values based on the systemic orders of the global assessment possible to recover based on the legal text, the case law and the views of the legal scholars. When solving the non-conformity of the values referring to the sources indicated proves impossible, it is assumed that should be determined in favour of the objective of the norm, as expressed by an interpretative presumption *in dubio pro fines.*

Another issue solved within the framework of the model discussed is the question of the scope of the permitted modification of the linguistic interpretation when referring to functional interpretation and giving a new meaning to the specific expression (not provided for in the linguistic system). Such a modification is allowed if the new meaning remains in the semantic field of one of the existing meanings of the expression interpreted and such expression in this new meaning is not excluded from the scope corresponding to the meaning indicated by the semantic rules of the language system.

3.3 Basic Features of the Model

At this point, a number of remarks should be formulated, allowing to emphasize the most important features of the approach discussed above and to place it in a wider theoretical perspective.

First of all, it should be pointed out that the aforementioned model is of normative, not descriptive, nature. Thus, it presents a vision, based on certain presumptions, how a model interpreter should act and not the manner in which the law enforcement bodies act in practice. However, it does not mean that the interpretative practice of the law enforcement bodies was not taken into consideration. Such practice has been considered, however only to the extent that allows to speak of developing a relatively homogeneous pattern within this framework. In the light of the research of the interpretative practice carried out in the Polish theory of law it may be stated that although certain patterns of interpretation can be observed, they are fragmented and far from sufficient to define an overall model of the functional interpretation. In order to formulate such model, it was necessary to consider a number of other findings, related, for example, to the features of the legal text and language, characteristics of values or basic methodological rules.

Subsequently, it should be noted that the presented model is of a formal nature, i.e. it does not indicate which actual values should be considered in the interpretation, which of the values take priority, etc. A certain exemption in this regard is the interpretative presumption *in dubio pro libertate*, directly referring to the value of the freedom from orders. However, it is a directive that is supposed to be used as a kind of "last resort" when reaching a conclusion by means of recourse to other arguments is not possible. Such presumption seems relatively easy to prove in the case of the legal systems of modern liberal democracies.

The formal nature of this approach consists in providing for a certain course of action, a certain procedure for determining the appropriate axiological solutions in a given case. These solutions are, in a way, a product of the application of this procedure, and not somehow provided 'in advance'. In principle, it is not possible to obtain such solutions without carrying out interpretation in accordance with the presented model. The formal nature of this model results from a formal approach to metaxiological issues. The approach discussed is based on the formal analyses of the structure of values, global assessments or the system of values, at the same time leaving aside the typically philosophical (metaphysical) issues – e.g. the question of the existence of the values or the subjective nature of justifying them – as well as pointing out the values that are "correct" in terms of ideology or worldview. The model discussed refers to the question how to recreate the values that can be attributed to the rational legislator, not how to justify the validity of certain values. In that scope, the approach discussed is as neutral as possible.

Obviously, the indicated ideological or philosophical neutrality is not absolute (if actually possible at all). The characterized model is based on certain evaluative assumptions, adopted without further justification as to what is appropriate. In the first place, it refers to the assumption that intersubjective conclusiveness of legal interpretation (ensured by the application of the model) is an extremely important value, instrumentally subordinated to the value of the state. In other words, the consistent implementation of a specific detailed model of interpretation is better from the point of view of the value of the rule of law than *ad hoc* or intuitive interpretation. The assumption that implementation of the formal justice (model application) is a necessary condition to obtain the material justice of the solution constitutes a foundation of the discussed approach.

The above remarks lead to more general questions: what concept of law and what philosophy of law is assumed in the discussed approach. It is certainly a certain subtle and moderate version of legal positivism. It is related to relying on a particular tradition (described earlier) of the Polish reflection over the legal interpretation, specifically derivative theory. The law itself is perceived as a set of norms established by the rational legislator (the norms, however, are not synonymous with the legal provisions). The concept of rational legislator is crucial here. It is a certain idealising conceptual design which allows not to identify it with the real legislator – the persons who affect the content of the legal provisions within the legislative bodies. The reconstructed global assessment is assigned to the rational legislator, although it does not have to be the same as the global assessment adopted by the real legislators. Specific form of legislation obviously has a very significant impact on the content of the recreated global assessment, it is not, however, the only factor influencing its content (other sources are also important). In fact, this content is the result of applying certain interpretative procedure, which assumes a significant role of the interpreter. Thus, despite the fact that it is the recreation which is mentioned in the discussed approach, it does not have solely "reproductive" character in relation to the real legislator. The content of the global assessment established through interpretation does not have to "mirror" the global assessment adopted by the real legislator (if there was any in the given case).

The assumption that the content of the norm and the related global assessment is the result of the interpretative process may be associated with the elements of hermeneutic approach to interpretation or Dvorkin-like approach. Therefore, it is worth noting that within the framework of the described functional interpretation there is a fundamental importance of the cultural dimension of interpretation (every process of interpretation is in a way immersed in a specific legal and general culture). The culture, however, is not coherent and contains axiological elements that are inconsistent with each other, especially nowadays, with the contemporary pluralism of the values and world view. From the legal point of view, a formal model seems necessary to "arbitrate" between them and reach conclusions in order to apply the law. In this aspect, the approach discussed reminds to certain extent the procedural theories of legal argumentation (legal discourse), however the interpretation is more of a monologue in this case (an intellectual process of the interpreter).

It is also worth emphasizing that pursuant to the discussed approach, considering the values and non-legal knowledge of the interpreter is also an indispensable element of any process of interpretation. It is not limited only to the linguistic situation of the ambiguity of the legal text. Hence, if we treat the directives of the interpretation as a part of the positivistic rule of recognition, it may be stated that pursuant to the discussed approach, the reference to values is its indispensable element.

The last properties of the discussed approach worth mentioning are as follows: systemic approach to the issue of values and the use of idealisation. They are significantly related to each other – treating the values as systemically interconnected and ordered in their entirety constitutes a certain idealisation itself. In fact, we are dealing with preferences which are usually partial, volatile, unspecific and thus do not constitute complex systems enabling unequivocal assessment of each case, but rather form more or less developed fragments of such systems (both in terms of particular persons and publicly manifested moral or social doctrine). It seems that the modern axiology focuses on the problems generated by the aforementioned areas of non-specificity, manifested by intensive consideration of issues such as disproportionality of values, their pluralism, etc. Thus, it may be stated that systemicity of values is to some extent a counterfactual idealizing assumption. The assumptions of idealisation may serve different functions. In natural sciences, idealisation – as methodological procedure – allows to simplify complex phenomena and thus find relevant regularities in them. In turn, within the framework of the approach discussed, idealizations regarding values serve the purpose of advocating performance of interpretation procedure, which will consider their essential formal features, in an ordered manner.

4 Axiological Interpretation

To sum up, it should be noted that another comprehensive study of the issue of the role of values in interpretation appeared in the most recent literature[22]. It constitutes a vast and complex analysis of the axiological aspect of interpretation based on the specific philosophical solutions – certain ontology and metaxiology. The aforementioned study focuses on the analysis of the phenomenology of values in law based on certain ontology and metaxiology – thus, in that sense it has a descriptive character (it does not formulate rules of interpretation). Nevertheless, many findings can be read in a normative way – as indicating what the interpreter should do in a given situation.

The discussed approach is also an expression of a formal attitude to axiological (metaxiological) issues as well as to the systemic perception of values – the approach is based on essentialism, i.e. the assumption that values in law are ordered by relations of domination. This approach broadly utilizes the concepts of idealizing theory of science and formal metaxiology and ontology developed in the Polish analytical philosophy by L. Nowak[23]. The approach represents axiological attributability, namely the concept that the objects which constitute the bundles of value-making properties are subject to valuation, whereas the elements of the real world (people, objects, situations) are exemplifications of the objects from the attributive universe.

Pursuant to the discussed approach, the axiological interpretation of law is aimed at the reconstruction of an element – and in the extreme case, the full

22 M. Zajęcki, *Aksjologiczna interpretacja prawa (studium z metodologii i teorii prawa)*, Warszawa 2017.

23 Ibid., pp. 42–171.

ideal – of law. The set of values affirmed in the law in their entirety constitutes the ideal of the law – the set of facts consisting in implementing the values to maximum extent. However, considering the conflict potential of values in law it is assumed that the ideal of law is a legal utopia – impossible to implement in the real world. In the light of the discussed approach, the values are recreated in the framework of the axiological interpretation of law by considering the axiological supposition and presupposition of the legal text. Supposition means that the legislator directly indicates the values in the legal text, whereas presupposition denotes indirect indication, consisting in such formulation of the content of the legal regulation, that the specific value becomes its axiological premise (axiological justification). Pursuant to the approach discussed, the information obtained as a result of axiological interpretation of law may – depending on the cognitive purpose – be applied in order to: (1) conduct functional interpretation, (2) explain legislative activities through a humanistic interpretation of these activities, (3) reconstruct the ideal social order affirmed in the legal system and – if necessary – to apply *de lege ferenda criticism*[24].

5 Summary

Rich tradition and achievements of the Polish theory of legal interpretation must be emphasized in summarizing the remarks contained in this study. The development of the Polish reflection over the legal interpretation was significantly related to the legal positivism and Polish analytical philosophy. Such origin had a significant influence on the fact that although the issue of the role of values in the interpretation of the law had not been overlooked, it was not the main subject of interest (which focused on the linguistic aspects of interpretation), and therefore no extensive, comprehensive study existed in the earlier period. Since the 1990s, under the influence of the change of the political system and the impact of theoretical and philosophical trends (other than positivism and analytical philosophy) on the Polish theory of law, there has been a significant increase in the interest in axiological issues of law interpretation.

The aforementioned achievements and tradition resulted in the presentation of a comprehensive normative approach (indicating the appropriate procedure) to functional interpretation, discussed in point 3, in the latest literature. This approach offers a detailed, yet comprehensive and sequentially ordered normative granting consideration to values (as well as non-legislative knowledge) when

24 Ibid., p. 341.

interpreting the law. It refers to the Polish analytical philosophy and is based on the legal positivism, however exhibits similarities to certain other philosophical and legal traditions as well. This approach reflects the formal, systemic and idealistic approach to the issue of values in law (as well as the issue of values in general). To sum up, it is worth emphasizing that although such approach is not the only one in the Polish theory of law, it is indeed the continuation of a certain (previously outlined) tradition and it specifies a certain significant research direction which may be evidenced by the development of another study of the issue of values and its role in interpretation (outlined in point 4), which may be considered an expression of the aforementioned approach.

M. Żbikowska

Recognition of Facts and Application of Law (Based on the Concept of Judicial Application of Law by Jerzy Wróblewski)

1 Introductory Notes

This outline presents the issue of determining the facts of the case by criminal court. This issue comprises the class of particular issues such as: the attitude of the court to the knowledge of the facts, the role of the court, the role of the court in obtaining information regarding the facts and the question of information which these facts provide, taking into account the types of facts of the case[1]. The following discussion is based on the concept of judicial application of law by Jerzy Wróblewski and translated into contemporary reflections on the Polish criminal law. It should be stated in advance that the concept of judicial application of law expressed by J. Wróblewski's and – within its framework – the reflections devoted to recognition of facts by the court, still remain valid to a large extent, due to their high cognitive value, and can be used effectively in the dogmatic and legal considerations, not only in the system of Polish law, but – because of their universal character – also in the system of other legal cultures.

In the analysis of the above issue, Wróblewski wrote:

> "(…) undoubtedly, one of the steps leading to a court decision is to establish the facts of the case. Each court decision of the judicial application of law has its factual grounds. The court establishes legal consequences of the facts considered confirmed. Establishing these facts, generally called <<facts of the case>> is one of the conditions for the accuracy of a decision"[2].

---

1 Such issues, among others, were raised by J. Wróblewski in his considerations[in:] *Sądowe stosowanie prawa,* Warsaw 1988, p. 193 et seq. Due to the limited framework of this publication, I have omitted the problem of the essence (course) of the procedural cognition in my deliberations. In, this regard see for example M. Zieliński, *Obiektywność ustalenia faktów jako element praworządności stosowania prawa,*"Ruch Prawniczy Ekonomiczny i Socjologiczny" 1979, no. 1, p. 31–41; R. Kmiecik (ed.), *Prawo dowodowe. Zarys wykładu*, Warsaw 2008, pp. 26–28.

2 Ibidem, 169.

Establishing the facts by the court (as the discussion refers only to judicial proceedings, however it is obviously possible to talk about recognition/establishment of the facts in preparatory proceedings) is the essence of the conducted evidentiary proceedings, aimed at learning the course of a "criminal event", meaning facts of the case (a particular fragment of social reality)[3]. Thus, learning the facts of the matter is the essence of the evidentiary proceedings carried out by the court and the condition for proper application of law. The relation between establishing the facts of the case and the judicial application of law may be defined as necessary (associated). Establishing the facts of the case constitutes the actual basis of judicial decision, while it is necessary to prove certain facts in order for them to become the grounds for judicial decision (it is worth mentioning that proof is one of the possible degrees of recognition by the determining authority in the course of legal proceedings). Pursuant to the provisions of Article 424 section 1 item 1 Code of Criminal Procedure, the statement of reasons to the judgment should contain concise indication of the facts the court has deemed proven or not, which evidence the court has relied on and why the court did not accept evidence to the contrary. Establishing the facts properly is thus one of the conditions for the accuracy of a judicial decision. When issuing a judicial decision, the determining authority shall formulate the following general **existential theorem**: "***The fact of the case F* exists in *t, p***"[4]. It means that fact of the case is subject to a general existential theorem presented above, subsequently formulated by the court[5]. In conclusion, it should be stated that the discussion over the recognition of facts in judicial proceedings, as well as the relation between recognition of facts and applying the law, is fundamental for the analysis of law in action.

---

3 In this paper, I assume - after J. Wróblewski - that the facts are recognizable, thus it is possible to get to know them. It does not mean, however, it is the only possible way of thinking. This issue has already been discussed in numerous philosophical works. For example, L. Wittgenstein wrote: "*We create images of facts. The image presents certain situation in a logical space - existence and non-existence of the matters of the case. (…) The image is the fact*". L. Wittgenstein, *Traktat logiczno – filozoficzny*, Vienna 1918, verse 2.11 et seq. At this point, however, I am leaving aside the whole philosophical argument whether the facts can actually be learned or whether it is only possible to develop a certain image of the fact.

4 J. Wróblewski, *Sądowe stosowanie…*, p. 193.

5 It refers to a general existential theorem, as this theorem is subject to certain modifications or extensions, depending on the type of the fact of the case. This issue will be discussed further herein.

A broader discussion of the issue of recognizability of the facts of a case and the application of the law requires the identification of a fundamental issue, namely determination of what the facts of the case are in general. J. Wróblewski indicated different types of the facts of the case and different procedures aimed at establishing them. The author has underlined the following:

> "The given term: <<**fact of the case**>> clearly indicates the relation between establishing the fact and the applicable law. The fact of the case does not exist in isolation from the law due to the necessary relation to the legal language. The approach proposed here probably corresponds to those views which stress <<inseparability>> of establishing the fact and its legal <<qualification>> - or, alternatively, <<legal>> or political assessment"[6].

The above statement clearly indicates that not every fact is a fact of the case, only the fact related to applicable law, the one which is significant for the case. Due to various types of the facts of the case, such a relation of the fact with applicable law may vary (as discussed further). Specifying such fact of the case and associating it with the findings of the court, therefore associating it with the evidentiary procedure, is identified in Polish criminal procedural law with specifying "**main fact**" and "**evidential fact**". The main fact is considered a circumstance which is to be finally proved in criminal proceedings (the main fact will therefore be the fact of committing the prohibited act by a specified person), while the "evidential fact" is a circumstance which constitutes the basis for concluding on the main fact or another evidential fact.[7] Therefore, the term "fact of the case" has a broader meaning than "main fact" or "evidential fact" and includes both these facts. When it comes to the issue of evidentiary procedure and evaluation of what is being evidenced, this procedure is not the same for each types of the facts of the case. Therefore, establishing facts of the case is not carried out in identical way for all types of facts. One of the differences is when (i.e. at which moment) the evidentiary procedure may be finished. In the case of the <<main fact>>, the evidentiary process may only end when evidenced, however some (what is important – not all) "evidential facts" only need prima facie evidence (thus the evidentiary procedure may end quicker)[8]. Another difference in establishing the facts of the case is whether it is necessary to refer solely to one

---

6 Ibidem,, pp. 173–174.

7 A. Gaberle, *Dowody w sądowym procesie karnym*, Cracow 2007, p. 27.

8 The degrees of recognition by the determining authority in legal proceedings have been discussed, i.a., by J. Nelken, *Dowód poszlakowy w procesie karnym*, Warsaw 1970, pp. 73–83; (the same:), *Uprawdopodobnienie w procesie karnym*,"Nowe Prawo" 1970, no. 4, p. 514; R. Kmiecik, *Uprawdopodobnienie w procesie karnym*,"Nowe Prawo" 1983, no. 5.

reference provision or to a bigger number of legal provisions. There are many more differences of this kind.

2 Recognition of the Facts Distinguished by Description and Facts Distinguished by Evaluation

J. Wróblewski have classified the facts of the case from different points of view. He indicated the following: (a) facts distinguished by description and facts distinguished by evaluation; (b) facts distinguished positively and facts distinguished negatively (depending on whether they are distinguished using a negation or directly); (c) facts distinguished directly and the facts distinguished relatively (thus the facts which do not require stating their compliance, or the lack thereof, with the legal norms and the facts which require determining their relation to such legal norm)[9]. Thus, referring to the first division, it may be stated that the "fact distinguished by description" may be expressed by the following existential theorem: "*x* exists in *t, p*", e.g. May be decoded from the following expressions: "whoever kills a man" (Article 148 Criminal Code), "depositing domestic currency for safekeeping" (Article 233 Code of Criminal Procedure), "the right to refuse to testify continues even upon cessation of marriage" (Article 182 section 2 Code of Criminal Procedure) and the "**fact distinguished by evaluation**" may be for example: "legitimate interest of the victim", "reasonable period" (Article 2, section 1 item 4 Code of Criminal Procedure) or "short-term use" (Article 289 Criminal Code). Not every expression representing the facts of the case may be this easily categorized as distinguished by description or evaluation[10]. J. Wróblewski indicated that proving the existential theorem referring to the fact distinguished by description does not require any evaluation, only the statement of the existence of other facts and – consequently – the existence of primary facts which are not subject to evidentiary procedure[11]. Evidentiary

9 J. Wróblewski, *Sądowe stosowanie…*, p. 177.

10 For example, there are certain disputes whether "strong emotions" ("strong agitation") may be considered a fact distinguished by description or evaluation. Ibidem, p. 178.

11 However, this is not an assumption that these original facts are universal statements (universal facts), only that these are the facts we no longer define, i.e. we accept the assumption of the lack of necessity to define them, e.g. assuming there is no need to define who a human being is. Therefore, at the stage of the process of reasoning, we decide to assume some base theorems at a certain point and not to define them any further. Such manner of logical reasoning which "stops" at certain base statements (obviously of relative nature) was initiated by K. R. Popper in: *Logika odkrycia naukowego*, Warsaw 2002, pp. 99 et seq.

process conducted in such a manner is of logical nature, where both the premise and conclusion of such reasoning is a particular fact, whereas the final conclusion of this reasoning is a **so-called original fact.** In the process of reasoning, those original facts are sometimes specified as **the so-called base theorems**, i.e. the ones that are not identified any further (e.g. a human being, linear descendant, body [e.g. In a phrase: "body harm"]). It should only be emphasized, for the purpose of linguistic precision, that identifying the so-called primary fact as a so-called base theorem is an ellipsis, as facts cannot be theorems. In that case, the theorem of the existence of the original fact will constitute a basic theorem. Some claim that the final conclusion in the reasoning on the facts distinguished in a descriptive manner is the original fact, while others conclude that it is the so-called base theorem on the existence of the original fact; this difference results from adopting different methodological approaches – for the former, the subject of evidence are the facts; for the latter, the subject of evidence are claims on the existence or non-existence of certain facts. Leaving aside this methodological dispute here[12], and stating – for the purpose of this study – that the claims of the existence of certain facts are proved, it can be concluded (in a very simplified way) that the aforementioned scheme of conclusions could be presented in the following way:

T[F1] ⟶ T[F2] ⟶ T[F3] ⟶ T[F4] ⟶ T[Fpw], i.e.
[P1] ⟶ [W1/P2] ⟶ [W2/P3] ⟶ [W3/P4] ⟶ [W4],

where: T denotes theorem, F1 denotes fact 1, F2 – fact 2, F3 – fact 3, Fpw – original fact, T[Fpw] denotes base theorem, i.e. Theorem on the existence of the original fact, P1 – premise 1, W1 – conclusion 1, P2 – premise 2 etc., "/" means that the particular theorem is both a conclusion and a premise.

---

12 At this point, I am leaving aside the dispute whether these are the facts or the statements of the existence of certain facts the are proved, due to limited framework hereof. The answer to that question would require previous explanation what reasoning means and this issue is also perceived in more than one way in Polish literature. Briefly signalling this problem, it is possible to indicate such scientific studies in which the issue has been discussed in various ways. Cf. e.g.. M. Zieliński, *Poznanie sądowe a poznanie naukowe*, Poznań 1979; Z. Kwiatkowski, *Zakazy dowodowe w procesie karnym*, Kraków 2005, pp. 34–35; J. Nelken, *Przedmiot postępowania dowodowego w procesie karnym,*"Nowe Prawo" 1968, no. 5, pp. 762–763; M. Cieślak, *Polska procedura karna. Podstawowe założenia teoretyczne,* [in:] *Marian Cieślak – dzieła wybrane, Vol. II, ed.* S. Waltoś, Kraków 2011, p. 334. I am also leaving aside the whole issue of the types of reasoning in the process of reasoning.

In turn, in the case of the court becoming acquainted with "facts distinguished by evaluation", the case is complicated due to the necessity of distinguishing between the fact and the value/evaluation – in order to establish the fact[13]. Thus, the expression: "fact distinguished by evaluation" is complex in nature. J. Wróblewski underlined that the word "exist" with reference to the statement: "*x* is a descriptive fact" and the statement "*x* is an evaluatory fact" (thus: "descriptive fact exists" and "evaluatory fact exists") has a different meaning (what is important, it adopts an anti-cognitive stance)[14]. It is worth mentioning the direct stance of the author:

> "(...) the statement on the existence of the fact distinguished by evaluation is of complex nature. First of all, it establishes the existence of something which is the subject of evaluation and, secondly, the subject is defined by value judgment. Distinguishing these two elements is by no means a psychological description of formulating this theorem. Neither it is an attempt at any ontological value which would require distinction between a substrate <<neutral in terms of value>> and value as the sense of this substrate. It is only a manner of presenting the issue of facts distinguished by evaluation in the law, where the most appropriate form is the one provided by the so-called hybrid theory of values"[15].

Thus, it should be emphasized that the author makes clear distinction between the facts and values (evaluation) for the purpose of the analysis of the law. Thus, the author departs from the complicated dispute over the general possibility of such a division, expressed in philosophical terms (we assess this fact immediately when talking about facts, don't we? And, when evaluating any fact, do we deviate from this fact, or maybe it is indeed the performed evaluation what specifies a particular being as a fact?). Such approach by J. Wróblewki seems correct as Polish law clearly separates facts and evaluation and actually allows to valuate certain facts, to assess facts (specified by J. Wróblewski as "facts distinguished by evaluation"). Thus, the adopted "hybrid theory of values" allowing to separate values/evaluations from the facts, which may raise many doubts in general (philosophical) reflection over reality, may find effective application on the grounds of social science such as law. Thus, J. Wróblewski stated that the phrase: "*x* is *Fo*" (thus: "*x* is evaluatory fact") is the "conjunction" of the existential theorem "*x* exists in *t, p*" and the non-relativized assessment "*x* has a value in *w*", or, alternatively, the non-relativized assessment "*x* has a value *w* due to R"[16], whereby the

13 J. Wróblewski, *Sądowe stosowanie...*, p. 178.
14 Ibidem, p. 179.
15 Ibidem, 180.
16 Ibidem, p. 180.

non-relativized assessment means the evaluator's experience, and the relativized assessment means its reference to the system of values adopted by a rational legislator, or the system of values adopted by the judge.[17] Therefore: $Fo = F \wedge O$, and $T(Fo) = T(F \wedge O)$. Only the determination of the existence of both segments of this "conjunction", thus the determination that some fact *x* exists in time *t* and space *p*, as well as determination that this fact *x* has a value *w*, allows to assume that we are dealing with a "fact distinguished by evaluation". Thus, recognition of the fact distinguished by evaluation is of complex nature.

When referring to the examples of "evaluatory facts" given above, it can be concluded that the interest of the victim is considered first, followed by establishing whether it is justified. Also, first it is established if a time limit exists, followed by establishing whether such limit is reasonable.[18] As an example of a "facts distinguished by evolution", J. Wróblewski indicated the existence of the fact of "action under the influence of extreme emotional agitation justified by the circumstances" (Article 148, paragraph 4 of the Criminal Code), indicating that this requires determining the occurrence of a strong agitation and the excusatory evaluation. Only establishing both elements of this "conjunction" allows to determine that the given fact is "distinguished by evaluation". Without evaluating certain fact from the perspective of a certain legal regulation providing for this fact, it is not possible to claim the existence of this fact in the legal reality. This means it is only the evaluation of a certain legal fact which gives such fact a legal significance. In turn, the subsequent review of the "fact distinguished by evaluation" comprises both the review of the occurrence of the fact *x* in time *t* and space *p*, as well as the relativized or non-relativized evaluation of this fact. Therefore, the process of learning "facts distinguished by evaluation" is inherently more complicated than the process of learning "facts distinguished by descriptors", due to the complex nature of such recognition, including not only theorems, but also their evaluation. This, in turn, is significant from the point of view of justifying the decision on the judicial application of law. In the case of the "facts distinguished by description", both the substantiation of the judicial

17 Ibidem, p. 182. It should only be noted that the evaluation relative to the system of values of the judge, is of controlled nature, ss it should comply with the system of values adopted in a given social group. Hence, it does not refer to every system of values of the judge.

18 It should be mentioned that J. Wróblewski has not identified his stance - as he indicated himself (Ibidem, p. 181) – with the introspective psychological statement by the judge: "I experience: *x* has value *w*", which would lead to a radical form of ideology of a free judicial decision.

decision and its review – from the point of view of the facts of the case – is a one-stage process, namely establishing that "x exists in t, p". In the case of the "facts distinguished by evaluation", as already indicated above, both the substantiation and the review is a two-stage process, consisting in establishing that "x exists in t, p" and "x has a value in w". In the latter case, due to the complicated process of recognizing facts as well as the process of justifying judicial decisions, the process aimed at establishing such facts is more complicated. It is due to the fact that the situations where it is established that "*x* exists in *t, p*" and "*x* does not have *w* value" are not excluded. Thus, establishing the lack of "conjunction" between the established fact and its legal evaluation determines establishing that a certain fact is not – by law – a "fact established by evaluation" and such a statement may already cause various legal consequences.[19]

3 Recognition of the facts distinguished positively and the facts distinguished negatively

Other facts classified by J. Wróblewski were **"facts distinguished positively"** and **"facts distinguished negatively"**[20], which was directly associated with the manner of distinguishing these facts by the legal norm (thus, certain facts are not simply "positive", or "negative". These are only mental shortcuts.[21]). Legal provision may formulate certain fact in a positive way, therefore without using a negation, or in a negative way – thus using the negation. The author – referring to negative facts – wrote:

> "Provision N expresses the fact of the case in a negative manner through the name expressing the lack of any fact specified with a positive name. Therefore, a negative name occurs, consisting of a negated name of a positive fact or a formula which can be reduced to such a name. The following examples of the negatively-distinguishing names can be found in legalese: <<Who does not provide assistance… (<<person not providing assistance>>), <<who is not authorised to…>> (unauthorised to>>) etc."[22].

The regulation of "negative facts" by the legislator in specific legal provisions depends on the legislator, but also on the richness of the language in which the

19 For example, in order to agree that the conditions provided for in Article 30 Criminal Code are fulfilled (mistake of law) it should be established that someone commits an act prohibited by law unaware of this fact and such unawareness is justified. The process aimed at such conclusions is a two-stage process and is reviewed as such.

20 Ibidem, p. 182.

21 Ibidem.

22 Ibidem.

legal texts are formulated as the duty of any action may be defined both as an obligation to act and as a ban on omission.[23] In both cases, however, the legal sanction would apply to the negative consequences of omission if there was an obligation to act (consequently, only the person who was obliged by the legal norm to act in specific situations may be held criminally liable for the omission).[24] It has been pointed out in the literature that the analysis of "negative facts" is actually the analysis of "positive facts" specified with a negative name. [25]. Otherwise, in view of J. Wróblewski' assumptions, we would arrive at false assumptions consisting in the necessary analysis of the non-existence of facts.

---

23 I am leaving aside here the problem and, at the same time, the controversial element in the considerations of W. Wolter and J. Wróblewski regarding the question whether every omission is a form of action. With reference to the legal analysis of omission cf. e.g. J. Wróblewski, *W związku z zagadnieniem przyczynowości zaniechania*,"Państwo i Prawo" 1955, no. 7–8, pp. 266–271; W. Wolter, *O tzw. przyczynowości zaniechania*,"Państwo i Prawo" 1954, no. 10–11. The indicated Authors concentrated on the issue of "causation of omission". Thus, J. Wróblewski in a certain way complements the argumentation of W. Wolter, (pp. 266–267): *"It is not a coincidence that negation is usually used for distinguishing between the action and omission (hence the lack of action). Actions are usually directly specified with names without negation. (…) This can be explained with reference to the nature of the negative names. Negative name designations are a set of objects which are not the designations of this name without negation - it is a<<complementary range>> with respect to the scope of this name without negation. (…) It is directly related to the issue of omission as a specified lack of action. The name <<not providing assistance to a drowning person>> means all those actions which are not providing assistance the drowning person, but which would be practically impossible to enumerate as it would consist in listing all the actions which are not providing assistance the drowning person"*. Also cf. the considerations of Ł. Pohl, *O niemożności wykonania nakazanego działania spowodowanej zachowaniem się zobowiązanego do działania (przyczynek do analizy zaniechania w prawie karnym)* [in:] *Professor Marian Cieślak – osoba, dzieło, kontynuacje*, eds. W. Cieślak, S. Steinborn, Warszawa 2013, pp. 447–455, as well as L. Kubicki, *Przestępstwo popełnione przez zaniechanie. Zagadnienia podstawowe*, Warsaw 1975 and W. Patryas referring to the views of the theorists and scholars of criminal law (including the deliberations of W. Wolter) [in:] "*Przyczynek do zagadnienia przyczynowości zaniechania*,"Ruch Prawniczy Ekonomiczny i Socjologiczny 1992, no. 3, pp. 1–9; (the same:) *Zaniechanie. Próba analizy metodologicznej*, Poznań 1993 together with the literature indicated therein.

24 J. Wróblewski, *Sądowe stosowanie…*, p. 183.

25 Ibidem, p. 183.

Thus, the phrase "positive fact" and "negative fact" is of linguistic – not ontological – importance, as the fact either exists or not. Consequently, J. Wróblewski indicated:

> "(...) the following construction should be adopted, with variable G symbolizing the fact specified positively and variable <<Pn>> denoted a negative name: <<x is named [Fn] due to provision N>> means that (a) x is G; (b) x exists in t, p; (c) provision N names as [Fn] everything that is not F; (d) G is named [Fn] due to provision N"[26].

However, this case is not that easy to resolve, especially in view of the problem related to the recognizability of a "negative fact", which may be a crime committed by omission[27]. The extremely complicated nature of the cognition of such "negative facts", which can be described as facts of omission, is already indicated by the volume of the widely developed literature on the subject. Judicial recognition of the "facts distinguished negatively" is associated with the issue of the possibility to hold the perpetrator criminally liable for their failure to act. The views of the legal scholars[28], indicate an objective proximate cause consisting in a relation between the objectively existing cause and subjectively existing result, thus establishing the inability to accept "causality of the omission". If we were to consider that we were dealing with "causality of omission", it would mean that, assuming an objective causal relationship, the omission ("negative fact") could not mean "non-existence" (could not denote "nothing"), because in such case it could not entail any consequences (as "something" could not come out of "nothing"). Due to adopting such a position, it should be concluded that since each omission may be considered also as an act different than the one which should have occurred, such a notion of "causality of the omission" would be defined as causality of an act other than the one which should have occurred and the effect which would not have occurred if the appropriate action had taken place (also if other circumstances had not occurred, not only those related to that other action).[29] Consequently, against this background of "proximate cause", we

---

26 Ibidem.

27 It should be noted, however, this is only one example of the so-called negative facts. Moreover, for the purposes of the considerations presented in this outline, the problems of omission indicated here have been extremely "simplified". My aim as not to analyse the crimes by omission (which have already been extensively analysed in the literature referred to herein), only presenting the relationships between the concept of recognizability of "negative facts" by J. Wróblewski and the issue of crimes committed by omission.

28 J. Wróblewski, *W związku z zagadnieniem...*, p. 268.

29 Ibidem.

would distinguish an action other than that which should have occurred (cause) and a state which would not have occurred if an appropriate action had been taken (effect). Even such rudimentary outline proves that the indicated "proximate cause" is not such cause at all, as such a specific reason does not result in such a specific effect (for example, the fact that person A catches fish in a lake does not result in the drowning of person B, whom person A saw in that lake). Therefore, it is necessary to adopt a different understanding of the problem of "causality of omission", and hence of the recognizability of "negative facts" – understood as crimes by omission (discussed further in the text).

The above rudimentarily outlined deliberations indicate that recognition of the "negative fact" (referring to omission) by the court has to start with placing such fact in a specific situational context, as it is not possible to claim the occurrence of a "negative fact" understood as omission if the person had not obliged to act in the first place. As it has already been underlined in the introduction, establishing facts of the case may occur only when the "legal qualification" of this fact is taken into consideration. However, as emphasized by W. Wolter, the omission is not merely a human judgment about the absence of a certain action; that is to say, it is not just a thought developed by the judge in charge of the case, but is objective in nature, namely it can be placed in the "objective reality"[30]. What constitutes an objective equivalent of reality for negative judgments is the complementary reality[31]. The author wrote:

> "Omission, meaning lack of action, necessarily does not entail causality, but the lack thereof. Therefore, omission is related to the lack of causality in a certain direction (interesting for us). This direction is marked out by the omitted action. If there were an action, causality would run in the opposite direction to that which occurred in the absence of action."[32] (**the so-called contrary causality theory** [33]).

Therefore, the court, recognizing a "negative fact" which constitutes an omission, not only sets such fact in the specific situational context, but also determines the absence of "contrary causality" of the effect which occurred although it should not have occurred due to a legal norm providing for a prohibition of the omission of a specific act existing in the legal system. The statement of the lack of "contrary causality" can only be made once the objective

30 W. Wolter, *O tzw. przyczynowości…*, p. 522.

31 Ibidem.

32 Ibidem, p. 523.

33 It has emerged as competitive for the so-called negative theory of causality. The so-called contrary causality theory has been fully supported herein.

reality of events has been established. Thus, the court does not establish the "non-existence" of a fact ex ante upon learning the "negative facts" followed by application of law, but establishes the complementary reality first. Learning the "negative fact" is done through learning objective reality of events which took place (as it is not possible acquire knowledge on "nothing"). The knowledge of objective reality by the court, assuming the "contrary causality" in omission, also requires stating the lack of the existence of such "contrary causality". Therefore, it should be considered that it is a certain kind of action[34] that should not have resulted in an effect which had occurred – although such effect should not have occurred, had it not been for that action. Thus, if such action occurred, the effect would not have occurred and the lack of such causality is indeed the recognition of a "negative fact" being an omission. It should be concluded, as emphasized in the criminal law literature, that establishing the lack of "contrary causality" may occur only when such "contrary causality" was possible in a certain arrangement of events (thus, it is not about any hypothetical causality, only the real causality). Thus, recognition by the court has to include specifying the real possibility of the occurrence of such "contrary causality".[35] Hypothetically, it is sometimes possible to imagine such causality, but in the case of a real arrangement of events such causality would not be possible (e.g. if – hypothetically – person A could jump to the water and save drowning person B, however in reality due to a high level of disability of the person A, he or she would not be able to jump into the water at all, thus would not be able to save a drowning person)[36].

---

34 It is usually not specified by the legislator. For example, the legislator does not specify how to assist a person who needs help (for example someone who is drowning). It is irrelevant. What is important here is the fact hat some (no matter what) action is taken in order to save a given person (although I am again oversimplifying the problem here). However, giving more insight to this issue, it could be concluded that the manner in which we act is significant. If person A undertakes actions aimed at saving the drowning person B, but this action is going to consist in, for example, throwing a lifebelt too far from the drowning person, it would be significant in terms of holding person A criminally responsible.

35 As in: W. Wolter, *O tzw. przyczynowości…*, p. 532.

36 At this point, I am leaving aside the whole issue of establishing/recognizing the elements of the subject of the offence.

4 Recognition of the Facts Distinguished Directly and the Facts Distinguished Relatively

According to J. Wróblewski, "facts distinguished directly" narrow down to the following statement: "*x* exists in *t*, *p*" and in order to formulate a statement about simple facts, it is not necessary to state the relationship between x and a given provision. On the other hand, a "**fact distinguished relatively**" is a fact for which it is necessary to determine the compliance or, relatively, non-compliance with a specific provision, i.e.:

> "I define the relative fact Fs by explaining the phrase <<x is Fs>> as <<conjunction>> of existential theorem <<x exists in t, p>> and the phrase <<x is consistent with the provision N>>".[37].

The author gives the following examples of "facts distinguished relatively": "valid act", "act contrary to the law", "authority of the state exceeding its competence". Other examples of "relatively distinguished facts" under the applicable Code of Criminal Procedure include, e.g., the fact specified in Article 171, paragraph 7 of the Code of Criminal Procedure, according to which "*Explanations, testimonies and statements made in the conditions excluding freedom of expression or obtained in contravention of the prohibitions set forth in Article 5 may not constitute evidence" or Article 170, paragraph 1, subparagraph 1 of the Code of Criminal Procedure, according to which "A motion for evidence shall be dismissed if the taking of evidence is inadmissible*". Analysing the "relatively distinguished facts", the author emphasized that the statement determining the compliance or non-compliance of the fact with the provision of law is called a "**relative phrase**"[38], zaś:

> "'Relative phrase' qualifies conduct Z as compliant with <<reference provision N>>. The reference provisions determine the characteristics of relative phrases to a great degree. (…) the reference provision is a rule of conduct which links the obligation to follow the consequences K with the occurrence of a fact (<<situation>>, <factual situation>>, etc.), by which I understand the appropriate conduct of certain persons"[39].

---

37 Ibidem, p. 185.

38 Ibidem.

39 Ibidem, p. 186. It should also be noted that the Author made a number of assumptions, e.g. the "obligation" in the statement: "in the conditions of the occurrence of fact F, conduct K should follow" should be considered an order, prohibition or permission. Moreover, the Author's understanding of "fact", "obligatory conduct K" was broad enough to cover all types of reference provisions.

Moreover, if a specific fact occurs, the specific person should behave in a specific manner. These conducts may involve the use of the competence granted to the given legal entities and were described by Mr Wróblewski as "**competence conducts**" (Kk), while all other conducts which do not confer competence on specific entities have been classified as "**regular conducts**" **(Kz)**[40]. In the case of "ordinary conduct", in principle there is no major problem in determining whether the conduct K determined by the reference provision has occurred. In order to establish this, it is necessary to examine whether a specific fact, provided for by a given legal provision, has occurred (and therefore whether a specific conduct K is provided for [e.g. ordered] by a specific legal provision which has been examined), followed by determining whether that conduct complies with the reference provision in question.[41] For example, in accordance with the provision of Article 12 § 1 Code of Criminal Procedure *in principio "In the cases concerning crimes prosecuted on complaint, proceedings are pending ex officio at the moment of filing the motion."* Here, conduct K will be filing the motion for prosecution. Therefore, first of all, the reference provision should be precisely defined, i.e. – in this case – the understanding of the content of Article 12(1) of the Code of Criminal Procedure should be established, followed by determining whether the observed conduct K is marked in the legal language by the name of Kz (in this case such name will be "filing a motion for prosecution"), and then – based on the aforementioned relative phrase – whether the conduct of a specific person is consistent with the content of Article 12(1) of the Code of Criminal Procedure, i.e. whether it is conduct consisting in the filing a motion for prosecution. Similarly, in order to determine whether there is conduct constituting human homicide (Kz), it is necessary to determine whether the conduct K observed[42] is conduct *Kz* provided for by the appropriately interpreted reference provision – Article 148 § 1 of the Criminal Code. ("whoever kills a man").

"Competence conduct" causes many more difficulties. J. Wróblewski pointed out that in such a case a mere comparison of the content of a given reference provision with the observed conduct K was not sufficient, as the rules of such behaviour had to meet a number of conditions laid down in numerous legal provisions.

---

40 Ibidem.

41 Despite quite simple scheme of determining conduct K, the process aimed at such determination is not always uncomplicated. It refers especially to "negative facts" (crimes of omission).

42 The term "observed behaviour" is not literal in the considerations. It is not the issue of a direct observation of the phenomena, but - e.g. with reference to the provision of Article 148 of the Criminal Code - an observation based on the collected evidence.

The author specified the regulations which provide for such conditions as "**complement provisions**"[43]. For example, pursuant to the provisions of article 412 Code of Criminal Procedure, *"Once the voting has been completed, the court shall immediately issue a written judgment."* In such a case, if the voting is finished, the court is obliged to make a judgment in writing. However, it is not sufficient to establish that the conduct observed – the written judgment – is consistent with the content of the reference provision (here: consistent with the provision of Article 412 of the Code of Criminal Procedure, e.g. it is not sufficient to establish that the written judgment is delivered following the voting), but it is necessary to establish that the conduct K – the written judgment – is in fact that conduct. On the other hand, in order to establish that the observed conduct constitutes a written judgment, it is necessary to determine the competence of a specific authority to draw up a written judgment (Kk) in certain situations. If the conditions laid down by several legal provisions ("complement provisions") are not satisfied, the conduct in question is not the conduct consisting in a written judgment. Determining and decoding these "complement provisions" is an extremely complicated task, as nowadays emphasized in the literature on criminal proceedings.[44] In addition, failure to meet the conditions set forth in the "complement provisions" or their defective implementation may have various legal consequences. Indeed, violation of such conditions will not always involve acknowledging that a specific legal act has not been performed. It is also worth mentioning that the author of the concept analysed here, when considering "regular conducts" and "competence conducts", also referred to language degrees, considering that the names describing "regular conducts" are formulated in the first-degree language, whereas the names defining "competence conducts" are formulated in the second-degree language, as – in the latter case – prior reference to the "complement provisions" is necessary.[45]. To sum up this fragment of the considerations, it should be considered that learning "facts distinguished relatively" is generally more complicated than learning "facts distinguished

43 Ibidem, p. 187.

44 A detailed analysis of the related issues from the point of view of formalization and conventionalization of procedural acts in criminal proceedings was carried out by B. Janusz-Pohl [in:] *Formalizacja i konwencjonalizacja jako instrumenty analizy czynności karnoprocesowych w prawie polskim*, Poznań 2017. See also the deliberations of S. Czepita (in:) *Reguły konstytutywne a zagadnienia prawoznawstwa*, Szczecin 1996; (the same:) *Formalizacja a konwencjonalizacja działań w prawie* [in:] *Konwencjonalne i formalne aspekty prawa*, ed. S. Czepita, Szczecin 2006.

45 J. Wróblewski, *Sądowe stosowanie…*, p. 187.

directly", since establishing them requires a conclusion that '*x* exists in *t*, *p*' and that '*x* complies with rule *N*', while determining this compatibility requires reference to a number of other legal provisions. Thus, recognition of the "relatively distinguished facts" is of complex – two stage – nature.

In conclusion, it is also worth noting that the following considerations discussed by J. Wróblewski concerning "relative facts" involve considerations of constitutive rules and the rules of conventional operations, whereas the "relative facts" are sometimes referred to as "institutional facts"[46]. Although J. Wróblewski's reflections on "relatively distinguished facts" – in the perspective of a contemporary, detailed concept in Polish criminal procedural law, concerning the formalization and conventionalization of procedural acts in criminal proceedings[47] – are of secondary importance, their value, compared to the whole of his analysis of the facts of the case, is still appreciated and can be effectively used in dogmatic and legal deliberations.

5 Summary

The above discussion allows to assume that the concept of Jerzy Wróblewski's judicial application of the law and the view on the types of facts of a case and their recognition by a court expressed within this concept can – and is – extremely useful for contemporary dogmatic and theoretical legal analyses. Due to its universal nature it may be used not only in the system of Polish law, but also in the other legal cultures. J. Wróblewski's analysis of the recognisability of the facts of a case may constitute both a starting point and a complementary element of many considerations including material and procedural issues of criminal law, such as the issue of value/evaluation in a criminal proceeding, the issue of crimes committed through omission or the issue of constitutive rules and rules of conventional operations in law. It also proves the heterogeneous nature of the recognition of the facts of the case, depending on their type. This is also illustrated by the multi-stage process of reasoning by the court and, therefore, by the highly complex process of justifying a judicial decision and its subsequent legal review.

---

46 It was stressed by J. Wróblewski himself [in:] *Sądowe stosowanie…*, p. 184, footnote 38.

47 Here I refer the Reader to a detailed concept dedicated to this subject created by B. Janusz-Pohl expressed, [in:] *Formalizacja i konwencjonalizacja jako instrumenty analizy czynności karnoprocesowych w prawie polskim*, Poznań 2017.

K. Gmerek, M. Peno

On the Concept of Conventional Actions in Law

When considering the aquis of the Polish legal theory, the concept of conventional actions in law cannot be ignored. Undoubtedly, it is a sophisticated concept – set in the broadly understood analytical philosophy, thus leaning towards the modern philosophy, operating with highly developed methodology. Therefore, it pursues the requirement of practising theory of law in as scientific (and thus universal) manner as possible. This concept is also considered original[1] and unprecedented on a global scale[2]. In this sense, it is undoubtedly a contribution of the Polish legal theory to a global legal thought and at its current level of development, this concept requires a broader discussion, i.e. a global debate ensuring further evolution.

These are, obviously, not the only reasons. In any case, vivid interest in this concept of the general theory of law[3] in Poland constitutes the evidence of its importance for the Polish legal science – expressed in creative development and modification of its elements and the specific legal sciences – consisting in using this concept as theoretical and methodological basis in the studies on the applicable law.

Both phenomena indicated in the previous sentence have been occurring in parallel over the years. In order to preserve the transparency of the structure of this chapter, we are going to begin with discussing the basic assumptions of the concept of conventional actions in law elaborated by the law theorists from Poznań. Further on, we will be presenting the suggestions for developing this concept, taking into consideration how such development has progressed. Thus, the starting point will include particular issues prompting (in chronological

---

1 S. Czepita, *Reguły konstytutywne a zagadnienia prawoznawstwa*, Szczecin 1996, p. 116.

2 B. Janusz-Pohl, *Formalizacja i konwencjonalizacja jako instrumenty analizy czynności karnoprocesowych w prawie polskim*, Poznań 2017, p. 21.

3 Understood as a set of expressions primarily containing certain generalizations significant for the jurisprudence as a whole or referring to various legal institutions present in different branches of law, O. Bogucki, M. Zieliński, *Rozdział 1. Zasady prawa z perspektywy ogólnej teorii prawa*, in: *System prawa karnego procesowego. Volume III. Zasady procesu karnego*, ed. P. Wiliński, Warsaw 2014, p. 53.

order) raising the issues related to conventional actions in law. To conclude, we will refer to the examples of applying the concept of conventional actions in law to analyse the issues specific for particular legal sciences.

1 Conventional Actions in Law – Base Concept

The concept of conventional actions in law was developed by the law theorists from Poznań in 1972 in the publication *Czynności konwencjonalne w prawie*[4]. It should be noted that the authors suggested the manner of addressing conventional actions as such in general, only later transferring their findings to legal considerations[5]. According to the authors, the term "conventional action" means a cultural action (thus also a rational action), at the same time focused on someone's interpretation[6]. "Cultural action" is a rational action taken on the grounds of knowledge containing information on the rules of cultural interpretation regarding this action (in other words, the knowledge which is a component of a cultural system)[7]. Specific terminology used in the above definitions refers (with certain modifications) to terminological grid, and thus the conceptual network, developed within the concept of humanistic interpretation[8]. A certain benchmark for the concept of conventional act is the assumption of rationality of the undertaken actions. The activity is deemed rational on the grounds of someone's knowledge and preferences[9], when (in accordance with this knowledge) it leads to realization of the state of affairs preferred by such

4 L. Nowak, S. Wronkowska, M. Zieliński, Z. Ziembiński, *Czynności konwencjonalne w prawie*, „Studia Prawnicze", z. 33, 1972, pp. 73–99. As indicated by the authors, Polish and global literature at that time offered the elaboration on certain general issues regarding performance of the conventional actions (in the works of: Czesław Znamierowski, Alfa Ross, Georg von Wright and Herbert Hart), which did not, however, exceed a certain level of exploration of the problem, ibidem, s. 74.

5 It is also a specific feature of the later developments of the discussed concept. Thus, in the further part of this publication we usually talk about "conventional actions" without specifying them as "at law". On the other hand, the explicit reference of issues concerning conventional activities to legal problems proves the particular importance and originality of the approach proposed by the authors of *Czynności konwencjonalnych w prawie*, S. Czepita, *Reguły...*, op. cit., p. 127.

6 L. Nowak, S. Wronkowska, M. Zieliński, Z. Ziembiński, *Czynności konwencjonalne...*, op. cit., p. 82.

7 Ibidem,, p. 81.

8 First of all contained in: J. Kmita, L. Nowak, *Studia nad teoretycznymi podstawami humanistyki*, Poznań 1968.

9 For this reason, they are sometimes described as "subjective-rational activities".

person to the greatest extent[10]. Pursuant to the above definition, the conventional actions are the cultural actions aimed at interpretation, i.e. one of the outcomes of performing such action (as believed by a person undertaking this action) will be its interpretation[11], namely an appropriate reconstruction of its meaning[12], on the grounds of the specific cultural system.

There are different types of actions in the class specified by the meaning of the term "conventional action", starting with nodding as a form of greeting or rook movement in a game of chess, followed by particularly significant conventional actions consisting in formulating expressions in a given language, through the actions specific for legal reality – adopting a bill, passing a judgment or entering a purchase agreement. Within this class, the authors of *Czynności konwencjonalne w prawie* distinguish a class of particularly significant conventional actions, specified as those *which are prescribed or prohibited by a rule of law, or the execution of which is part of a situation falling within the scope of* [13]*a rule of law*[14]. Moreover, the level of conventionalization may differ for various conventional actions[15](namely they can be conventional actions of a different degree)[16]. It is also emphasized that the conventional actions in law are usually at least the second-degree conventional actions, whose first degree of conventionalization is a linguistic action[17].

---

10 L. Nowak, S. Wronkowska, M. Zieliński, Z. Ziembiński, *Czynności konwencjonalne…*, op. cit., p. 76. At the same time, there rationality of actions taken by particular persons may be of a different degree and, moreover, it is always discussed from the point of view of the knowledge and preferences of these persons and not the perspective of a third person (the observer).

11 Ibidem, p. 78.

12 "The sense of a rational action" (and thus of the conventional action as well) is specified by the authors as the aim of a person behaving in a rational manner, associated with performing this activity in itself (ibidem, p. 76); however, the authors also write about the "sense of a conventional activity" also in the context of recognizing the given psycho-physical activity as a conventional action of a certain type; the dual nature of this approach was also observed by S. Czepita in: S. Czepita, *Reguły…*, op. cit., pp. 128–130.

13 Circumstances in which a given norm is applied.

14 L. Nowak, S. Wronkowska, M. Zieliński, Z. Ziembiński, *Czynności konwencjonalne…*, op. cit., p. 73.

15 However, the authors of *Czynności konwencjonalne w prawie*, did not use the term "conventionalization" in this publication.

16 Ibidem,, p. 84.

17 Ibidem,, p. 86.

To conclude the outline report on the concept of conventional actions in law developed by law theorists from Poznań, we are going to refer to the issue of a semiotic status of the expressions specified by the authors as "the rules of meaning of conventional actions". This term refers to the expressions which *indicate how to attribute specific meaning to the specific psychophysical (or lower-level conventional) activities*[18]. In the case of conventional actions, assignment (attribution) of a specific meaning is of "conventional" nature in such a sense that it is not determined by natural causal dependencies[19]. A particularly important fact, from the perspective of legal considerations, is that the authors noticed the semantic status of the rules of meaning of conventional actions – different from the teleological (technical) directives and norms of conduct – and the relation between these actions and these types of expression. Teleological directive referring to a given conventional action would indicate how to perform the particular conventional action (i.e. what should be done in order to carry out the conventional action of a certain type)[20]. The basic relations between a conventional action of a certain type (and the rules of meaning of such action) and the legal norms (as a type of the norms of conduct) consist in the following: (1) legal norm prescribes a specific addressee, and in specific circumstances, to perform a certain conventional legal action (in accordance with the rules of meaning) or (2) as a consequence of performing a certain conventional legal action (in accordance with the rules of meaning) by the entitled entity, the duties of a certain person are formed or updated[21].

Zygmunt Ziembiński and Maciej Zieliński, developing the issues regarding conventional actions, including the rules of these actions (refraining from associating them with the humanist interpretation[22]), specify the "rules of meaning" as "the rules of performing (constructing) conventional actions"[23]. They also specify their characteristics, assuming that these rules force assigning a new meaning to certain psychophysical activities, understanding them in a certain way, whereas the expression "prescription of understanding" is an ellipsis referring to setting out specific terminology[24]. Consequently, the aforementioned

18 Ibidem,, p. 88.
19 Ibidem,, p. 83.
20 Ibidem,, p. 88.
21 Ibidem,, p. 92.
22 cf. S. Czepita, *Reguły…*, op. cit., p. 123.
23 M. Zieliński, Z. Ziembiński, *Uzasadnianie twierdzeń, ocen i norm w prawoznawstwie*, Warszawa 1988, p. 60 et seq., Z. Ziembiński, M. Zieliński, *Dyrektywy i sposób ich wypowiadania*, Warszawa 1992, p. 46 et seq.
24 Z. Ziembiński, M. Zieliński, *Dyrektywy…*, op. cit., p. 51.

authors tend to recognize the rules of meaning as a specific form of nominal definitions[25]. This approach will de creatively developed in the 1990s by Stanisław Czepita (see point 3).

2 The Issue of (In)validity of Conventional Actions

First of all, it must be stated that the conventional actions (legal actions may be perceived as conventional actions) may be either „valid"/"invalid". Psychophysical activities are not subject to valuation referring to (in)significance (picking a pen from the floor leads to placing it on a table or not, however it would not be significant or insignificant in such a manner in which we are intuitively ready to speak about raising a hand during voting on adoption of a bill). Such issues are discussed due to the fact that conventional actions (please note: of legal significance) are the example of deliberate actions, aimed at producing such an effect and not another. Such an effect may only be achieved once the particular conditions have been fulfilled. They are related to cultural rules, as the effect is also a part of a world of culture[26]. What does that mean and what impact it has on the legal science and practice?

With reference to the issue of invalidity of the conventional actions, the concept of conventional actions has evolved; at first, the concept has not been very elaborate, but in terms of legal practice – which the Polish legal theory has always been very sensitive to – it constituted an important catalyst for thoughts on various situations where the actions were encumbered with various faults. Besides, it is evidenced *prima facie* that those faults and their impact on the action are gradable.

Legal dogmatics, especially the studies of civil law, divides the legal actions into valid and invalid, whereas these actions constitute the models of legally significant conventional actions. Does the invalid legal activity exist at all? When developing certain concepts of conventional actions, T. Gizbert-Studnicki concluded that the action is either in line with the rules of performing a given conventional action or not – and if so, it may have certain effect (still remaining a conventional action) or it may simply not constitute a conventional action on the ground of a given system of rules. However, there are no grounds to deem legal

25 Ibidem,, p. 47.

26 L. Nowak, S. Wronkowska, M. Zieliński, Z. Ziembiński, *Czynności konwencjonalne…*, p. 82 et seq.; K. Radzikowski *Skutki wadliwości czynności cywilnoprawnej w świetle ustawy o podatku od czynności cywilnoprawnych*, „Ruch Prawniczy, Ekonomiczny i Socjologiczny" 2008, z. 1, pp. 133–134.

action invalid in that case. This means the invalid conventional action is not a legal action. Therefore, the "invalid legal action" means an event which is not a legal action. However, the case is not as easy as it may seem at first.[27]

It was observed in the original version of the concept of conventional actions that this concept sets new perspective in the studies on the defects of the legal actions, where the problem of (absolute) invalidity of the legal actions played an important role from the point of view of the civil law studies. Moreover, even delivery of a ruling is a conventional action. The issue of non-existing rulings appeared in this scope[28].

Solutions to the issues appearing herein have been sought in the analysis of the so-called constitutive rules (see point 3). A non-existing legal action characterized with reference to the conduct violating constitutive norms, i.e., the rules specifying the conditions which have to be fulfilled due to the meaning of the name of a given activity in a given language. Constitutive rules referring to a certain type of action determine the recognition of someone's conduct as a conventional action of such type. For example, in the so-called connotative approach, the content of the name (connotation) of a given type of conventional action will be decisive. Otherwise, conventional rule may be approached in two ways: i.e. selectively or globally. The first approach divides the constitutive rules into the ones subject to the sanction of invalidity and the ones not sanctioned this way (on the grounds of a given set of rules), whereas not all rules of the construction of legal actions are constitutive in nature (even if their violation would result in invalidity). The second approach considers the constitutive rules to be generally of homogenous nature and the rules of conducting legal actions subject to strict invalidity are constitutive in nature[29].

When characterizing a conventional action of a given type, in a certain simplification, it is possible to distinguish specific elements, namely material substrate (someone's action, conduct), specific name characteristic for this conventional action (in a given language) and the consequences of performing this action (in the light of this or other system of rules). For the validity of a conventional action it is necessary to carry it out pursuant to these rules (constitutive rules),

27 For more information see T. Gizbert-Studnicki, *O nieważnych czynnościach prawnych w świetle koncepcji czynności konwencjonalnych*, „Państwo i Prawo" 1984, Vol. 6, pp. 70-82.

28 L. Nowak, S. Wronkowska, M. Zieliński, Z. Ziembiński, *Czynności konwencjonalne...*, p. 93 et seq.

29 S. Czepita, *Reguły konstytutywne ....*, p. 150 et seq.

including the rules specifying the competence of a given entity to perform a given conventional action.

From the very beginning of the functioning of the conventional action it has been noted that there are cases of actions only which are seemingly a substrate of the given conventional action, which, consequently, is not carried out, (therefore it does not have any effect), as well as the ones which have different effects than in the case of a non-valid action, due to non-compliance with the rules of carrying out the conventional action of a given type.

The analysis of the problem of non-existing rulings in legal theory is a good illustration of this issue, as there is a question regarding specifying the border between the faults resulting in a particular action not being treated as the delivery of a ruling, and the faults which does not have such a serious effect. It seems that the meaning of the phrase "delivery of a ruling" was considered conclusive. Th ruling is delivered on the grounds of specific rules regarding the performance of this conventional action. A distinction between a defective existing and a non-existent decision will be made in reference to the name "ruling". On the grounds of Polish language, as well as legal language (including the views of the legal scholars), a statement by a body which is not a court (e.g. the Sejm) will not be deemed delivery of a ruling – the ruling will not exist; however, if no substantiation of the ruling issued by the court is made, such action will remain a ruling even if the rules for issuing the rulings require such substantiation (it will be defective, but existing). Similarly, the ruling which has not been signed (even if such requirement exists) by some members of the adjudicating body, although there are other issues in this case (as the meaning of the word "ruling" in Polish language does not provide clear distinction whether it is the ruling in this case, or not)[30].

In the legal practice and from the point of view of theoretical model it is essential to link together various elements constituting the given concept. How are the issues of (non)existence, (in)significance and (in)effectiveness of action related from the point of view of the concept of conventional actions? Undoubtedly, the typically conventional actions are performed for a specific reason, namely in order to achieve the intended effect. Such effect will only be achieved when the given action is deemed valid. Obviously, only the existing action may be valid[31].

---

30 Cf. S. Czepita, *Zagadnienie orzeczeń nieistniejących w postępowaniu cywilnym w świetle koncepcji czynności konwencjonalnych…*, p. 139 et seq.

31 B. Janusz-Pohl, *op. cit.*, p. 60; M. Zieliński, *Wykładnia prawa…*, p. 28.

It has already been pointed out that the concept of constitutive rule is significant for the issue of validity (invalidity) of conventional action. Thus, the constitutive rules of conventional actions should be specified in more detail.

3 Constitutive Rules of the Conventional Actions. Classification of the Meaning of the Term "conventional action"

The important moment within the framework of the scientific deliberations on the subject of conventional actions in law (and the conventional actions in general) was publishing the monography by Stanisław Czepita[32], where the author had developed and modified various elements of the concept of conventional actions in law, granting consideration to both its original form and later developments[33]. The core of S. Czepita's considerations is the characteristics of constitutive rules of the conventional actions; however, prior to presenting these characteristics in a necessary simplified manner, we are going to refer to the definition of "conventional action", which, according to the author, is a consequence of clarification of the components of the content of this name[34]. Czepita's definition is specific, as the author explains the term "conventional action" by indicating the requirements of defining this term through the characteristics of its designates. The requirements are as follows: (1) a given conventional activity must be legitimized with a material substrate in the form of the conduct of a particular human being [35](although its accomplishment may be attributed to a subject other than a human being)[36]; (2) for each conventional action, a term constituting its name may be indicated in a given language; (3) for any conventional action, the rules determining the consequences of its performance may

32 S. Czepita, *Reguły…*, op. cit.

33 S. Czepita preceded the adoption of a specific way of perceiving the rules of constitutive conventional activities with a thorough analysis of Polish and foreign literature in the field of constitutive rules. He clearly drew inspiration primarily from the concept of constitutive and regulative rules by John Searle, p. 18 et seq and p.1 44, i.a.

34 Ibidem, p. 145.

35 However, acting is considered by the author to be a conscious and voluntary conduct or omission to do so, ibidem, s. 146.

36 …and in the case of particularly complex conventional activities, such as court proceedings, even a few entities, S. Czepita, *O koncepcji czynności konwencjonalnych w prawie*, in: *Wykładnia Konstytucji. Aktualne problemy i tendencje*, ed. M. Smolak, Warszawa 2016, p. 127.

be indicated[37], as the action is conventional only if its performance affects the normative situation of the entity performing the particular conventional action, or the situation of the other entities[38]. As emphasized by the author himself, this definition clarifies the selected elements of the content of "conventional action", however maintaining the vagueness of its scope.[39].

S. Czepita also indicates the relation between the definition he formulated through requirements and the definition formulated by the authors of *Czynności konwencjonalne w prawie*[40], as he discloses that the concept of conventional actions he adopted leads to limiting the scope of these actions to the ones which are of at least minimum social significance. Therefore, the concept of the law theorists from Poznań seems to be broader, according to the author[41].

The characteristics of conventional actions perceived in the aforementioned manner should, according to S. Czepita, consider the rules of performing certain activity (constructional rules) and the rules specifying the consequences of its performance (consequential rules)[42]. Those aforementioned rules whose violation result in a given action not being recognized as conventional action of a given type due to the linguistic content (connotation) of its name[43] are called constitutive rules[44]. Such meaning, pragmatically understood as a manner of using particular name[45], establishes the connotation of the name, however is

---

37 For the record, it should be pointed out that in his newer publication, the author introduces some exceptions in this regard, e.g. with reference to expressions as the acts of speech, S. Czepita, *O pojęciu czynności konwencjonalnej i jej odmianach*, „Ruch Prawniczy, Ekonomiczny i Socjologiczny" 1/2017, p. 85 et seq

38 S. Czepita, *Reguły…*, op. cit., pp. 146–147.

39 Ibidem, p. 146.

40 L. Nowak, S. Wronkowska, M. Zieliński, Z. Ziembiński, *Czynności konwencjonalne…*, op.cit., p. 73 et seq

41 In order to explain the difference in the scope of definitions adopted in both approaches compared, the author gives the example of playing solitaire, which is hardly a socially significant activity, S. Czepita, *Reguły…*, op. cit., p. 149–150.

42 Ibidem, p. 148. It should be noted here that the author adopts certain terminology and resigns from talking about the "rules of sense", only the "constructive rules" and "consequential rules".

43 The author's understands the concept of "connotation of the name" similar to Kazimierz Ajdukiewicz, as a specific set of characteristics of the designates of a name, allowing to identify a specific object as a designate of a given name, S. Czepita, *Reguły…*, op. cit., p. 155.

44 Ibidem, p. 151, idem, *Formalizacja a konwencjonalizacja…*, op. cit. p. 13.

45 In this draft, we leave aside the issue of the characteristics of a language in which the names of legally significant conventional actions have been shaped. We only indicate

not equivalent to this name[46]. *It is the meaning of the expression "bow" which determines how to perform the action we define as a bow and also how to react to such a bow*[47]. S. Czepita specified such manner of perceiving constitutive rules as "connotative approach". He also indicated the relation between the constructive rule he distinguished, as well as the consequent conventional actions, and the rules of meaning developed by the law theorists from Poznań (see point 1): *It seems that in this terminology, the rules defined as the rules of meaning of the conventional actions by L. Nowak, S. Wronkowska, M. Zieliński i Z Ziembiński, are the constitutive rule for a given type of conventional actions which have the character of rules of construction of this type of actions - obviously, provided that (...) we understand the rules of meaning as the rules of recognition, and not explanation, of conventional actions*[48].

To sum up, we would like to point out that S. Czepita presented not only the theoretic development of various issues regarding conventional actions, but also the way of applying his approach towards the constitutive rules of conventional actions to the characteristics of the action of entering into marriage as a conventional action in family law.[49].

4 Conventionalization and Formalization of Conventional Activities

Maciej Zieliński has differentiated, in terminological and also conceptual terms, between ,conventionalization and formalization of conventional actions[50]. The theoretical development of the concept was the contribution of Stanisław Czepita[51].

---

that S. Czepita focuses his attention on the legalese understood as a language (sociolect of an ethnic language) used by lawyers in a social role specific to them, ibidem p. 177.

46 Ibidem,, p. 155.

47 Ibidem,, p. 151.

48 Ibidem,, p. 157.

49 Ibidem, p. 210 et seq.

50 A. Choduń, S. Czepita, *Profesor Maciej Zieliński. Uczony, Nauczyciel, Wychowawca*, in: *W poszukiwaniu dobra wspólnego. Księga jubileuszowa Profesora Macieja Zielińskiego*, ed. A. Choduń, S. Czepita, Szczecin 2010, p. 32–33 and S. Czepita, *Czynności konwencjonalne i formalne w prawie a proces prawotwórczy i rola Trybunału Konstytucyjnego*, „Państwo i Prawo", 12/2014, p. 7.

51 Especially in: S. Czepita, *Formalizacja a konwencjonalizacja działań w prawie*, in: *Konwencjonalne i formalne aspekty prawa*, ed. S. Czepita, Szczecin 2006, p. 9 et seq

Conventionalization of a given action consists in the fact that the execution of this action in a specific way, the appropriate rules prescribe assigning [52] the meaning of the execution of a specific conventional action.[53]. In turn, formalization of a certain action[54] consists in specifying by the proper norms of conduct the manner of performing a given action, while the activity carried out against the rules of formalisation remains a given type of activity[55].

Obviously, conventionalization of a given action is connected with constitutive rules, the "violation" of which (meaning: acting in a manner different than the one determined by the rules constituting a given activity) in this activity not being recognized as a conventional activity of a specific type[56], e.g. as a greeting, delivery of a judgment or interrogation.[57]. Obviously, psychophysical activities may be conventionalized on various levels, as has already been pointed out, using different terminology, in the original version of the concept (see point 1). However, in order to speak of the legal conventionalization of a given act, the rules of recognizing it as a conventional, legally important act must be formulated in law – explicitly in the legal regulations – or must be a part of the legal culture.[58]. At the same time, legal conventionalization is superstructured over

52 Subject to the specific meaning of this and similar expressions, as already discussed in point 1.

53 S. Czepita, *Formalizacja i konwencjonalizacja w systemie prawnym*, in: *System prawny a porządek prawny*, ed. O. Bogucki, S. Czepita, Szczecin 2008, p. 109.

54 Obviously, both the conventional and psychophysical activities can be formalised, but the latter issue is not relevant in this discussion.

55 Ibidem, idem, *Formalizacja a konwencjonalizacja…*, op. cit., p. 11.

56 Idem, *Formalizacja i konwencjonalizacja…*, op. cit., p. 110. Let us note that the idea of distinguishing the phenomenon of conventionalization and formalization of conventional activities is closely related to the assumption that not all the rules constituting conventional actions of a given type are constitutive, which S. Czepita clearly pointed out in his earlier works, distinguishing constitutive rules from the class of all constructional rules and consequential conventional actions., cf. idem, *Reguły…*, op. cit., p. 151.

57 For example, let us point out that the conventionalizing rules (of legal proceedings) in procedural law usually include: the existence of proceedings (criminal, civil) or its stage, the basic elements of the characteristics of the subject and the existence of a given action in a specific sequence of actions, idem, *Formalizacja i konwencjonalizacja…*, op. cit., p. 114, J. Wieczorkiewicz-Kita, *Zagadnienie wyrokowania w procesie karnym w świetle koncepcji czynności konwencjonalnych*, w: *Konwencjonalne…*, op. cit., pp. 57–59, B. Janusz-Pohl, *Formalizacja…*, op. cit., p. 616.

58 Idem, *Formalizacja i konwencjonalizacja…*, op. cit., p. 111.

conventionalization at the level of a particular cultural system and, above all, the language as its element[59].

Formalization of a given action may take two forms: (1) formalization through designating an obligation – the standards prescribe (prohibit) the performance of an action in a specific manner and (2) formalization through designating the consequences – performance of an action in a specific manner will have positive consequences which will not occur if the action is performed against the rules of formalization, or if the performance of an action differently than provided for in the rules of formalization will give rise to specific negative consequences[60]. Both forms of formalization do not exclude one another.

The boundary between conventionalization and formalization of conventional actions is obviously evident only in the model approach. Recognizing the rules conventionalization and formalization of conventional action of a given type is associated with the necessity to decide which constructive and consequent rules are constitutive for this action. As of legal analyses, the case is even more complicated as there may be a different relation between the rules conventionalization and formalization of a legally significant conventional action and the law (legal norms)[61]. In particular, the legislator might add an extra rule to the set of rules constituting a certain conventional action in a given culture, assuming that only the action performed pursuant to all rules is significant for a legal system[62]. It is also possible that the rules specified on the ground of a legal system do not constitute a specific conventional legal action, only formalize the action conventionalized at the level of a cultural system, e.g. by specifying that if this action is performed in a certain manner, it will have specific legal effect[63]. Deciding, whether this "extra" rule (rules) specified by the legislator is conventionalizing or (only) formalizing conventional action of a certain type can be problematic. The boundary between conventionalization and formalization is blurred when the rules set by the legislator are assigned a different status.[64].

59 Ibidem.

60 Ibidem, s. 109–110, idem, *Formalizacja a konwencjonalizacja…*, op. cit., p. 12.

61 Idem, *Formalizacja a konwencjonalizacja…*, op. cit., pp. 15–16.

62 Ibidem,, p. 16. The author indicates that the requirement of a form of a notarial deed constitutes such rule indicated by the legislator, which co-constitutes the action of entering into agreement of the transfer of ownership of the property.

63 Ibidem.

64 Ibidem,, p. 17.

5 The Concept of Conventional Actions in Law as Theoretical and Methodological Basis for Legal Studies

The representatives of general theory of law, specific legal sciences, or even legal practice, have been applying the concept of conventional actions in law. This concept (in its original form) was used first in considerations of substantive civil law[65] and has continued to constitute a methodological basis for many works on civil law[66]. The increased interest in the concept of conventional actions of the specialists in legal proceedings[67], civil[68] and administrative[69], has been noticeable since this concept was complemented with the issue of formalization of conventional actions[70].

---

65 Z. Radwański, Teoria umów, Warsaw 1977. As the author wrote in *Zakończenie [Conclusion]* of his work: First of all, it has been noted that the "representations of will" of the parties is a conventional action of a social significance, ibidem, p. 256 Please note this work has played significant role in the studies on civil law, A. Olejniczak, *Profesor Zbigniew Radwański 1924–2012*, „Nauka" 1/2013, pp. 174-175.

66 np. S. Czepita, Z. Kuniewicz, *Spór o konwalidację nieważnych czynności prawnych*, „Państwo i Prawo", z. 9, 2002, p.79 et seq., K. Mularski, *Czynności podobne do czynności prawnych*, Warszawa 2011, p. 103 et seq.

67 E.g. J. Wieczorkiewicz-Kita, *Zagadnienie wyrokowania…*, op. cit., p. 55 et seq., eadem, *O konwencjonalnych i formalnych aspektach procesu karnego*, in: *W poszukiwaniu…*, op. cit., p. 754, B. Janusz-Pohl, *O konstrukcji niedopuszczalności czynności karnoprocesowej*, Ruch Prawniczy, Ekonomiczny i Socjologiczny 4/2014, p. 161 et seq, eadem, *Formalizacja…*, op. cit.

68 E.g. O. Bogucki, *Przeprowadzanie dowodów w postępowaniu cywilnym z perspektywy czynności konwencjonalnych*, in: *Konwencjonalne…*, op. cit., p. 103 et seq, S. Czepita, *Zagadnienie orzeczeń nieistniejących w postępowaniu cywilnym w świetle koncepcji czynności konwencjonalnych*, in: ibidem, p. 139 et seq, G. Szacoń, *Proces cywilny na tle koncepcji czynności konwencjonalnych – formalizacja czynności faktycznych i konwencjonalnych*, in: ibidem, p. 87 et seq., J. Jaśkiewicz, *Poznanie faktów w postępowaniu cywilnym*, Warszawa 2013, p. 55 et seq., K. Markiewicz, *Zasady orzekania w postępowaniu nieprocesowym*, Warsaw 2013, p. 21 et seq, K. Gmerek, *Udzielanie pouczeń przez sąd w postępowaniu cywilnym. Uwagi na tle wykładni przepisu art. 5 Kodeksu postępowania cywilnego.*

69 T. Kiełkowski, *Nabycie prawa na mocy decyzji administracyjnej*, Warsaw 2012, p. 134 et seq.

70 Indicated in the context of criminal proceedings: J. Wieczorkiewicz-Kita, *O konwencjonalnych…*, op. cit., p. 754, B. Janusz-Pohl, *O konstrukcji…*, op. cit., p. 162.

6 Summary

If the intention of the authors of *Czynności konwencjonalne w prawie* was to create a universal tool of analysing various legal phenomena of the same genus – in the form of a conventional action – then, undoubtedly, this aim has been achieved. Presenting their arguments in favour of the choice of the subject of research, the author claims as follows: *If we abandoned a more general theoretical concept regarding conventional acts, or even a definition regulating this term, required to define a concept constituting a genus for a large number of various legal acts (...), we would renounce the possibility of some consistent, based on a uniform theoretical basis, solutions to problems arising in legal practice with reference to the performance of such or other conventional actions causing the legal effects of different type.*[71] Thus, this tool might serve (and serves, as evidenced by numerous publications, including the ones listed in item 5) as theoretical and methodological basis of the analyses conducted in the science of law, but also solving the factual problems.

This does not mean, however, that the process of constructing conventional actions in law has finished. The concept of conventional actions is still under development in a way. However, especially as an attempt to answer the needs of legal practice, the new thought will appear in the near future, as evidenced by the cases of application and development of this concept in the area of criminal and administrative proceedings, not to mention civil law[72]. It turns out this task is undertaken not only by law theorists[73] but also the representatives of particular legal sciences, who sometimes apply this universal tool, in some aspects, to the analyses they conduct[74].

---

71 L. Nowak, S. Wronkowska, M. Zieliński, Z. Ziembiński, *Czynności konwencjonalne...*, op. cit., 75.

72 B. Janusz-Pohl, *Formalizacja...*, op. cit., p. 57.

73 Undoubtedly, from the point of view of the general theory of law, detailed issues related to the consistency of the concept of conventional actions in law (in its present form) with Maciej Zieliński's derivational concept of law interpretation, which otherwise takes into consideration elements of the concept of conventional actions in law within its framework. The current form of derivative concept may be found in: M. Zieliński, *Wykładnia prawa. Zasady, reguły, wskazówki*, 7th edition, Warsaw 2017.

74 Some of the actions of this type may lead to the enrichment of the actual concept of the conventional actions in law, provided that they are conducted with due care as regards methodological tools. More universal thoughts (i.e. the ones which can refer to a wider class of conventional actions than the actions related to criminal proceedings discussed by the author) may be found in: B. Janusz-Pohl, *Formalizacja...*, op. cit., p. 62 et seq.

Bibliography

1. Andrejew I., *Zagadnienia typizacji przestępstw*, "Studia Iuridica" 1981, Vol. 10.
2. Arlen J., Talley E., *Experimental law and economics*, "NYU Law and Economics Research Paper" 2008, No. 08–30. Available at SSRN: https://ssrn.com/abstract=1144086.
3. Banakar R., *Who Needs the Classics? – On the Relevance of Classical Legal Sociology for the Study of Current Social and Legal Problems*, [in:] *Retssociologi*, eds. O. Hammerslev and M.R. Madsen, Copenhagen 2012.
4. Barczak-Oplustil A., *Zasada koincydencji winy i czynu w Kodeksie karnym*, Kraków 2016.
5. Biernat A., *Poglądy filozoficzne Leona Petrażyckiego i ich interpretacje*, Toruń 2002.
6. Bloch J., *Kodeks pracy. Ustawy, rozporządzenia, dekrety, orzecznictwo. Komentarz*, Warsaw 1936.
7. Bogucki O., *Model wykładni funkcjonalnej w derywacyjnej koncepcji wykładni prawa*, Szczecin 2016.
8. Bogucki O., *Przeprowadzanie dowodów w postępowaniu cywilnym z perspektywy czynności konwencjonalnych*, [in:] *Konwencjonalne i formalne aspekty prawa*, ed. S. Czepita, Szczecin 2006.
9. Bogucki O., Zieliński M., *Rozdział 1. Zasady prawa z perspektywy ogólnej teorii prawa*, in: *System prawa karnego procesowego. Volume III. Zasady procesu karnego*, ed. P. Wiliński, Warsaw 2014.
10. Bosiacki A., *Wstęp*, [in:] *Leon Petrażycki, Polityka prawa cywilnego i ekonomia polityczna*, ed. A. Bosiacki, Warsaw 2017.
11. Bougette P., Deschamps M., Marty F., *When Economics Met Antitrust: The Second Chicago School and the Economization of Antitrust Law*, "GREDEG Working Papers" 2014, No. 23, pp. 1-35.
12. Brożek B., *Rationality and Discourse: Towards a Normative Model of Applying Law*, Warszawa 2007.
13. Brzęk W., *Regulation Impact Assessment (RIA) at Poland and at some EU countries*, "Procedia – Social and Behavioral Sciences" 2014, No. 109,pp. 45–50.
14. Chmielewski J., Hoff W., *Regulatory Impact Assessment (RIA) and Rationality of Law – Legal Aspects*, "Management and Business Administration. Central Europe" 2015, Vol. 23, No. 2. pp. 92-108.

15. Choduń A., Czepita S., *Profesor Maciej Zieliński. Uczony, Nauczyciel, Wychowawca*, [in:] *W poszukiwaniu dobra wspólnego. Księga jubileuszowa Profesora Macieja Zielińskiego*, ed. A. Choduń, S. Czepita, Szczecin 2010.
16. Cieślak M., *Polska procedura karna. Podstawowe założenia teoretyczne*, [in:] *Marian Cieślak - dzieła wybrane*, Vol. II, ed. S. Waltoś, Kraków 2011.
17. Cieślak W., Steinborn S. (ed), *Profesor Marian Cieślak - osoba, dzieło, kontynuacje*, Warszawa 2013.
18. Cooter R., Ulen T., *Ekonomiczna analiza prawa*, Warsaw 2009.
22. Czepita S., *Koncepcja polityki prawa Leona Petrażyckiego a koncepcje współczesne*, "Państwo i Prawo" 1977, Vol. 7, pp. 46-56.
24. Czepita S., *Metodologiczna charakterystyka ewolucji koncepcji polityki prawa Leona Petrażyckiego*, "Zeszyty Naukowe". Vol. 27. Prace Studium Administracyjnego. Vol. 1, Szczecin 1978. pp. 99 - 120.
27. Czepita S., *Reguły konstytutywne a zagadnienia prawoznawstwa*, Szczecin 1996,.
20. Czepita S., *Formalizacja a konwencjonalizacja działań w prawie*, [in:] *Konwencjonalne i formalne aspekty prawa*, ed. S. Czepita, Szczecin 2006.
23. Czepita S. (ed.), *Konwencjonalne i formalne aspekty prawa*, Szczecin 2006.
28. Czepita S., *Zagadnienie orzeczeń nieistniejących w postępowaniu cywilnym w świetle koncepcji czynności konwencjonalnych*, [in:] *Konwencjonalne i formalne aspekty prawa*, ed. S. Czepita, Szczecin 2006.
21. Czepita S., *Formalizacja i konwencjonalizacja w systemie prawnym*, [in:] *System prawny a porządek prawny*, ed. O. Bogucki, S. Czepita, Szczecin 2008.
19. Czepita S., *Czynności konwencjonalne i formalne w prawie a proces prawotwórczy i rola Trybunału Konstytucyjnego*, „Państwo i Prawo“ 2014, Vol. 12, pp. 3–19.
25. Czepita S., *O koncepcji czynności konwencjonalnych w prawie*, [in:] *Wykładnia Konstytucji. Aktualne problemy i tendencje*, ed. M. Smolak, Warszawa 2016.
26. Czepita S., *O pojęciu czynności konwencjonalnej i jej odmianach*, „Ruch Prawniczy, Ekonomiczny i Socjologiczny“ 2017, Vol. 1, pp. 85–102.
29. Czepita S., Kuniewicz Z., *Spór o konwalidację nieważnych czynności prawnych*, „Państwo i Prawo“ 2002, z. 9, pp. 79- 87.
31. Daszkiewicz K., *Przestępstwo z premedytacją*, Warszawa 1968.
30. Daszkiewicz K., *Przestępstwa z afektu w polskim prawie karnym*, Warszawa 1982.
32. De Francesco F., Radaelli C. M., Troeger V. E., *Implementing regulatory innovations in Europe: the case of impact assessment*, "Journal of European Public Policy" 2012, Vol. 19, No. 4, pp. 491-511.

33. Dereń E., Polański E., *Wielki słownik języka polskiego*, Kraków 2015.
34. Drabik L., Sobol E., *Słownik języka polskiego*, PWN, Warszawa 2007.
35. *Diritti umani e genere. Fondamenti scientifici, antropologici, storici e filosofico-giuridici del modello dell'uguaglianza nella differenza – Stelle inquiete. Interventi e confronti*, ed. A.C. Amato Mangiameli, Turin 2017.
36. *Estudios sobre género y derecho. Hacia un modelo de género de la igualdad en la diferencia*, ed. A. Aparisi Miralles, Navarra (Pamplona) 2016.
37. Evju S., *Labour is Not a Commodity: Reappraising the Origins of the Maxim*, "European Labour Law Journal" 2013, No. 4, pp. 222-229
38. Fenichel Z., *Zarys polskiego prawa robotniczego*, Krakow 1930.
39. Fittipaldi E., *Everyday legal ontology. A psychological and linguistic investigation within the frame of Leon Petrazycki's theory of law*, Milan 2016.
40. Flasche K., Lorenz A., Riechers W., *Die Ausarbeitung, Einführung und Handbung des Gehaltsgruppenkatalogs*, Berlin 1959.
41. Florek L., *Ochrona praw i interesów pracownika*, Warsaw 1990.
42. Frydman S., *Dogmatyka prawa w świetle socjologii*, [in:] *Ogólna nauka o prawie*, ed. B. Wróblewski, Vilnius 1936.
43. Gaberle A., *Dowody w sądowym procesie karnym*, Kraków 2007.
44. Garlicki L., *Przesłanki ograniczania konstytucyjnych praw i wolności (na tle orzecznictwa Trybunału Konstytucyjnego)*, "Państwo i Prawo" 2001 Vol. 10, pp. 3-18.
45. Giaro T., *Leon Petrażycki i ekonomiczna analiza prawa. Materiały do dalszych rozważań*, [in:] *Nauka i nauczanie prawa. Tradycja i przyszłość. Konferencja na dwóchsetlecie Wydziału Prawa i Administracji Uniwersytetu Warszawskiego*, ed. H. Izdebski, Warsaw 2009.
46. Giedrewicz-Niewińska A., *Projekt kodeksu pracy z 1949 r.*, Oświęcim 2015.
48. Giezek J., *Strona podmiotowa czynu zabronionego a model i kryteria subiektywnego przypisania*, [in:] *Obiektywne oraz subiektywne przypisanie odpowiedzialności karnej*, eds. J. Giezek, P. Kardas, Warszawa 2016.
47. Giezek J., Kardas P., *O kryteriach obiektywnego oraz subiektywnego przypisania z punktu widzenia podstaw odpowiedzialności karnej - uwagi wprowadzające*, [in:] *Obiektywne oraz subiektywne przypisanie odpowiedzialności karnej*, eds. J. Giezek, P. Kardas, Warszawa 2016.
49. Giezek J., *Świadomość sprawcy czynu zabronionego*, Warszawa 2013.
50. Gil D., Pikuła Ł. (eds.), *Prawo i nauka w poglądach Leona Petrażyckiego*, Lublin 2013.
51. Gmerek K., *Udzielanie pouczeń przez sąd w postępowaniu cywilnym. Uwagi na tle wykładni przepisu art. 5 Kodeksu postępowania cywilnego* [in print].

52. Gniewek E., P. Machnikowski (ed.), *Kodeks cywilny. Komentarz, do art. 1 nb. 4*, Legalis 2017 (access: 14.02.2018).
53. Goldštejn M., Korotkov V., *Garantijnye i kompensacionnye vyplaty rabocim i sluzascim*, Moscow 1960.
54. Goździewicz G., *Szczególne właściwości norm prawa pracy*, Toruń 1988, passim;
55. W. Szubert, *Szczególne właściwości prawa pracy, Studia Prawno-Ekonomiczne* 1970, vol. IV.
55. Grantt H.L., *Travail, salaires et bénéfices*, Paris 1921.
56. Gronowski S., *Polskie prawo antymonopolowe. Zarys wykładu*, Warszawa 1998.
57. Groszyk H., Korybski A., *O programie tworzenia nauki polityki prawa Leona Petrażyckiego*, "Annales Universitatis Mariae-Curie Skłodowska. Sectio G" 1981, Vol. XXVIII, pp. 1-36.
58. Grzybowski P. (ed.), *System prawa cywilnego. Cześć ogólna. Vol. 1*, Wrocław-Warszawa-Kraków-Gdańsk 1974.
59. Grzybowski S., *Wspomnienia*, Krakow 1999.
60. Gurvitch G., *Le Temps Présent Et l'Idée du Droit Social*, Paris 1931[1932].
61. Gutowski M. (ed.), *Kodeks cywilny. Komentarz. Art. 1-449*[11], Vol. I, Warszawa 2016.
62. Habrat A., *Ideał człowieka i społeczeństwa w teorii Leona Petrażyckiego*, Rzeszów 2006.
63. Harmsen H., *Lohnzahlungen bei Betriebsstockungen: ein Versuch zur Lösung des Problems aus dem Wesen des Arbeitsvertrages*, Berlin 1925.
64. Helios J., *Metody psychologiczne w prawie. Szkic problemu*, "Wrocławskie Studia Erazmiańskie" 2014, No. 8, pp. 199–214,
65. Jan Paweł II, *Veritatis splendor* [in:] *Encykliki Ojca Świętego Jana Pawła II*, Kraków 1997.
66. Janusz – Pohl B., *Formalizacja i konwencjonalizacja jako instrumenty analizy czynności karnoprocesowych w prawie polskim*, Poznań 2017.
67. Janusz-Pohl B., *O konstrukcji niedopuszczalności czynności karnoprocesowej*, "Ruch Prawniczy, Ekonomiczny i Socjologiczny" 2014, Vol. 4, pp. 161–173.
68. Jaśkiewicz J., *Poznanie faktów w postępowaniu cywilnym*, Warszawa 2013.
69. Jerzak M., Kitala M., *Prawo w gospodarce. Metodyka oddziaływania prawa na gospodarkę*, "Materiały i Studia NBP" 2012, No. 276. pp. 2–28.
70. Jędrzejewski Z., *Bezprawność jako element przestępności czynu. Studium na temat struktury przestępstwa*, Warsaw 2009.

71. Jędrzejewski Z., *Uwagi o pojęciu przestępstwa w projekcie kodeksu karnego*, "Państwo i Prawo" 1993, Vol. 10, pp. 90-97.

72. Jolls C., Sunstein C., Thaler R., *A behavioral approach to law and economics*, "Stanford Law Review" 1998, Vol.. 5, pp. 1473-1548

73. Kaczor J., *Zasada autonomii woli w świetle filozofii liberalnej*, "Ruch Prawniczy, Ekonomiczny i Socjologiczny" 2001, No. 1–2, pp. 1–25.

74. Kaczor J., *Zasada autonomii woli z perspektywy teorii prawa*, "Acta Universitatis Wratislaviensis. Przegląd Prawa i Administracji" 2005, No. 69, pp. 67-82.

75. Kahneman D., Tversky A., *Prospect Theory: An Analysis of decision under risk*, "Econometrica: Journal of the Econometric Society" 1979, No. 2, pp. 263-291.

76. Kant I., *Krytyka czystego rozumu. Tom II*, Warsaw 1986.

77. Kardas P., *Teoretyczne podstawy odpowiedzialności karnej za przestępne współdziałanie*, Kraków 2001.

78. Kidyba A., *Kodeks cywilny. Komentarz. Art. 1-449[11], Vol. III*, Warszawa 2014.

79. Kiełkowski T., *Nabycie prawa na mocy decyzji administracyjnej*, Warsaw 2012.

80. Kirkpatrick C., Parker D., Zhang Y.F., *Regulatory Impact Assessment in Developing and Transition Economies: A Survey of Current Practice*, "Centre on Regulation and Competition, Working Papers" 2004, No. 83, pp. 1–14.

81. Klein A., *Elementy zobowiązaniowego stosunku prawnego*, Wrocław 2005.

82. Kmiecik R. (ed.), *Prawo dowodowe. Zarys wykładu*, Warszawa 2008.

83. Kmiecik R., *Uprawdopodobnienie w procesie karnym*, "Nowe Prawo" 1983, No. 5, pp. 45-59.

84. Kmita J., *Z metodologicznych problemów interpretacji humanistycznej*, Warsaw 1971.

85. Kmita J., Nowak L., *Studia nad teoretycznymi podstawami humanistyki*, Poznań 1968.

86. Kojder A., *Idee społeczno-prawne Leona Petrażyckiego i ich współczesne kontynuacje*, http://www2.wpia.uw.edu.pl/files/Idee_spoleczno-prawne_LP.pdf?short=, access 20.02.2018.

87. Kojder A., *Idee społeczno-prawne Leona Petrażyckiego i ich współczesne kontynuacje* [in:] *Klasyczna socjologia polska i jej współczesna recepcja*, eds. J. Mucha, W. Wincławski, Toruń 2006.

89. Kojder A., *Przedmowa*, [in:] L. Petrażycki, *O nauce, prawie i moralności. Pisma wybrane*, ed. A. Kojder, Warsaw 1985.

88. Kojder A., *Godność i siła prawa*, Warsaw 2001.

90. Kojder A., Timošina E.V., *Bibliografi ja opublikowanych trudov L.I. Petražickogo*, [in:] *Teorija i polityka prava. Izbrannyje Trudy*, ed. L.I. Petražickij, Sankt-Peterburg 2010.

91. Kopińska G., *Najważniejsze wnioski i rekomendacje*, [in:] *Tworzenie i konsultowanie rządowych projektów ustaw*, eds. G. Kopińska, G. Makowski, P. Waglowski, M., Wiszowaty M. *Raport z badania nad sposobem prowadzenia konsultacji publicznych i tworzenia dokumentów towarzyszących rządowym projektom ustaw w 2012 roku*, http://www.batory.org.pl/upload/files/Programy%20operacyjne/Odpowiedzialne%20 Panstwo/Tworzenie_i_konsultowanie.pdf [access 20.02.2018].

92. Koranyi K., *Powszechna historia państwa i prawa. Tom I. Starożytność*, Warsaw 1961.

93. Kordela M., *Zasady prawa. Studium teoretycznoprawne*, Poznań 2012.

94. Kowalczyk A., *Ochrona wynagrodzenia za pracę. Prawo rzymskie a współczesne regulacje prawa pracy*, "Zeszyty Naukowe Uniwersytetu Rzeszowskiego" 2014, No. 82, pp. 61–77.

95. Król-Bogomilska M., „*Formy winy w prawie karnym w świetle psychologii*, Warszawa 1991.

96. Kubicki L., *Przestępstwo popełnione przez zaniechanie. Zagadnienia podstawowe*, Warszawa 1975.

97. Kwiatkowski Z., *Zakazy dowodowe w procesie karnym*, Kraków 2005.

98. Laserson M., *The Work of Leon Petrazhitsky*, "Columbia Law Review" 1951, No. 1, pp. 41–63.

99. Leszczyna H., *Hermeneutyka prawnicza – rozumienie* i *interpretacja tekstu prawnego*, Warszawa 1996.

100. Leszczyna H., *Petrażycki*, Warsaw 1974.

101. Locke J., *Dwa traktaty o rządzie*, Warszawa 1992.

102. Małecka M., O behawioralnym podejściu do badania prawa, paradoksie, do którego prowadzi i sposobie jego przezwyciężenia, "Nauka i Szkolnictwo Wyższe" 2013, No. 1, pp. 19–42.

103. Markiewicz K., *Zasady orzekania w postępowaniu nieprocesowym*, Warsaw 2013.

104. Matczak M., *Summa Iniuria. O błędzie formalizmu w stosowaniu prawa*, Warszawa 2007.

105. Matraszek L., *Socjologiczne pierwiastki teorii prawa Leona Petrażyckiego*, "Ruch Prawniczy, Ekonomiczny i Socjologiczny" 1975, z. 3, pp. 227-240.

106. Mącior W. *O finalizmie w prawie karnym*, "Państwo i Prawo" 1971, Vol. 6, pp. 970-985.
107. Mącior W., *W związku z dyskusją na temat finalizmu*, "Państwo i Prawo" 1972, Vol. 5, pp. 108-112.
108. Mereżko A., Teoria Leona Petrażyckiego w kontekście rosyjskiej filozofii prawa (uczniowie i kontynuatorzy), "Przegląd Prawno-Ekonomiczny" 2009, No. 6, pp. 5-19..
109. Mędrala M., *Funkcja ochronna cywilnego postępowania sądowego w sprawach z zakresu prawa pracy*, Warsaw 2011.
110. Milewski R., Kwiatkowski E. (eds.), *Podstawy ekonomii*, Warszawa 2005.
111. Mojak J., Kidyba A., *Zdolność prawna przedsiębiorstw państwowych w świetle ustawy z dn. 25 września 1981 o przedsiębiorstwach państwowych*, "Annales Universitatis Mariae Curie Skłodowska. Ius" 1982, Vol. XXIX, pp. 253-265.
112. Morawski L., *Filozofia prawa*, Toruń 2014.
113. Motyka K., *Wpływ Leona Petrażyckiego na polską teorię i socjologię prawa*, Lublin 1993.
114. Mularski K., *Czynności podobne do czynności prawnych*, Warszawa 2011.
115. Muszalski W., Ogólna refleksja o rozwoju prawa pracy i jego uwarunkowaniu, "Studia Iuridica Lublinensia" 2015, Vol. XXIV, pp. 59-67.
117. Nelken J., *Przedmiot postępowania dowodowego w procesie karnym*, "Nowe Prawo" 1968, No. 5, pp. 760-775.
116. Nelken J., *Dowód poszlakowy w procesie karnym*, Warszawa 1970.
118. Nelken J., *Uprawdopodobnienie w procesie karnym*, "Nowe Prawo" 1970, No. 4, pp. 514-529.
119. Neumann J., Morgenstern O., *Theory of games and economic behavior*, Princeton 1947, as cited in M. Peterson, *An introduction to decision theory*, Cambridge 2009.
121. Niedośpiał M., *Autonomia woli w części ogólnej prawa cywilnego*, "Państwo i Prawo" 1984, No. 12, pp. 64-73.
120. Niedośpiał M., *Swoboda czynności prawnych*, Bielsko-Biała 2004.
122. Nizioł K., E*konomizacja prawa finansowego – nowy trend w polskim i unijnym prawie finansowym* [in:] *Prawo finansowe wobec wyzwań XXI wieku*, eds. J. Gliniecka, A. Drywa, E. Juchniewicz, T. Sowiński, Warszawa 2015.
123. Niżnik-Mucha A., *Zakaz naruszania konstytucyjnych wolności i praw w Konstytucji Rzeczypospolitej Polskiej*, Warsaw 2014.

124. Nowacki J., *O stosunku prawa intuicyjnego do prawa pozytywnego w teorii Leona Petrażyckiego*, [in:] *Z zagadnień teorii prawa i teorii nauki Leona Petrażyckiego. Studia opracowane dla upamiętnienia stulecia urodzin*, ed. K. Opałek , Warsaw 1969.

125. Nowacki J., *O rozróżnieniu prawa i moralności w teorii Leona Petrażyckiego*, "Studia Filozoficzne" 1981, Vol. 5, pp. s. 51-62.

126. Nowak L., Wronkowska S., Zieliński M., Ziembiński Z., *Czynności konwencjonalne w prawie*, "Studia Prawnicze". 1972, **No.** 33(2), pp. 73–99.

127. Ohanowicz A., *Wolność umów w przyszłym polskim kodeksie cywilnym*, "Ruch Prawniczy, Ekonomiczny i Socjologiczny" 1926, No. 3, pp. CXLVII– XLII.

128. Olejniczak A., *Profesor Zbigniew Radwański 1924–2012*, "Nauka" 2013, Vol. 1, pp. 169-180.

129. Organiściak W., Prawo pracy II Rzeczypospolitej. Szkic dla celów dydaktycznych, "Prace Naukowe Uniwersytetu Śląskiego" 2009, No. 2704, pp. 233-257.

130. Osiecka-Chojnacka J., *System oceny skutków regulacji w Pols*ce, "Biuro Analiz Sejmowych, Indos" 2008, No. 2, pp. 1-4.

131. Parisi F., Klick J., *Functional Law and Economics: The Search for Value-Neutral Principles of Lawmaking*, "Chicago-Kent Law Review" 2004, No. 79. , pp. 431- 450.

132. Patryas W., *Interpretacja karnistyczna. Studium metodologiczne*, Poznań 1988.

136. Patryas W., *Przyczynek do zagadnienia przyczynowości zaniechania*, "Ruch Prawniczy, Ekonomiczny i Socjologiczny" 1992, Vol. 3, pp. s. 288-300.

138. Patryas W., *Zaniechanie. Próba analizy metodologicznej*, Poznań 1993.

137. Patryas W., *Rozważania o normach prawnych*, Poznań 2001.

133. Patryas W., *Jeszcze w sprawie normy sankcjonowanej w prawie karnym*, "Ruch Prawniczy, Ekonomiczny i Socjologiczny" 2006, Vol. 4, pp. 187-189.

134. Patryas W., *Na polemikę dra Łukasza Pohla – odpowiedź*, "Ruch Prawniczy, Ekonomiczny i Socjologiczny" 2006, Vol. 4, pp. 177-180.

135. Patryas W., *„Norma sankcjonowana w prawie karnym (…) – kilka uwag do artykułu Łukasza Pohla*, "Ruch Prawniczy, Ekonomiczny i Socjologiczny" 2006, Vol. 1, p. 66, pp. 65-67.

139. Pazdan M., *Specjalna zdolność prawna osób prawnych (uwagi de lege lata i de lege ferenda)*, [in:] *Prace cywilistyczne. Księga ku czci prof. Jana J. Winiarza*, ed. P. Wójcik, Warszawa 1990.

140. Pazdan M., *Podmioty bez osobowości prawnej po nowelizacji Kodeksu cywilnego z 2003 roku*, [in:] *W kręgu teoretycznych i praktycznych aspektów prawoznawstwa. Księga jubileuszowa Profesora Bronisława Ziemianina*, ed. M. Zieliński, Szczecin–Poznań 2005.

141. Petrażycki L., *Die Lehre von Einkommen: Vom Standpunkt des gemeinen Civilrechts unter Berücksichtigung des Entwurfs eines bürgerlichen Gesetzbuches für das Deutsche Reich*, Berlin 1895, Vol 2.

142. Petrażycki L., *O dopełniających prądach kulturalnych i prawach rozwoju handlu*, Warsaw 1936.

146. Petrażycki L., *Teoria prawa i państwa w związku z teorią moralności*, Warsaw 1959, Vol. 1.

148. Petrażycki L., *Wstęp do nauki prawa i moralności*, Warszawa 1959.

147. Petrażycki L., *Teoria prawa i państwa w związku z teorią moralności*, Warsaw 1960, Vol. 1.

143. Petrażycki L., *O nauce, prawie i moralności. Pisma wybrane*, Warszawa 1985.

144. Petrażycki L., *O pobudkach postępowania i o istocie moralności i prawa*, Warszawa 2002.

145. Petrażycki L., *Polityka prawa cywilnego i ekonomia polityczna*, ed. A. Bosiacki, Warsaw 2017.

149. Piątkowski J., Prawo do Kodeksu pracy czy konieczność jego posiadania, "Studia z zakresu prawa pracy i polityki społecznej" 2017, No. 1, pp. 1-16.

150. Pietrzykowski K., *Kodeks cywilny. Komentarz. Art. 1-449^{11}, Vol. I*, Warszawa 2013.

151. Piotrowski M., *Normy prawne imperatywne i dyspozytywne*, Warszawa 1990.

152. Płeszka K., *Reguły preferencji w prawniczych rozumowaniach interpretacyjnych*, [in:] *Studia z filozofii prawa*, ed. J. Stelmach, Kraków 2003, Vol. 2.

153. Pohl Ł, *Obiektywna istota sprawstwa w ujęciu polskiego prawa karnego (Uwagi na marginesie lektury pracy P. Kardasa „Teoretyczne podstawy odpowiedzialności karnej za przestępne współdziałanie"),* "Ruch Prawniczy, Ekonomiczny i Socjologiczny" 2004, Vol. 2, pp. 187-293.

154. Pohl Ł., *O kulturze prowadzenia dyskusji i jej meritum słów kilka – uwagi na marginesie artykułu Piotra Kardasa „Sprawstwo kierownicze i polecające – wykonawcze czy niewykonawcze postaci sprawstwa?"*, "Przegląd Sądowy" 2006, Vol. 11–12, pp. 257-266.

157. Pohl Ł., *Podmiotowe znamiona czynu zabronionego w strukturze przestępstwa*, "Państwo i Prawo" 2006, Vol. 2, pp. 56-68.

160. *Pohl Ł., Zawartość normatywna przepisu art. 18 § 1 k.k., "Prokuratura i Prawo" 2006, Vol. 2*, pp. 19-24.

159. Pohl Ł., *Struktura normy sankcjonowanej w prawie karnym. Zagadnienia ogólne*, Poznań 2007.

155. Pohl Ł, *O niemożności wykonania nakazanego działania spowodowanej zachowaniem się zobowiązanego do działania (przyczynek do analizy zaniechania w prawie karnym)*, [in:] *Profesor Marian Cieślak – osoba, dzieło, kontynuacje*, eds. W. Cieślak, S. Steinborn, Warszawa 2013.

158. Pohl Ł., *Prawo karne. Wykład cześci ogólnej*, Warsaw 2015.

156. Pohl Ł., *O znaczeniu refleksji naukowej Profesora Tomasza Kaczmarka*, "Państwo i Prawo" 2017, Vol. 12, pp. 88-99.

161. Poli R., Libardi M., *Logic. Theory of Science and Metaphysics According to Stanislaw Lesniewski*, "Grazer Philosophische Studien" 1999, No. 57., pp. 183–219.

162. Popper K.R., *Logika odkrycia naukowego*, Warszawa 2002.

163. Raczyński A., *Polskie prawo pracy*, Warsaw 1930.

164. Radwański Z. (ed.), *System Prawa Prywatnego. Prawo cywilne – część ogólna, Vol. 2*, Warszawa 2008.

166. Radwański Z., *Teoria umów*, Warszawa, 1977.

167. Radwański Z., *Uwagi ogólne o autonomii woli*, [in:] *II Kongres notariuszy Rzeczypospolitej Polskiej. Referaty i opracowania*, ed. R. Sztyk, Poznań 1999.

165. Radwański Z., *Prawo cywilne*, Warszawa 2005.

168. Radzikowski K., *Skutki wadliwości czynności cywilnoprawnej w świetle ustawy o podatku od czynności cywilnoprawnych*, "Ruch Prawniczy, Ekonomiczny i Socjologiczny" 2008, issue 1, pp. 133-154.

169. Rejsner M.A., *Sowremennaia jurisprudencjia i uczenie L.I. Petrażyckogo (Современная юриспруденция и учение Л.И. Петражицкого)*, Russkoje bogatstwo (Русское богатство) 1908, p. 59, as cited in: A. Mereżko, Teoria Leona Petrażyckiego w kontekście rosyjskiej filozofii prawa (uczniowie i kontynuatorzy), Przegląd Prawno-Ekonomiczny 2009, No. 6, pp. 5-19.

170. Renda A., *Impact Assessment in the EU. The State of the Art and the Art of the State*, Brussels 2006.

171. Rogowski W., Szpringer W., *Problemy metodologiczne oceny skutków regulacji w Polsce – czy powstają nowe perspektywy ekonomicznej analizy prawa?*, [in:] *Ocena skutków regulacji – poradnik OSR, doświadczenia, perspektywy*, eds. W. Szpringer, W. Rogowski, Warszawa 2007.

172. Safjan M. (ed.), *System Prawa Prywatnego. Prawo cywilne – część ogólna,. Vol. 1*, Warszawa 2012.

173. Skąpski M., *Ochronna funkcja prawa pracy w gospodarce rynkowej*, Krakow 2006.

174. Skoczyński J., *Prawna ochrona wynagrodzenia za pracę*, Warsaw 1995.

175. Słotwiński Sz., *Status prawny energii elektrycznej jako wyznacznik stosunków umownych w polskim prawie prywatnym*, Warszawa 2017.

176. Smoczyński P.J., *Oceny i normy postępowania w psychologistycznej koncepcji prawa i moralności Leona Petrażyckiego*, "Etyka" 1984, No. 21, pp. 71-102.

177. Smolak M., *Wykładnia celowościowa z perspektywy pragmatycznej*, Warszawa: Wolters Kluwer, 2012.

178. Sobczyk A., *Prawo pracy w świetle Konstytucji RP. TOM I. Teoria publicznego i prywatnego indywidualnego prawa pracy*, Warsaw 2013.

179. Sobell R.S., *Welfare Economics and Public Finance*, [in:] *Handbook of Public Finance*, eds. J.G. Backhaus, R.W. Wagner, Boston 2005.

180. Sorokin, Doroga dalniaia: Awtobiografia (Дорога дальняя: Автобиография), Moscow 1992, p. 56, as cited in: A. Mereżko, Teoria Leona Petrażyckiego w kontekście rosyjskiej filozofii prawa (uczniowie i kontynuatorzy), Przegląd Prawno-Ekonomiczny 2009, No. 6.

182. Sośniak M., *Znaczenie zgody uprawnionego w zakresie cywilnej odpowiedzialności odszkodowawczej*, „Zeszyty Naukowe Uniwersytetu Jagiellońskiego. Prace Prawnicze" 1959, z. 6, pp.127-173.

181. Sośniak M., *Rozwój historyczny konstrukcji umowy obligacyjnej*, Katowice 1986, pp. 128–136.

183. Špiljak M., *La repartition du revenu de l'entreprise et le systeme de remuneration en Yougoslavie*, Belgrad 1961.

184. Spyra T., *Granice wykładni prawa*, Kraków 2006.

185. Stabryła A., Trzcieniecki J. (ed.), *Organizacja i zarządzanie. Zarys problematyki*, Kraków 1986.

186. Stanek J., *Rosyjski realizm prawny. Psychologiczna koncepcja prawa – powstanie i rozwój*, [in:] *Naturalizm prawniczy. Stanowiska*, eds. J. Stelmach, B. Brożek, Ł. Kurka, K. Eliasza, Warsaw 2015.

187. Stanek J., *Teoria Nikołaja Korkunowa. Pierwsza próba psychologicznego ujęcia prawa*, [in:] *Naturalizm prawniczy. Stanowiska*, eds. J. Stelmach, B. Brożek, Ł. Kurka, K. Eliasza, Warsaw 2015.

188. *Stawecki* T., O *praktycznym zastosowaniu hermeneutyki* w *wykładni prawa*, [in:] *Teoria i praktyka wykładni prawa*, ed. P. Winczorek, Warszawa 2005.

189. Stefanowcz J.A., Szamałek K., *Analiza skutków regulacji prawnych w obszarze prawa geologiczno-górniczego*, "Zeszyty Naukowe Instytutu Gospodarki Surowcami Mineralnymi i Energii PAN" 2010, No. 79, pp. 43-55.

192. Stelmach J., *Współczesna filozofia interpretacji prawniczej*, Kraków 1995.

191. Stelmach J., *Kodeks argumentacyjny dla prawników*, Kraków 2003.

190. Stelmach J., Brożek B., Załuski W., *Dziesięć wykładów o ekonomii prawa*, Warszawa 2007.

193. Stelmachowski A., *Wstęp do teorii prawa cywilnego*, 1st edition, Warszawa 1969.

194. Stelmachowski A., *Wstęp do teorii prawa cywilnego*, 2nd edition, Warszawa 1984.

195. Stelmachowski A., *Zarys teorii prawa cywilnego*, Warszawa 1998.

196. Szacoń G., *Proces cywilny na tle koncepcji czynności konwencjonalnych – formalizacja czynności faktycznych i konwencjonalnych*, in: *Konwencjonalne i formalne aspekty prawa*, ed. S. Czepita, Szczecin 2006.

197. Szadok-Bratuń A., O dwóch koncepcjach prawa naturalnego polskich filozofów prawa okresu międzywojennego, "Przegląd Prawa i Administracji" 2015, No. 3661, pp. 233-251.

198. Szahaj A., *Zwrot antypozytywistyczny dopełniony (zamiast wstępu)*, [in:] *Filozofia i etyka interpretacji*, eds. A. F. Kola, A. Szachaj, Kraków 2007.

199. Szczepaniak I., Rola małych i średnich przedsiębiorstw w gospodarce (na przykładzie przemysłu spożywczego), "Equilibrium" 2009, No. 1, pp. 71–81.

200. Szymczak M. (ed.), *Słownik języka polskiego*, Warszawa 1978, Vol. I.

201. Szyszkowska M., *Filozofia prawa i filozofia człowieka*, Warsaw 1989.

202. Ślipko T., *Zarys etyki ogólnej*, Kraków 2004.

203. Śliwa R., Żaba-Nieroda R., *Ocena skutków regulacji jako element procesu regulacyjnego*, "Rocznik Administracji Publicznej" 2017, Vol. 3, pp. 364-379.

204. Święcicki M., *Prawo wynagrodzenia za pracę*, Warsaw 1963.

205. Tkacz S., *O „pozytywności" i „oficjalności" w teorii prawa Leona Petrażyckiego*,"Ruch Prawniczy, Ekonomiczny i Socjologiczny" 2005, Vol. 1, pp. 75–92.

206. *The Making of Labour Law in Europe. A comparative Study of Nine Countries up to 1945*, ed. B. Hepple, London – New York 1986.

207. *The Transformation of Labour Law in Europe. A comparative Study of Nine Countries 1945–2004*, ed. G. Hepple, Oregon 2009.

208. Timasheff N., Право как коллективно-психологическая реальнос ть, [in:] Труды русских ученых за границей. Берлин, Berlin 1923, Vol. 2.

209. Tversky A., Kahneman D., Judgment Under Uncertainty, "Heuristics and Biases, Science" 1974, No. 4157, pp. 1124-1131.

210. Tobor Z., *W poszukiwaniu intencji prawodawcy*, Warszawa 2013.

211. Ulman P., *Praca człowieka i godne jej wynagradzanie w świetle encykliki Centesimus annus*, [in:] *Polityka społeczna wobec "rzeczy nowych". 25-lecie encykliki Centesimus annus św. Jana Pawła II*, ed. Jan Mazur, Krakow 2016.

212. Walicki A., *Filozofia prawa rosyjskiego liberalizmu*, Warsaw 1995.

213. Waltoś S. (ed.), *Marian Cieślak – dzieła wybrane*, Tom II, Kraków 2011.

214. Walulik J., *O relacjach regulacji ekonomicznej i ochrony konkurencji – próba podsumowania debaty*, [in:] *Wyzwania dla ochrony konkurencji i regulacji rynku. Księga Jubileuszowa dedykowana Profesorowi Tadeuszowi Skocznemu*, eds. M. Bernatt, A. Jurkowska-Gomułka, M. Namysłowska, A. Piszcz Warszawa 2017.

215. Waśkowski E., *Teoria prawa cywilnego*, Warszawa 1936.

216. Weddeburn L., Rood M., Lyon-Caen C., Däubler W., Van Der Heijden P., *Labour law in the Post-Industrial Era. Essays in Honour of Hugo Sinzheimer*, Dartmouth *1994*.

217. Wieczorkiewicz-Kita J., *O konwencjonalnych i formalnych aspektach procesu karnego*, [in:] *W poszukiwaniu dobra wspólnego. Księga jubileuszowa Profesora Macieja Zielińskiego*, ed. A. Choduń, S. Czepita, Szczecin 2010.

218. Wieczorkiewicz-Kita J., *Zagadnienie wyrokowania w procesie karnym w świetle koncepcji czynności konwencjonalnych*, [in:] : *Konwencjonalne i formalne aspekty prawa*, ed. S. Czepita, Szczecin 2006.

219. Wiszniewski J., *Specjalna zdolność prawna osób prawnych*, "Studia Prawnicze" 1970, No.26–27, pp. 326-221. Wojtczak S., O niewspółmierności wartości i jej konsekwencjach dla stosowania prawa, Łódź : Wydawnictwo Uniwersytetu Łódzkiego, 2010.348.

220. Wittgenstein L., *Traktat logiczno – filozoficzny*, Vienna 1918.

221. Wojtczak S., O niewspółmierności wartości i jej konsekwencjach dla stosowania prawa, Łódź 2010.

221. Wojtyczek K., *Zasada proporcjonalności jako granica prawa karania*, "Czasopismo Prawa Karnego i Nauk Penalnych" 1999, Vol. 2, pp. 33–52.

222. Wojtyła K., *Osoba i czyn*, Lublin 2000.

223. Wojtyła K., *O metafizycznej i fenomenologicznej podstawie normy moralnej. Na podstawie koncepcji św. Tomasza z Akwinu i Maxa Schelera*, [in:] *Zagadnienia podmiotu moralności*, ed. K. Wojtyła, , Lublin 2001.

224. Woleński J., *Leon Petrażycki o prawie i moralności*, "Rocznik Polskiej Akademii Umiejętności" Kraków, 2016/2017, pp. 171-182.

225. Woleński J., *Marian Smoluchowski i Leon Petrażycki*, [in:] *Historia filozofii polskiej*, eds. J. Skoczyński, J. Woleński, Kraków 2010.

226. Wolter A., Ignatowicz J., Stefaniuk K., *Prawo cywilne*, Warszawa 1998.

227. Wolter W., *Czynnik psychiczny w istocie przestępstwa*, Kraków 1924.

228. Wolter W., *O tzw. przyczynowości zaniechania*, "Państwo i Prawo" 1954, No. 10–11, pp. 520-534.

229. Wratny J., Prawo do wynagrodzenia za pracę w świetle zasad sprawiedliwości i równości, "Annales Universitatis Mariae Curie-Skłodowska" 2015, Vol. LXII, pp. 297-315.

230. Wronkowska P., Zieliński M., Ziembiński Z., *Zasady prawa. Zagadnienia podstawowe*, Warszawa 1974.

231. Wróbel W., Zoll A., *Polskie prawo karne. Część ogólna*, Kraków 2010.

234. Wróblewski J., *W związku z zagadnieniem przyczynowości zaniechania*, "Państwo i Prawo" 1955, No. 7–8, pp. 266-271.

235. Wróblewski J., *Zagadnienia teorii wykładni prawa ludowego*, Warszawa 1959.

232. Wróblewski J, *Sądowe stosowanie prawa*, Warszawa 1988.

233. Wróblewski J., *Rozumienie prawa i jego wykładnia*, Wrocław 1990.

236. Zajęcki M., *Aksjologiczna interpretacja prawa (studium z metodologii i teorii prawa)*, Warszawa 2017.

237. Zakolska J., *Zasada proporcjonalności w orzecznictwie Trybunału Konstytucyjnego*, Warsaw 2008.

238. Zieliński M., *Interpretacja jako proces dekodowania tekstu prawnego*, Poznań 1972.

240. Zieliński M., *Obiektywność ustalenia faktów jako element praworządności stosowania prawa*, "Ruch Prawniczy, Ekonomiczny i Socjologiczny" 1979, No. 1, pp. 36–52.

241. Zieliński M., *Poznanie sądowe a poznanie naukowe*, Poznań 1979.

239. Zieliński M., *Konstytucyjne zasady prawa*, [in:] *Charakter i struktura norm konstytucji*, ed. J. Trzciński, Warszawa 1997.

242. Zieliński M., *Wykładnia prawa. Zasady, reguły, wskazówki*, Warszawa 2017.

243. Zieliński M., Ziembiński Z., *Uzasadnianie twierdzeń, ocen i norm w prawoznawstwie*, Warszawa 1988.

246. Ziembiński Z., *Przepis prawny a norma prawna*, "Ruch Prawniczy, Ekonomiczny i Socjologiczny" 1960, No. 1, pp. 1–15.

244. Ziembiński Z., *Logiczne podstawy prawoznawstwa*, Warsaw 1966.

245. Ziembiński Z., *Metodologiczne zagadnienia prawoznawstwa*, Warsaw 1974.

247. Ziembiński Z., *Zarys zagadnień etyki*, Poznań-Toruń 1994.

248. Ziembiński Z., Zieliński M., *Dyrektywy i sposób ich wypowiadania*, Warszawa 1992.

249. Ziemianin B., Kuniewicz Z., *Prawo cywilne – część ogólna*, Poznań 2007.

250. Zirk-Sadowski M., *Hermeneutyka a problemy filozofii prawa*, „Studia Prawno-Ekonomiczne" 1982, Vol. XXVIII, pp. 7-25.

251. Zirk-Sadowski M., *Rozumienie ocen w języku prawnym*, Łódź 1984.

252. Znamierowski C., *Oceny i normy*, Warsaw 1957.

253. Znamierowski C., *Z rozmyślań teoretyka prawa*, "Ruch Prawniczy, Ekonomiczny i Socjologiczny", 1929, Vol. 2, pp. 178–182.

254. Zoll A., *O normie prawnej z punktu widzenia prawa karnego*, Krakowskie Studia Prawnicze, 1990, Vol.XXIII, pp. 69-95.

255. Zoll F., Prawo pracy w biegu wieków, Rocznik Prawniczy, Wileński 1930.

256. Zubek R., *Jak i dlaczego reformować ocenę skutków regulacji w Polsce?* https://www.rpo.gov.pl/pliki/12180262910.pdf [access 20.02.2018].

257. Zyzik R., Czy *Leon Petrażycki był prekursorem behawioralnej ekonomicznej analizy prawa?*, "Forum Prawnicze" 2017, No. 1, pp. 21–33.

258. Zyzik R., *Ideał społeczny w polityce prawa Leona Petrażyckiego. Perspektywa ewolucyjna*, "Archiwum Historii Filozofii Myśli Społecznej" 2015, Vol. 60, pp. 175–178

Lex et Res Publica
Polish Legal and Political Studies

Edited by
Anna Jarón

Vol. 1 Anna Jarón: Socio-Economic Constitutional Rights in Democratisation Processes. An Account of the Constitutional Dialogue Theory. 2012.

Vol. 2 Stanisław Filipowicz: Democracy – The Power of Illusion. 2013.

Vol. 3 Teresa Dukiet-Nagórska (ed.): The Postulates of Restorative Justice and the Continental Model of Criminal Law. As Illustrated by Polish Criminal Law 2014.

Vol. 4 Agnieszka Kupzok: Enforcement of Patents on Geographically Divisible Inventions. An Inquiry into the Standard of Substantive Patent Law Infringement in Cross-Border Constellations. 2015.

Vol. 5 Alicja Jagielska-Burduk / Wojciech Szafrański: Legal Issues in Cultural Heritage Management. A Polish Perspective. 2016.

Vol. 6 Maciej Mataczyński (ed.): The Takeover of Public Companies as a Mode of Exercising EU Treaty Freedoms. 2017.

Vol. 7 Maciej Barczewski (ed.): Value of Information. Intellectual Property, Privacy and Big Data. 2018.

Vol. 8 Pawel Smoleń, Marcin Burzec: Introduction to Polish Tax Law. 2018.

Vol. 9 Łukasz Pohl, Konrad Burdziak: Judicial Interpretation of the 1997 Criminal Code Provisions on Self-Defence. 2019.

Vol. 10 Adam Szot: Court as a "Guard" and "Navigator". Judical Review of Administrative Discretion. 2019.

Vol. 11 Michał Peno / Konrad Burdziak (eds.): The Concept of Modern Law. Polish and Central European Tradition. 2019.

www.peterlang.com

www.ingramcontent.com/pod-product-compliance
Ingram Content Group UK Ltd.
Pitfield, Milton Keynes, MK11 3LW, UK
UKHW021832100926
8556IPUK00004B/305